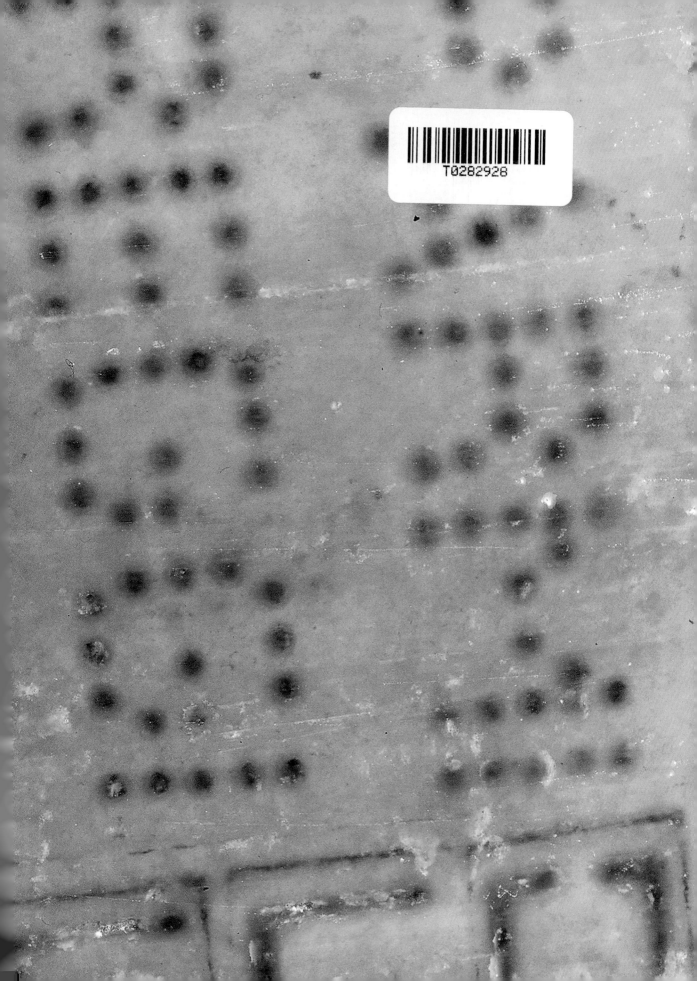

T0282928

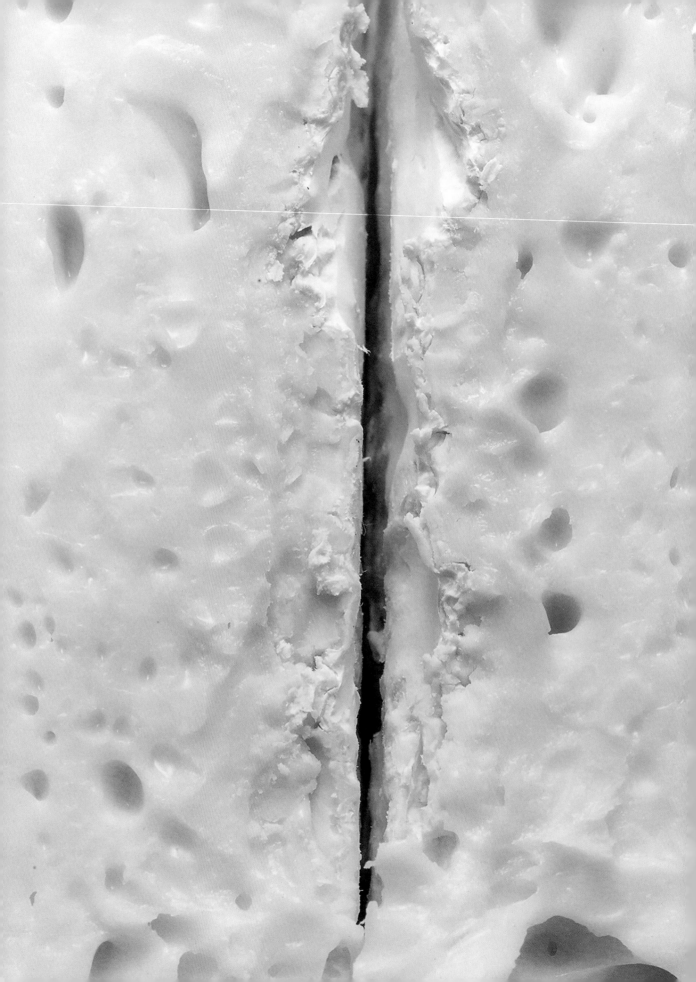

'Everybody knows the moon is made of cheese.'

– Wallace & Gromit

For Stella, may you grow up in a world full of good humans and good cheese.

The best things in life are CHEESE

How to buy it, store it, cook with it and
wow your guests with it

ELLIE & SAM STUDD
THE STUDD SIBLINGS

plum. Pan Macmillan Australia

CONTENTS

INTRODUCTION

We have looked up at the night sky, more than once, nodding in strong agreement that the myth of the moon being made of cheese is wrong. Not for the obvious reason that it's not actually made of cheese (sadly), but because if you're going to compare cheese with anything celestial, you should probably say that it's a galaxy within the infinite cosmos, with its endless diversity of aromas, flavours, types, textures, colours and shades. And the 'big bang' of this cheese galaxy? It can be attributed to just four ingredients: milk, salt, rennet and cultures. Doesn't that blow your mind?

Cheese gets under people's skin. Its consumption ignites an intriguing combination of unabashed pleasure and grounding nourishment in our bodies, our hearts, our beings. Cheese was born out of necessity for humans; it was a discovery that transformed a perishable product (milk) into a nutritious, preserved food source. Yet cheese represents so much more than nourishment – it encapsulates human craftsmanship and culinary artistry in its purest form. Perhaps it's this combination of cheese's foundational existence and its artistry that echoes deep within our genes and creates a feeling that, together, we belong to something greater. With one bite, cheese can teleport us to the Franche-Comté mountain pastures in full bloom, with tinkling cowbells in the distance … or it can transport us to an Italian nonna's kitchen, where she makes a simple ricotta for her evening pasta. We can even hear her humming under her breath while she does it.

Like many ancient agricultural products, the history of cheese is full of rich stories. Tales of the alchemy of turning liquid milk into curds; of the passion, skill, resilience and innovation of cheesemakers and affineurs – those who have paved the way before us, as well as those making magic now and forming the blueprint for those to come. Stories of landscapes, mountains, deserts, grasslands, animals and the pastures they graze on; of microbes, and all the visible and invisible actors essential to creating a cheese's final form and flavour. Stories of traditions, cultures, families, communities, language and heritage. And, yes, stories of people happily munching on cheese, and sharing it with their loved ones.

This book is a celebration of these stories, and by sharing them with you, we hope you feel a little bit more alive, educated and inspired to pass them on! Because (here comes the tough news) the diversity of cheese, and the ancient artisan practices employed to create it, are under threat and in need of preservation.

Like never before in history, we live in a world that vibrates on a frequency of fast, mass-produced industrial consumerism. Cheesemaking has not been spared, and traditional cheese is fighting for its life. You only have to visit the supermarket to see dairy shelves stuffed full of five-dollar bland, industrial cheeses that all taste the same. Close your eyes when you eat them and it's hard to tell the difference between the white, fluffy, moulded cheeses on offer. Artisanal cheese, both traditional and contemporary, is becoming rarer and rarer. If we're not careful, future generations won't have any choice but to eat those 'same same' supermarket cheese options.

The biggest threats facing traditional artisan cheese are industrial giants buying out small producers; strict and complicated government regulations; reduced utilisation of naturally occurring cultures in raw milk and increased dependency on centralised culture houses; and the painstaking labour and steep costs required to produce the cheese. Whether it be younger generations of shepherds wanting a less gruelling lifestyle, or an established small producer working 24/7 just 'for the love of cheese', the challenges are immense.

Luckily, as with many complex messes in the world, there is a counter culture of reaction and movement against this industrial takeover. Many people are curious and seeking to learn the origins and practices of traditional food-making. There is a demand for food that reflects a genuine taste of place. Our hope is that by telling the stories of artisanal cheese, we can contribute to this growing revolution and widen this crack of hope so more light can get in.

On a less flowery, more practical note, our goal in writing this book is to share the basic concepts of cheese, and to celebrate all the things that make artisan cheese special. We want to give you the tools for how to buy it, store it, snack on it, wow your guests with it, and how to cook using cheese as a star ingredient for all kinds of occasions. Cheese can seem intimidating, and so we hope this book is accessible and entertaining. We want to nudge you to explore cheeses you may have avoided before – the ones whose names you might be afraid to pronounce – or to try something outside your comfort zone, like putting together a fabulous cheese board.

In the recipe section, we want you to melt, ooze and be pulled in new ways (cheese-pull pun very much intended). Our aim is always to respect the quality of the cheese, centring the taste and aroma, rather than hiding it behind bolder flavours. We have consciously selected cheeses for our recipes that are accessible and won't break the bank, saving the higher-end artisan varieties for you to showcase on a cheese board, or enjoy with a considered pairing on a special occasion. We've brought you a combination of bougie slow-Sunday experiences, trashy snackies, yummy brunch go-tos and many other cheese dishes that are appropriate at any time, on any occasion. Because everyone knows it's all about balance, even when getting swept off your feet into a brand new and amazing galaxy.

WHO WE ARE

We were born into a cheese family. Our father, Will Studd, is a passionate and committed cheese specialist – since the 1970s, he has lived, breathed, imported, tasted, written about and even made a long-running TV show about cheese. The joke in our family is that there's probably more brie than blood running through our veins. Our earliest memories of cheese are vivid and very pleasant (and they do start early!), and we're super grateful to our parents for raising us and our sister Fleur to taste, understand and appreciate delicious, fascinating and authentic cheeses.

It's possible a few too many school lunches involved a baguette stuffed with tomato and stinky French Camembert (no real complaints there – Sammy still eats one every Sunday). We'd definitely whine, 'Why do we have this?' and 'I don't want to be "Smelly Ellie!"', on school report day, when our mum Bonnie would strategically fill our schoolbags with cheese to give to our teachers. The other kids eating Vegemite sandwiches found it a little bit weird, and extremely stinky. While it seemed odd to others at the time, we recognise how fortunate we were to have a fridge heaving with specialty Australian and European cheeses, often casually moving a 4 kg hunk of clothbound cheddar aside so we could get to the cucumbers.

Our dad's quest to find the world's best, most interesting cheeses, and his mission to protect consumer choices and raw milk cheese, was palpable, even in our very young years, and we'll never forget the look on Mum's face the day he came home and told us he'd been threatened with ten years in jail for importing Roquefort! And yet, our interest or professional involvement in cheese was never discussed or encouraged. After high school, Ellie studied to become an adolescent clinical nurse consultant, and it wasn't until her ten-year long service leave that she decided to take the leap into the professional world of cheese. Sam also took a circuitous path to the family business, studying marketing, riding motorbikes in India and Bali, then managing bars in the US, before passion and curiosity inspired him to delve deeper into cheese and its possibilities.

Our individual 'calling' to work in cheese happened organically and after much deliberation. Serendipitously, we arrived there around the same time. Our dad wasn't convinced at first – perhaps he thought it would be a short-lived phase – but we threw ourselves into it, working in cheese shops and affinages around the globe, with stints at Jasper Hill Farm (Vermont), Neal's Yard Dairy (London), Kirkham's Lancashire (Preston, UK), Spring Street Grocer (Melbourne) and Nimbin Valley Dairy (Byron Bay).

We both took on the gruelling task of passing the American Certified Cheese Professional (CCP) exam, an intense theory-based exam that's one of the only recognised certificates for cheese professionals. And we have also learned an incredible amount from our exceptional mentors, including Cathy Strange and Lisa Zografos (global cheese buyers), David Gremmels from Rogue Creamery and Mateo Kehler from Jasper Hill Farm. In recent years, we've even been on the road with our dad while he films his documentary series *Cheese Slices*, which has given us privileged behind-the-scenes insights into some of the world's rarest cheeses.

Today, we both work in the family business, hand-selecting artisan cheeses that form the 'Selected by Will Studd' range, which we sell into the Australian and US markets. We run masterclasses for cheesemongers, as well as cheese lovers who want to learn more, and we write for several food publications, including our monthly column in *delicious.* magazine. And what we've both humbly and happily recognised is that the more you learn about cheese, the more there is to learn.

This book feels like the natural progression of our cheese journey. With it, we of course hope to continue our family's legacy, but we also hope to get as many people as possible enthused and a little more educated about cheese. Cheese can be complicated, but it doesn't have to be. It can be expensive, but there are ways to enjoy it without overly stretching the budget. It can also be an intimidating topic if you don't know where to start, but all you have to do is take that first step, which in this case means turning the page and starting your own cheese journey. So, let's do this! It's going to be hella delicious and fun.

A BRIEF ORIGIN STORY

Cheese is a simple and nutritious food source that originated due to the human race's determination to thrive. Its origins can be traced back to the earliest attempts to preserve a seasonal surplus of milk using the process of fermentation.

The oldest written record of cheese we have dates back approximately 5000 years and comes by way of a diligent Sumerian stock breeder.[1] This ancient would-be accountant meticulously kept records of his herd's reproduction and the amount of cheese and butter they yielded on clay tablets in a logo-syllabic script called cuneiform (similar to Egyptian hieroglyphs and looking a lot like something Indiana Jones would pilfer from a tomb). Although we don't know this industrious individual's name, it is the first hard evidence we have of cheese and butter production.

However, cheese was around long before this. The jury is out as to the exact date, but historians and archaeologists suggest its inception began in the vicinity of 8000 years ago in the Mediterranean fertile belt, which is modern-day Turkestan and Iran.[2] The first cheese is thought to have resembled a brine-cured feta or something similar.

Since its discovery, many ancient civilisations have highly valued and even worshipped cheese. In Egypt, a pharaoh would be buried with cheese, the literature of the ancient Greeks is littered with references to its health benefits, and cheese even turns up in the Old Testament.

But cheese really began to hit its stride when humans started to cultivate cereal crops and develop essential pasture management and agriculture techniques. While traditional free-roaming flocks of goats and sheep had been a staple of nomadic people, humans began to domesticate and manage the once wild-tempered cattle. Cattle offered extended lactation periods and, although they demanded more extensive pasture lands, they also offered up larger volumes of milk.

The expansion of the Roman Empire from the 1st century BC helped spread the knowledge of cheesemaking through the Mediterranean, Asian minor and northern Europe, as every legionnaire was provided with a small cake of salted cheese as part of their daily rations. No doubt, these cheese cakes were hotly traded for other goods in a Romanesque equivalent to today's schoolyard lunchbox swaps. Cheesemaking began to evolve in monasteries and feudal systems, and techniques were adapted to suit their terroir, which allowed for a wonderful diversity of cheese to blossom into existence.

Small bloomy cheeses were produced by farms and households with a small number of animals, while larger hard cheeses, such as Gruyère, were made by cooperative milk pooling, and were able to be transported further. As time went on, cheese gradually became an essential

part of the daily diet for the poor, but also evolved into a respected artform for the rich. Most cheese at this time was handmade by women.

After the Roman Empire collapsed, the world entered the Dark Ages. Unrest, conflict and frosty environmental factors resulted in large transient movements of people and their animals. During this time, much cheese knowledge was lost, apart from a small group of remote mountain communities and highly guarded religious organisations who maintained their cheesemaking practices. These organisations later made refinements to their processes and developed techniques to generate income for their monasteries by selling cheeses to the public.

Skip forward a few hundred years and we hit the Industrial Revolution. Sadly, this was a dull period for artisan cheese as production sped up exponentially with the rise of the factory. By the 1850s, American dairies began to adopt systems by which farmers were contracted to provide milk to centralised modern processing facilities. Over the next 100 years, factory production continually increased, with many small farmhouse cheese manufacturers becoming obsolete. The introduction of sophisticated and dependable cheesemaking technologies, fast and reliable transport, refrigeration and globalisation marked the beginning of the end for most small producers.

World War II further devastated the beautiful diversity of artisan cheese with a drain on resources and workforce.

We continue to nurse the hangover of these blindly embraced technological advances and geopolitical skirmishes, as much of the cheese available today remains mass-produced and severely lacks any proper flavour or sense of belonging. These lost decades of cheesemaking have spawned cheeses grappling with identity crises.

Happily, though, recent years have seen a resurgence in artisan cheesemaking, which brings some hope for cheese tragics like us (and you, we're assuming). Now is a period of introspection and revolution, if you will. Some of us are hungry for knowledge. People want to know about cheese, its origins and the intricacies of its production, and are willing to seek it out and take steps toward reviving and preserving this ancient art form. The European Union's support of the PDO name appellation system (see page 291) is a clear sign of respect and acknowledgment of the importance of traditional cheesemaking.

The most exciting cheeses exhibit a fundamental link between a farmer's skill, the cheesemaker's traditional craft, and the complex influences of local, seasonal soils and geography. It's a long and exciting story from animal husbandry to the cheese counter. Before we delve into the details, let's first explore the basic steps of cheesemaking.

HOW CHEESE IS MADE

MILK + CULTURES + RENNET + SALT

Cheese is essentially four ingredients: milk, cultures, rennet and salt. The aim of cheesemaking is to concentrate the nutrients in milk for it to become portable and storable. Milk consists of approximately 87 per cent water, and cheesemaking is basically removing the water from milk. We like to think of the cheesemaker as a chef who manipulates the milk to a desired taste, texture and shape. Cheesemaking involves capturing and solidifying the milk (fat, protein, minerals) and removing the liquid (whey). The process can be broken down into six steps, and tweaking these steps and adding different cultures results in an endless array of cheese types.

1. Heat the milk

The first step in cheesemaking is to heat the milk to prepare it for the addition of starter cultures. There are three different heat treatments for milk: unpasteurised, pasteurised and thermalised (see Curd Nerd Terms on page 290 for explanations of these).

2. Add cultures

Next, the cheesemaker adds starter cultures to the milk to begin the acidification process.

The role of these microbes is to eat the milk sugars (lactose) and 'fart out' lactic acid, which in turn acidifies the milk.

3. Add rennet

The cheesemaker then adds rennet to coagulate the milk. Coagulation is when the milk changes from a liquid to a solid (curd).

Rennet causes the proteins in the milk to clump together, trapping the fat and concentrates to form a curd. The curd is firm and looks like soft tofu when it's ready to be cut (see Curd Nerd Terms on page 290 for more on rennet).

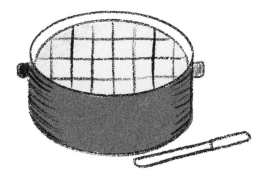

4. Cut the curds

After coagulation, the curds are cut to release whey, with the aim of reducing moisture. The size of the curd cut depends on the type of cheese being made. As a general rule, large cuts (walnut size) make for soft, high-moisture cheeses, such as brie, while tiny cuts (rice size) create hard, low-moisture cheeses, such as Grana Padano. The curd can be further manipulated through heating and stirring to expel more moisture.

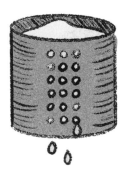

5. Drain, press & salt

The curds are poured into moulds with holes in them to drain the remaining whey, a process called 'hooping', which gives the cheese its final shape. Some cheeses are pressed using their own weight or with the help of a cheese press, to knit and squash the curds together. After this happens, the cheese is turned regularly to ensure even drainage. Cheeses are then dry rub salted, left in a brine bath or wrapped in cloth to cure. Salting helps preserve the cheese, draw out whey, form the rind, enhance taste, balance flavours and manage flora growth.

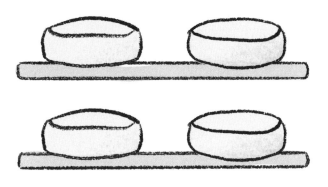

6. Affinage

Cheeses are stored in a cheese cave or humid room to mature. The time varies from a few days to weeks and even years, depending on the type of cheese being made. The cheese needs to be flipped regularly and carefully cared for by the affineur.

RAW MILK CHEESE

Raw milk cheese is made from milk in its purest natural form that has not been heat treated or pasteurised (if you'd like the technical nitty gritty, see Curd Nerd Terms on page 290).

When raw milk is used to make cheese, its natural bacteriological enzymatic characteristics and natural flora are fully utilised. In essence, raw milk is the foundation of traditional cheesemaking and allows the cheese to carry an authentic microbial fingerprint, reflecting its region of origin in every organoleptic sense (taste, sight, smell and touch). It is the premise of the overused and misunderstood term 'terroir'.

It's important to note that raw milk and raw milk cheese are two entirely different products and the risks of consuming them are often confused. Raw milk is fluid milk that is not processed or heat treated and can harbour harmful bacteria if not sourced from healthy animals and properly regulated. However, raw milk cheese is simply *made* from raw milk. During the cheesemaking process, there are many hurdles and safeguards to create an environment where pathogenic bacteria are unable to survive. These steps include heating the milk, acidification, fermentation, salting and affinage.

There is a mounting evidence to support the idea that microbes in raw milk play an important role in helping to ensure the safety of cheese, as well as improve its sensorial properties (see *Reinventing the Wheel* and *Ending the War on Artisan Cheese* for further reading).[3,4]

When milk is pasteurised, 98 per cent of all micro-organisms are killed. This includes harmful pathogens that may or may not be present but everything else in milk too, including the beneficial bacteria, natural flora, vitamins and enzymes responsible for flavour and identity. To make up for this loss, modern cheesemaking supplements cheese with added industrial cultures.

When making cheese with either raw or pasteurised milk, a cheese's potential is dictated by the quality of the milk. Raw milk cheeses are not necessarily better than pasteurised milk cheeses, but they have far more integrity and links to place. Their complexity of flavour, diversity and deep traditional history are worth supporting. Moving forward, we believe there needs to be a more sophisticated approach based on scientific evidence to separate pathogen-free food (including raw and pasteurised milk cheeses) from bacteria-free food.

What's the deal with raw milk cheese in Australia?

Australia's laws around the production, importation and sale of raw milk cheese are bound with red tape and are deeply confusing. While most of the world recognises and supports the production and sale of raw milk cheese, the Australian Food Standards and state food authorities do not, through limiting the types that can be produced and sold. This is especially the case for high-moisture raw milk cheeses. To make things even more confusing for the everyday consumer, Food Standards Australia New Zealand classifies cheeses such as Parmigiano Reggiano, Gruyère, Emmentaler, Comté, Section28 Monforte Reserve and Bruny Island C2 as 'cooked curd cheeses', rather than raw milk cheese, like the rest of the world. Outside of this cooked curd cheese classification, Australia has a few exceptions, including Roquefort, Ossau-Iraty and 12 British raw milk cheeses.[5,6]

Australian cheesemakers are legally allowed to make some raw milk cheeses; however, they must be produced under very strict, costly and impractical regulations. At the time of writing, Prom Country and Pecora Dairy are the only non-cooked raw milk cheesemakers that meet these regulations. As one of our dear cheesemaker friends, who shall remain nameless, pointed out: 'Making raw milk cheese in Australia is 90 per cent paperwork and legislation, 5 per cent animal husbandry, care and milking, and 5 per cent cheesemaking. It's a complete nightmare and should be the opposite.'

There is still a long, bumpy road ahead for Australian consumers and cheesemakers. But the good news is that through the gumption of domestic producers and strong rallying from passionate consumers and organisations (such as Will Studd, the Australian Specialist Cheesemakers' Association and Neal's Yard Dairy), the doors for access to raw milk cheese are slowly opening.

CHEESE ANATOMY

1. Rind

The rind protects a cheese from the outside world. It's formed by the community of microorganisms in the cheese, which are deliberately chosen by the cheesemaker to protect the cheese, control ripening and add flavour. The type of rind (such as its thickness and colour) can indicate the age of the cheese and its edibility (see page 43).

2. Creamline

The creamline is the layer between the rind and the paste that can be seen in soft cheeses rather than hard. The soft layer can vary in thickness and be translucent, giving clues to the cheese's ripeness. It is a physical manifestation of the breakdown of fats and proteins.

3. Paste

The paste is the edible interior of the cheese. Look at the colour and feel the texture. How the paste presents depends on the fat and protein breakdown of the cheese. Its colour can indicate the milk type and animals' diet, but use it as 'information' and not gospel (see page 39 for more on paste colour).

4. Eyes

Holes in cheese paste are called 'eyes'. They vary in size and are usually intentionally created by the cheesemaker by the addition of a bacteria called *Propionibacterium shermanii*. This starter culture basically eats lactic acid in the cheese and releases carbon dioxide, which makes the holes, a process also known as 'secondary fermentation'. The size of the eyes is controlled by the cheesemaker and the humidity and temperature of the ageing room. *P. shermanii* thrives especially well in low-acid cheeses and warmer temperatures. Some examples of cheeses with eyes are Emmentaler, Gouda, Havarti and Tilsit. Cheeses with no eyes are called 'blind cheeses'.

5. Crystals

Cheese crystals can appear in two main forms: tyrosine and calcium lactate.

Tyrosine crystals are found on the inside of aged cheeses (usually longer than nine months) and they give a euphoric crunch when you bite down on them. Tyrosine is an amino acid that occurs when the protein in the cheese breaks down and forms crunchy clusters. People often think these little pockets of crunch are salt, but they are, in fact, flavourless. A cheese will usually be saltier and have more depth of flavour due to ageing, rather than these guys. Tyrosine crystals are harder and grainier than calcium lactate crystals. Cheese crystal experiences include Le Gruyère, Parmigiano Reggiano, Rogue River Blue, aged Comté, L'Amuse Signature Gouda and Cornish Kern.

Calcium lactate crystals are softer than tyrosine crystals and are usually found on the inside and surface of aged cheeses as a white powdery layer or pale dots. The crystals build up as the cheese ages, due to a reaction with calcium and lactic acid. They are flavourless and do not crunch, and are often confused with mould growth by consumers. Calcium lactate crystals are more common than tyrosine crystals.

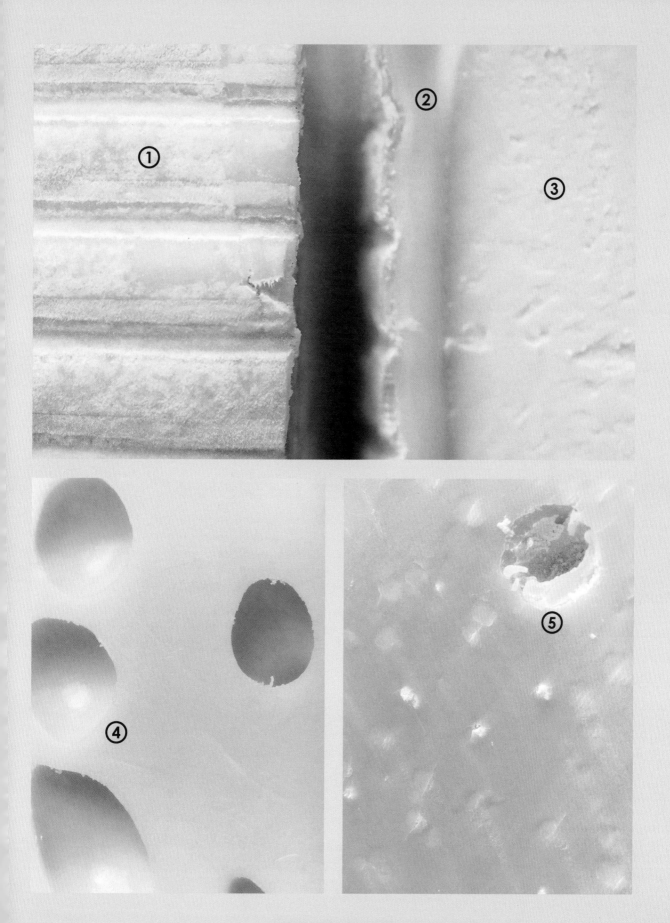

CHEESE ESSENTIALS

HOW TO BUY CHEESE

Walking into a specialist cheese shop can be an intimidating experience, not only because there are so many cheeses to choose from, but because it will often involve a conversation with a cheesemonger who knows a lot more about the topic than you do. But it doesn't have to feel like travelling in Paris when you don't speak French. Buying cheese can, and should, be a fun, rewarding and enlightening experience. Here are some tips to help demystify how to buy cheese and open the whiffy, but exciting, door wider into this fascinating world.

Have a fling with your cheesemonger

To start this new relationship, your first step is to find a specialty cheese shop, deli or independent supermarket with a cheese counter. Be prepared for an immersive sensory experience when you walk into a cheese shop; your nostrils will be whooshed and walloped with the full spectrum of cheese aromas – from wet hay and damp river pebbles, to sweet buttered popcorn. Your cheeks may encounter air that is cool and humid. Your eyes should be met with a small selection of quality cheeses with a high turnover (rather than hundreds of cheeses in dubious condition, or bargain bins that are advertising three cheeses for $10).

As with most flirtatious exchanges, it's good to have a few one-liners up your sleeve to break the ice. You don't have to know much about cheese to know where you might want to start. Some examples of opening lines might include: 'I love the creaminess of brie. What can I try that's similar?' Or: 'I'm in the mood for something strong and funky. What do you suggest?' Or even: 'I want something that reminds me of a warm summer's night in Greece. Take me there!'

Consent is sexy, so it's also good to know and express what you don't like. Taste is personal, contextual and cultural. Your boundaries around cheese may stay consistent throughout this journey, or they may shift as you grow more confident and explore more complex cheeses. A good cheesemonger will be highly skilled in helping you navigate this romance. And if you're ever feeling wild and adventurous, you can always ask them what they love or are most excited by at the moment and give it a whirl.

Cheesemongers are the sommeliers of the cheese world. A good monger will be knowledgeable about the land, animals, terroir, seasons and artisan producers behind each cheese. They love to talk cheese when there is time, and they should make you feel comfortable and curious, not silly or intimidated. Take your time chatting and selecting your cheese – it should be a pleasurable fling after all!

One of the best parts of visiting a cheese shop is hearing the stories of the passionate people who created the cheese, and mongers should be able to tell them to you. Sometimes a cheese comes from a small family dairy that has been operating for centuries; other times a young renegade just took an interest in cheesemaking and started up a dairy of their own. Understanding the history and hard work behind a cheese makes you appreciate it even more, and enables you to make better informed and educated choices as a consumer. It also gives you some fun bits of information to share with friends as you munch on the cheese that night!

As with any fling, sometimes it's the wrong fit. Sometimes the enthusiasm and knowledge just isn't there, and the person behind the counter may act aloof or too cool to help you. Trust your intuition when this happens, and don't take it personally.

Set your intentions

Are you cooking with cheese? Or planning to wow some friends at a Sunday picnic in the park? Making sandwiches? Having the in-laws over? Planning a fondue party? Nailing the best four-cheese pizza your town has ever seen? Your cheesemonger is there to help guide you. If you're cooking with cheese, they may suggest some classic melters. If you're assembling a cheese board, they can help you select different textures, milk types and in-season cheese.

Flavour comes first

If possible, always ask to taste a cheese before you buy it. Like fruit and vegetables, cheese is seasonal, so be guided by your monger about what is good at the moment.

Buy cheese as close as possible to the day you plan to eat it. Traditional cheese is a living, breathing, perishable food that requires certain storage conditions to stay at its best. A good cheese shop will provide this environment through controlled humidity and temperature, and a good monger should guide you on how best to house your cheese when you get it home. Consider buying cheese paper to extend a cheese's longevity (see page 26).

For mozzarella, ideally buy it on the day you will eat it. For bloomy cheeses and washed rinds, we like them close to their use-by date. The flavours are more pronounced, with the yeasts and mould being broken down. Larger, firmer cheeses, such as Comté and clothbound cheddar, taste best when cut straight from the wheel.

Less is more

It's better to buy less cheese, more often. Once a cheese is portioned it starts to deteriorate, so buying smaller amounts helps guarantee freshness and flavour. If you still have soft cheeses in the fridge after two weeks, it means you have bought too much. Larger portions of any cheese left in the fridge will taste different from the time you buy it to the time you eat it.

Trust us, one or three sensational cheeses in perfect condition are far better than four or five average cheeses sitting around on a cheese board. Don't compromise on the quality of your cheese – if it's not up to scratch, go without. Communicate your budget to the cheesemonger, so they can guide you to what's best, and remember that artisan cheese is often punchier in flavour than industrially made cheese, so you'll need less of it.

When buying for a group, as a general rule, aim for 50 g of cheese per person. If the cheese is a larger part of the meal, aim for 80 g. For a 'cheese only' dinner you'll need 120–200 g per person.

Good cheese is expensive, but still less than a bottle of wine …

You might have seen the meme floating around the internet or written in stone in Anne Saxelby's cheese handbook, *The New Rules of Cheese*:

> The two biggest shocks of adult life:
> 1. Everyone does cocaine
> 2. Cheese is fucking expensive

This makes us laugh every time, but inside we're also thinking to ourselves we actually can't believe cheese is so cheap! This is a sentiment that has been imparted to us by one of our mentors, Cathy Strange. Before you roll your eyes, let's take a look at everything that has to happen to get exceptional cheese into the hands of the person selling it to you – then you can make up your own mind.

Pasture: To make excellent artisan cheese you need to start with good-quality, unique milk. This begins with the quality of the soil and pasture on which the milking animals graze. This requires land upkeep, rotational grazing, and vegetation and biodiversity management.

Animal husbandry: Superior milk also demands that animals are healthy – firstly, because it's the right thing to do, and secondly because an animal's treatment and quality of life comes through in the milk. Factors, such as herd size and where the animals are housed and milked, need to be taken into account, and this adds to the cost of farming.

The farmer: Most animals are milked twice a day, every day of the year. Each milking can take up to two hours of the farmer's time.

The cheesemaker: As a general guide, 10 litres of milk makes 1 kg of cheese. Once enough milk is collected, the cheesemaker creates their cheese, which takes roughly eight hours from start to finish, depending on the type of cheese. This also requires meticulous upkeep of the cheesemaking facilities.

Affinage: The cheese is matured and then aged. Depending on the style of cheese, this can take anywhere from four weeks to four years. This process requires the skills of an affineur, and manual or mechanical labour for flipping cheese and regular brushing or brining.

Transport: The cheese then needs to make its way from the farm to its destination – sometimes cities, countries or continents away – all while being kept in a temperature-stable environment to avoid spoilage and damage.

The cheesemonger: The people selling you the cheese at your local cheese shop or specialty market have to pay their staff and cover the overheads of running a business, as well as being able to offer a variety of small-quantity cheeses.

So, as you can see, there is a significant amount of cost and labour involved in getting that farmhouse and artisan cheese to you. And, by purchasing it at a fair price that may be higher than the cost of the generic, industrially made cheese you'll find at the supermarket, you are supporting the time-honoured traditions and skills that went into crafting it.

Artisan cheesemaking is an endangered craft, and without it we would only have access to predictable, bland cheese. It is crucial to understand the enormous difference between artisan and farmhouse cheese, and mass-produced industrial cheese. When exploring the world of quality cheese, we always encourage people to think about what they are eating, the unique flavours and textures they're experiencing, and the stories, people and care behind it all, rather than just going by price or a name.

Buying cheese from unattended cheese counters

Maybe you don't have access to a specialty cheese shop or deli, or maybe you need to grab some cheese from the supermarket in a rush. Here are our tips for buying different cheeses when you're without a professional to bounce ideas off.

- Choose small, individually packaged cheeses in wooden boxes or well wrapped in waxy parchment paper.
- Buy Parmigiano Reggiano and not impersonator parmesan.
- Use visual and scent cues to assess if a cheese is up to scratch. Is the packaging bloated? Is the cheese damaged; for example, does it have bruising, are there any obvious cracks in the rind or paste, or is the rind mushy? Does it smell ammoniated? (See page 31 for further cues.) Look for cheese with an intact rind and a paste with even colouring.
- If creating a cheese board, balance it with cheeses of different textures and milk types.
- If the cheese has been cut from a wheel, have a look at the packing date to make sure it's as recent as possible (ideally within a week).
- Check the label and take into account where the cheese is made and the type of milk used.
- Keep your eyes peeled for a yellow and red stamp (PDO: Protected Designation of Origin) or another acronym after the cheese's name. This is highest form of certification in the EU and is a guarantee of authentic cheese.
- Never buy pre-grated cheese, even for cooking. It's inferior and contains unnecessary additives such as anticaking agents and preservatives.

Buying cheese online

Like everything else, quality cheese can be found and purchased online. Here are a few pointers to help you get the best out of your order without being able to smell or hold the cheese before clicking purchase.

1. Find a good cheese shop with reputable reviews as that usually means there is knowledge and expertise behind their selection and seasonality.
2. A good online cheese shop will have helpful information about how each cheese tastes and what it can be paired with. You can also google additional information about specific cheeses and cheesemakers, including looking at the dairy's website.
3. Look for a shop that sells bigger-format cheeses cut to order, and that wraps its cheese in wax paper, rather than vacuum-packing. Vacuum-packed cheeses often taste 'baggy' and can be soggy, which suggests the shop likely prioritises a cheese's longevity over quality.
4. Consider buying the 'cheesemonger's choice', if available, as this is a guide to what is in season. The aim here is to give you a similar experience as going to a shop and asking for a recommendation.
5. If you're not sure, call the shop to double-check your selection and ask them any questions you may have.
6. If creating a cheese board, follow the same rules you would in an IRL cheese shop. Choose a variety of milk types, textures and flavour profiles to keep your selection interesting. You should be able to buy individual cheeses, rather than be limited to a pre-packed box.
7. Check the shipping details to make sure it includes refrigeration and proper storage with insulation. You don't want your cheese arriving damaged or in bad condition, which could even pose a health and safety risk! The cheese should still be cold when you open the parcel. Make sure someone will be around to receive the order, so it's not left out too long, and put it in the fridge as soon as possible.

Buying cheese from the cheesemaker

A local farmers' market or a farmgate shop are both great places to buy local cheese. You may even get an opportunity to meet the producer and find out how the cheese was created and what makes it special. This is also an excellent way to experience the seasonality of small-batch production, plus it's the ultimate way to shop local.

How to read a cheese label

There are some key things to look for on a cheese label. Notice if a company is revealing more or less of the below information. Leaving out such details can be a strategic marketing tool by industrial giants:

- Place of origin
- Style of cheese
- How long the cheese was (or wasn't) aged
- Milk type
- Whether a cheese is raw or pasteurised

Use-by vs best-before dates

All Australian cheeses will display a use-by or best-before date. Here's what they mean:

Use-by: This means the date by which you must consume a cheese. It may not be safe to eat after this date – so consume at your own risk! You will more commonly see this on fresh and stretched-curd cheeses.

Best-before: This is the guide to when a cheese will be ripe. Personally, we think it's best to consume it as close as you can to this date, especially for washed rinds and bloomies. A cheese close to its best-before date will have a bolder flavour, as the fats and proteins have had more time to break down. Another bonus is that the cheese will often be on sale at a reduced price, but do keep your nose on alert for ammonia as a guide of just how far it's gone.

Key words & symbols on cheese labels

FARMSTEAD/FERMIER	A cheese that is made on the farm where the animals are milked and raised. Usually small-batch cheesemaking, made by hand.
GEOGRAPHICAL INDICATORS/ NAME-PROTECTED SYMBOLS OR ACRONYMS	Turn to Curd Nerd Terms on page 290 for a full list of these. The EU has a strictly regulated system for name-protected and geographically protected cheeses. Keep your eyes peeled for the highest certification: PDO (Protected Designation of Origin), which will appear after the cheese's name or as a red and yellow stamp on the label.
DOUBLE CREAM/TRIPLE CREAM	Cheeses that have added cream to the recipe, so expect them to taste rich and creamy.
CREAMY/SOFT/TANGY	The cheese will likely be milder in taste.
NUTTY/SHARP/STRONG	The cheese will likely be stronger in taste.
RENNET	The ingredients will state the type of rennet used. There are animal, microbial and vegetable rennets (see Curd Nerd Terms on page 290 for more information).
PASTURE-RAISED/GRASS-FED	Suggests that animals have been raised on pasture or fed grass when it's available. However, its meaning is not enforced by a regulatory body and it's up to the producer to define this.
CAVE-RIPENED/CAVE-AGED	The cheese is aged in a man-made or natural cave.
AGED	The meaning of 'aged' can vary but, generally, cheeses will often have a drier texture. Note: the term is sometimes added as a marketing trick to try to add value to a product – the age of the cheese is often missing in these instances.
RAW MILK CHEESE	Made from raw milk (read more about raw milk cheese on page 14).

HOW TO STORE CHEESE

Once you have purchased your cheese, you want to keep it happy. Cheese is alive, teeming with microbes such as bacteria, yeasts and moulds, and needs to breathe to taste its best. Like us, every cheese has unique characteristics and, as such, needs to be treated differently. For example, hard cheeses in their uncut form can age for several years and develop in flavour, aroma and texture over time. However, once that wheel is cut, that same cheese will begin to deteriorate and requires special care to stop the effects of its new environment. Only buying the amount you will eat over a few days is important; if you have some left over after two weeks, you have bought too much. Home storage of cheese should be temporary – just long enough for you to enjoy the cheese at its peak.

Remember, like us, cheese is meant to age, and it's up to us whether it ages gracefully or goes out with the slogan, 'live fast, die young'. If we treat cheese properly it will age like Iris Apfel; if we treat it like punk rock it will end up looking and smelling like Iggy Pop in his darkest hours. To slow down the deterioration of the taste, texture and appearance of your cheese, read on.

Create a cheese cave (for your fridge)

The best cheese in the world is often matured in climate-controlled affinage facilities. At home, this can be replicated in a cold, damp cellar, as well as garages and laundries, to create the perfect conditions. For those with neither an affinage cave nor cellar (which, let's face it, is most of us), the vegetable drawer in the fridge is the next best thing, due to the higher humidity and slightly warmer temperature. The optimum storage for most cheese is 10–14°C.

We suggest having a dedicated large plastic, glass or ceramic container with a tight-fitting lid for small portions of cheese. Leave the small air tab open for airflow. Make sure each cheese is wrapped individually so as to not cross-contaminate flavours and aroma, and keep your blue cheeses in a separate container.

Optional upgrade: non-porous materials tend to trap moisture, allowing water to accumulate as drops that cause surface mould and accelerate spoilage. To help prevent this (and take your cheese storage to the next level), line the bottom of the container with a damp tea towel, paper towel, cloth or sushi mat.

Invest in cheese paper

The reason cheesemongers tell you to buy cheese paper, rather than wax or parchment paper, is that it is better and, funnily enough, specifically designed for cheese. Cheese paper is a multi-layered paper with a wax coating on the outside and a thin, porous layer on the inside. The waxed outside prevents moisture from escaping but allows for oxygen exchange and for the cheese to breathe. The porous layer controls humidity and soaks up condensation that can develop on your cheese, but also prevents it from becoming dry. There are a lot of beeswax wraps for cheese available, but after testing them multiple times, we found they did not work for us. They were hard to seal, so air got in and the cheese dried out. The investment in cheese paper is worth it as it extends shelf life. To be cost efficient, make sure the size of the paper is appropriate for the piece of cheese and not larger than necessary.

Storing fresh cheeses

Spoiler alert: you shouldn't store fresh cheeses, such as mascarpone, ricotta and burrata, for very long as they don't have rinds to protect them and will quickly sour or grow mould when exposed to air. If the cheese is stored in brine it can be durable, but once exposed to air it will deteriorate quickly. This style of cheese is pretty much the only cheese where you don't want to see any colour. Any spots or specks are usually a sign that the cheese has spoilage. Here are our tips for keeping fresh cheese at its best.

- Eat ASAP. Fresh cheese doesn't want to wait around to grow old. Enjoy it for its youth.
- Keep the cheese in its original packaging, including brined cheeses – avoid breaking the seal until you are ready to consume it. Make sure you keep the brine as clean as you can (no double dipping with dirty knives), and consume the cheese within 1–5 days of opening.
- Oxygen is your worst enemy. If the cheese is sitting outside the brine, keep it tightly wrapped in plastic wrap.
- If the cheese is vacuum-packed, the package will say how many days after opening it can be consumed.
- Acidic fresh cheeses, such as chèvre, can be stored in airtight containers and have a slightly longer shelf life.

STUDD SIBLINGS
RECOMMEND

Our fave cheese paper
is Formaticum, which is
available online or from
cheese shops.

Storing bloomy & washed rind cheeses

Bloomy and washed rind cheeses are sensitive creatures with a limited shelf life. They are encased in a living rind that is constantly breaking down the fats and proteins as the cheese ages. How long your cheese will last depends on when you bought it during its shelf life. How ripe in taste you like it is personal preference, similar to people's preferences for how ripe they like to eat a peach.

BOXES

Not all boxes are created equal. If cheese, such as Camembert, comes in a traditional wooden box and wax paper, store it in its original packaging, even after you have eaten half of it. Wooden boxes are natural insulators and act as mini affinage facilities that keep your cheese at the perfect humidity. Cardboard cheese boxes can look pretty but they are a cheap alternative. They are usually paired with plastic-wrapped cheese and tend to dry out the cheese. We recommend avoiding buying cheeses like this.

CUT & WRAPPED

Often, when you buy a bloomy from the local supermarket or deli you will find that it has been cut from the wheel and smothered in plastic. If this is the only option, start by searching for the best-looking piece of cheese, and choose one that has been cut recently (often stated in small print on the label).

Once you get home:

- Remove the plastic wrap and let that sucker breathe again.
- Rewrap the cheese in cheese paper or parchment paper to allow for airflow and humidity.
- Place the cheese in an airtight glass or plastic container (make sure it is as close to the size of the cheese as possible to prevent it drying out).

Optional upgrades:

- Line the bottom of the container with a damp tea towel, paper towel, cloth or sushi mat.
- Air out the container every 2–3 days. Ensure the rind has some breathing space around it.

The above steps can also be taken for pieces of cheese that you cut into and don't finish. Realistically, any bloomy or washed rind cheese that has been cut from the wheel has about one week to live. If you notice small patches of green, blue or white mould developing, these should be scraped away or cut out; in all truth, however, this is an indication that the cheese has been stored too long in your fridge.

WHY SOFT CHEESE SHOULD NOT BE WRAPPED IN PLASTIC

- It makes the cheese soggy and smelly.
- It suffocates the cheese, leading to off flavours and textures.
- It traps moisture and makes the cheese sweaty and potentially mouldy.
- It lets in the light, which can cause oxidation and bland-tasting cheese.

CAN I STORE CHEESE IN THE FREEZER?

Please, for the love of God, don't freeze your cheese, okay? Dairy does not generally take well to freezing, especially soft or semi-firm cheeses. It affects the texture and flavour terribly. Cheese rinds are the only exception (see page 148 for how to use rinds).

Storing firm cheeses

The best way to store firm cheeses is similar to bloomy and washed rind cheeses:

- Remove the plastic wrap and let that sucker breathe again.
- Scrape off the sweaty layer with the back of a knife (do this now, and before eating it).
- Rewrap the cheese in cheese paper or parchment paper to allow for airflow and humidity. For larger wheels you can leave the rind exposed, if you wish.
- Place the cheese in an airtight container or plastic zip-lock bag (make sure it is as close to the size of the cheese as possible to avoid it drying out, and push the air out). Feel free to wash and reuse zip-lock bags.

Optional upgrades:

- In addition to the optional upgrades listed opposite, you can also buy a 'cheese vault' for firmer cheeses. We have tried and tested silicone cheese vaults for smaller wedges of hard cheese with pleasing results. The bonus is that you don't have to use cheese paper either. They can be purchased online.

FOR LARGER HARD HUNKS

A technique that some people use for storing large hunks of hard cheese, such as Parmigiano Reggiano, is to wrap it in several layers of dampened muslin cloth or cotton calico. Keep the cheese in the fridge, or garage or cellar, and check on the cloth every few days to see if it's still damp.

CONFESSION

If we have purchased an extra-large wedge of mature hard cheese, such as cheddar, Manchego or Parmigiano Reggiano, that we want to use over an extended period, we do wrap it in plastic wrap or quality plant-based wrap. We then cut off smaller workable bits for cooking and eating as we need it. If we do use this method, we scrape back the face of the cheese with a blunt knife before serving to remove any damage the plastic has made and bring the cheese back to life. (If we are the victims of a hit-and-run shortly after the publication of this book, you will know why … but we also believe in honesty.)

Storing blue cheeses

Most blues have a higher moisture content compared with other cheeses, which makes them more fragile. Store blue cheeses separately, as their mould and flavour can easily transfer to other cheeses.

Blues hate plastic more than any other cheese. The plastic sucks up the moisture and allows water to accumulate in drops that cause surface mould and accelerate spoilage. Your best bet is to stick to foil and avoid all plastic. Wrap firmer blues, such as Stilton, in wax or cheese paper before wrapping in foil; wrap wetter blues, such as Roquefort, straight into foil, loosely (due to the increased moisture). Fuzzy blue or green mould patches that form on the cheese's surface after a few days can be cut away.

Blue cheeses can be stored at a lower temperature than other cheeses, so they love the coldest part of your fridge (usually the bottom shelf, down the back).

Troubleshooting common cheese problems

Our inbox is regularly plagued by cheese lovers wondering why their cheese has created such an almighty stank in the fridge that it assaults anyone who opens the door. If that sounds like you, we're here to help. Read on to demystify this phenomenon and other cheese-related enigmas.

HELP! MY CHEESE IS MOULDY

Cheese is alive, so it is perfectly normal if it sometimes grows mould. In fact, it's an issue if it doesn't grow mould at some point. To remove mould, gently trim the cheese or scrape the mould off with the back of a knife. This rule does not apply to fresh cheeses such as mozzarella, ricotta and cottage cheese. Discard them.

HELP! MY CHEESE IS CRACKING

If a cheese paste looks cracked, this is usually a sign that it's too dry. You can attempt to revive the cheese by putting a damp cloth over it. However, this is most likely an indication that you haven't stored your cheese properly or you've bought too much.

For cheeses that should always be sticky, such as Époisses, if you notice it has dried out, you can mix 1 tablespoon of white wine with 125 ml (½ cup) of boiled and cooled water, and apply it to the cheese rind with your fingertips, until it glistens.

Hard, dry cow's milk cheeses can be repurposed by mixing with Parmigiano Reggiano and sprinkling on pasta. Dry goat's cheeses can be shaved over sourdough toast with tomato and herbs.

HELP! MY FRIDGE STINKS

Cheese stinks. Cheeses that have a particularly strong aroma include washed rind and blue cheeses. Here are a few ways to not piss off your family or housemates with a stinky fridge.

- Charcoal/charcoal drying eggs for your fridge.
- Airtight containers.
- Wrapping the real stinkers, such as genuine Camembert, in newspaper over the traditional box, then placing in an airtight container. It gives an extra layer for the smell to absorb. We also do this when we are travelling with it!
- Buy a separate bar fridge or dedicated 'cheese fridge' if space allows.

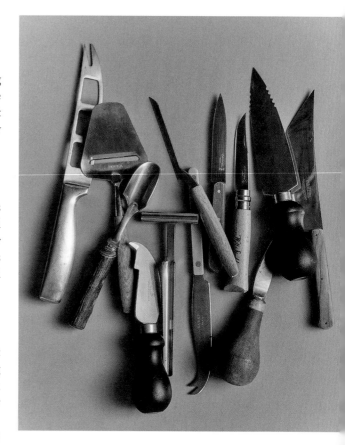

How can I tell if a cheese is destined for the bin?

If you see, smell or taste any of the below characteristics in your cheese, it is well and truly time to bin it.

RIND & PACKAGING

- Unopened, bloated packaging.
- Rinds that are cracked or dried-out and powdery.
- Soggy, slimy, overly chewy or mushy rinds. This can indicate the cheese has been frozen, poorly temperature-controlled or past its best-before date.
- Bloomies should not be covered in brown rinds.
- Dark discolouration under natural rinds can indicate the cheese has not been kept at the correct temperature.

AROMA

- Unpleasant aromas. Trust your nose. Fresh cheeses and bloomies should not smell off, sour or pungent.
- Washed rinds should smell vaguely like your partner's body odour, in that it's whiffy, but strangely alluring. It should not be obscenely putrid, smell of old Band-Aids or have the aroma of decay, which can be a sign that it's ammoniated, over-aged or has been kept in poor storage.
- Heavily ammoniated-smelling cheese, especially if the cheese has been unwrapped for an hour or more, indicates it's over-ripe.

PASTE

- Cheeses with a slimy surface or paste, which includes excess liquid coming out of the paste.
- For non-blue cheeses, avoid bright-pink, green, blue, bright-yellow and grey patches, moulds or splotches on the paste or rind. Sometimes you might see grey or black mucor (a type of mould family), known as 'cat fur', on the surface of mould cheeses. This is caused by humidity and the season. It's undesirable, but safe. Simply remove it or return it to your cheese retailer.
- Blue cheese that has yellow, brown, red or pink splotches. Pale-green or white patches usually indicate a secondary mould that is not intentionally part of the cheese. Scrape it off and the cheese can still be eaten.
- 'Frog skin', which is when the rind separates from the paste and the cheese oozes everywhere. Many people think this is a sign of a good cheese, but it's often due to poor cheesemaking. Look for spoonable, rather than liquid, pastes.
- Firm cheeses with dark, dry, cracked or excessively oily surfaces and pastes.

TASTE

- Cheese that tastes overly sour or has a funky flavour. Abort consumption if you detect soapy, bitter, fishy flavours or a burning sensation at the back of your throat.

WHERE DOES FLAVOUR COME FROM?

It is truly a miracle just how many flavours can be tasted in cheese when it is only four ingredients – milk, cultures, rennet and salt – that make up the infinite tapestry of cheese flavour profiles.

When a cheesemaker is creating their cheese, they will play with acidity and explore how they'd like their cheese to taste. Speak to many a cheesemaker and they'll tell you 'everything, everywhere, all at once' affects the taste of cheese. Some cheesemakers, such as David Gremmels from Rogue Creamery, would even go so far as to say that the mood of the cheesemaker or background music that is played impacts the final personality of a cheese. David puts the name of the record he was playing on some of his cheese wheels to propel this romantic notion. Our halloumi producers in Cyprus insist that halloumi should be folded by women for a gentle and calm character in the finished cheese.

Here are the main factors that affect the overall flavour of cheese.

Animals

The species, breed and welfare of an animal all influence the flavours in artisan cheese. Traditional breeds often produce less milk, but the fat and protein content will be higher. An animal's diet, living conditions and stress levels also impact on milk quality, as does seasonality. Milk produced in calm environments will be higher quality, and have a more desirable taste and flavour. Here are the some of the flavours found in cheeses made from different milks.

- **Cow:** Mild, sweet, creamy, smooth and buttery.
- **Goat:** Lemony, bright, fresh, herbaceous, less sweet and more acidic than cow's milk.
- **Sheep:** Rich, gamey, nutty, buttery, oily, more savoury in taste than cow's milk.
- **Buffalo:** Rich, tangy, slightly sweet, creamy, clean, richer and creamier than cow's milk.

Raw milk vs pasteurised

If the milk is pasteurised, the process kills most bad and good bacteria, enzymes and flavour compounds. This means flavour must be reintroduced by cultures.

Quality of the milk

This relates to the cheesemaker using fresh milk shortly after milking, as well as the animal's diet and environment.

Skill of the cheesemaker

This includes the tools used to cut the curd, how hard cheeses are pressed, intuition, care and orchestration.

Microbes & enzymes

Flavour and aroma are created by the fats and proteins and how they break down. Microbes and enzymes contribute to this breakdown and free the fatty acids into flavours and aromas we can recognise. Cheese is predominantly milk (sweet) that is fermented (sour/acid) with salt added, so these flavours often dominate in cheese. The cheese will taste different at various stages of ripeness.

FLAVOUR THEORY

FLAVOUR = TASTE + MOUTHFEEL + AROMA + MIND

Flavour is fascinating and complex. So what happens when you first see and then eat a piece of cheese? Put on your lab coat, it's time to strap in for some science.

We experience cheese through our five senses: sight, smell, taste, touch and sound. Wavelengths of light are converted to colours when we see the cheese, while molecules in the cheese are detected by receptors on our tongue and 8000 tastebuds, which perceive the five basic tastes of salty, sour, bitter, sweet and umami/savouriness. There is now evidence that the brain can actually detect fat as a flavour, but let's park that for now.[7] Fascinatingly, it is only in conjunction with the nose that we are able to discern specific aroma compounds, such as mushroom or nuts. In fact, aromas are responsible for 80 per cent of flavour perception. Molecules in the air are detected by the receptors in the nose and converted into aroma compounds, such as fruity, earthy and floral.

When we chew on cheese, a second layer of smell is triggered, as aromas and volatile compounds pass through our retronasal region (the back of the throat that connects the nose and mouth). Interestingly, smell is connected directly to our limbic system, the part of the brain where memories and emotions are stored. It helps us to navigate what we can eat, as well as steer us away from putrid and off foods as a form of survival. When we smell the cheese, our brain basically flips through a Rolodex of memories and aromas (up to 10,000) and compares it to an experience we have had before.

Touch is also processed by the brain through the temperature and texture of the cheese in our mouth, then converted to signals between neurons in the brain, as well as sound. This information is then woven together and integrated into our brain, which recognises and computes it as a conscious experience: 'I just ate cheese, and I liked it'. This is the intersect of flavour.

We also taste with our heart and spirit. And no, we haven't been consulting crystals for this one; research acknowledges neurological interpretations of food as a conscious and unconscious experience that can add bias to the way we perceive flavour and our enjoyment of food.[8] It includes how we prefer our mother's mascarpone pie over that of a Michelin-starred chef, and how there are long and passionate histories of traditional cuisines across the globe.

Cheese is also said to bring up emotional experiences from our primordial programming and mammalian diet.

Neuroscientist Dr Thomas Morell, in Max McCalman's *Mastering Cheese*, theorises that because cheese is energy and nutritionally dense, there could be a subconscious embedding from our ancestors to experience it as more pleasurable for survival.[9] A recent psychology review on food rewards reveals that the gut–brain pathway senses nutritive qualities in food and activates the brain reward circuit.[10] Another explanation for our attraction to cheese is due to it having high concentrations of tyrosine. This amino acid is responsible for regulating stress and mood, and needs to be supplemented in our diets as we have naturally low levels. When we eat cheese, our body breaks down the tyrosine further into casomorphin, a feel-good chemical that activates dopamine as well as the areas of the brain that respond to morphine and heroin. This could be your cheeky excuse to explain why your feet remain planted next to the cheese board at a party.

FLAVOUR &

A radial flavour wheel divided into categories, from outermost to innermost:

Fermented — fermented veggies, BO, armpits, gym socks, fermented grass, miso

Meat — bacon, smoky bacon, lamb chop, beefy, beef broth, salami, pancetta

Barnyard — leathery, wet leather, manure, wool, wet wool, gamey, hide, goaty, wet hay

Cellar — damp cellar, limestone, clay, cavey, wet stone, musty, mildew

Mushroom — fungal, button mushroom, porcini mushroom, pickled mushroom, truffle, soil, wet earth

Wood — forest floor, pine, eucalyptus, spruce, wet leaves, wood shavings

Brassica — cabbage, cooked cauliflower, brussels sprout, bitter greens, broccoli, braised greens, mustard greens

Herbs — thyme, rosemary, wild herbs, fresh herb bouquet, freshly cut grass, wet grass, fresh hay, wild grass, fresh pasture

Onion — shallot, garlic, leek, celery, caramelised onion, sautéed onion

Citrus — lemon, orange, grapefruit, pineapple, candied lemon, preserved lemon, yuzu

Apple — granny smith apple, fuji apple, pear, nashi

Stone Fruit — peach, plum, dried apricot

Floral — buttercup, daisy, wildflowers, clover, dandelion, honey, tea-like, violet

Grouped under the broader bands: **FUNKY**, **EARTHY**, **VEGGIES**, **FRUITY**

AROMA WHEEL

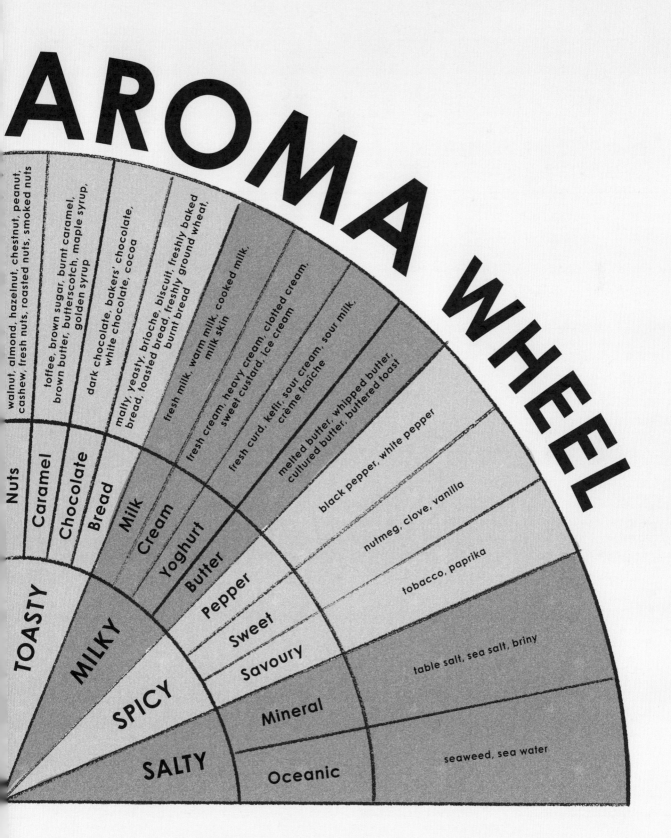

Nuts — walnut, almond, hazelnut, chestnut, peanut, cashew, fresh nuts, roasted nuts, smoked nuts

Caramel — toffee, brown sugar, burnt caramel, brown butter, butterscotch, maple syrup, golden syrup.

Chocolate — dark chocolate, bakers' chocolate, white chocolate, cocoa

Bread — malty, yeasty, brioche, biscuit, freshly baked bread, toasted bread, freshly ground wheat, burnt bread

Milk — fresh milk, warm milk, cooked milk, milk skin

Cream — fresh cream, heavy cream, clotted cream, sweet custard, ice cream

Yoghurt — fresh curd, kefir, sour cream, sour milk, crème fraîche

Butter — melted butter, whipped butter, cultured butter, buttered toast

Pepper — black pepper, white pepper

Sweet — nutmeg, clove, vanilla

Savoury — tobacco, paprika

Mineral — table salt, sea salt, briny

Oceanic — seaweed, sea water

TOASTY

MILKY

SPICY

SALTY

TEXTURE & MOUTHFEEL

The mouth has a perception of touch and can register texture and temperature which, in turn, affects flavour. Whether a cheese is light and fresh or full and lingering is often linked to its fat content. It is okay to have personal preferences when it comes to cheese texture. Some like soft, others hard.

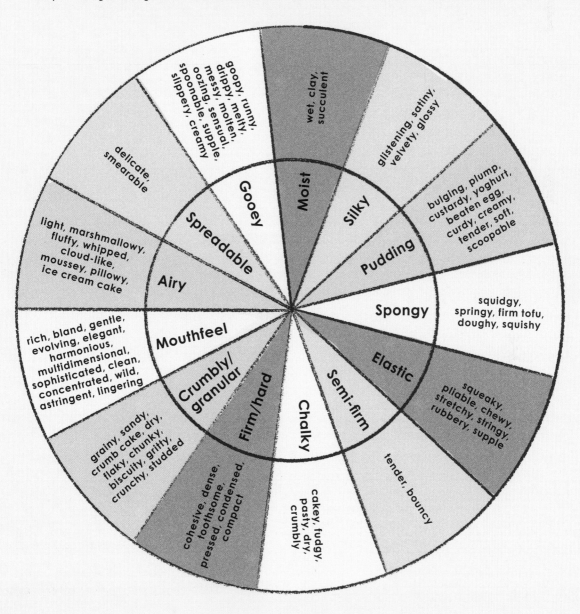

HOW TO TASTE CHEESE

We believe cheese should be treated with a little tenderness, because both you and your cheese deserve the careful attention it takes to coax out its inner beauty. Here's our guide to setting yourself up for a successful tasting, so that each cheese will grace your palate with the best version of itself.

Tasting cheese is like sex …

1. Set the scene. Just like preparing your boudoir for a sexy night ahead, get your environment ready and comfortable. Make sure your cheese is appropriately warmed up at room temperature. If you don't trust us, try doing a side-by-side taste comparison of the same cheese: one taken straight from the fridge; and one that has been left out for an hour. Like your cheese board, arrange them mild to wild for tasting.

2. Be fresh. Strong-flavoured foods and drinks will affect your ability to pick up on tastes and flavours. If you are trying a few cheeses, have freshly cut apple, baguette or crackers nearby to clear the acid and fat off your tongue. Beverages, such as soda water, champagne and beer, also assist. Cleanse your palate between cheeses with a small piece of your chosen cleanser as an intentional reset.

3. Use your senses to look, feel, smell and taste your cheese (see opposite).

4. Be present! It will make it better.

5. Write your experiences in your black book/ cheese book. This is not compulsory, but it can be a handy reference if you want to compare batches or learn more about a particular cheese. It also encourages you to connect your own experiences of what YOU are tasting and build your vocabulary. Jot down the taste, texture and whether or not you like it. You can describe cheese any way you like. Some people compare it to a piece of music or a celebrity or personality. If you can, when it comes to describing the cheese, stay away from overused terms such as sharp, strong, salty and lactic. They are umbrella terms and do not give a good indication of what the cheese actually tastes like. For inspiration, check out the flavour wheel on pages 34–5.

6. If you want to be super serious about this, don't wear perfume and make sure you have clean hands as they can conflict with the aromas of the cheese.

7. Use clean knives, preferably a different one for each cheese.

8. We are advocates of self-pleasure/eating cheese on your own, but we also believe tasting cheese can be more pleasurable with friends or a partner. With company and different palates, you have the opportunity to bounce around ideas and experiences. Sometimes we listen to a cheese podcast or watch an episode of *Cheese Slices* while we are eating a particular cheese, so we can consolidate information about where it's from and the stories behind it.

9. Remember, at the end of day, it's what you like and don't like and being able to articulate that. Don't overthink it.

10. Only after you have tried the cheese on its own, would we suggest exploring a pairing (see page 44) and seeing how that works.

Look

Be curious and look for clues that indicate what a cheese *might* taste like, as well as its age, milk type and what the animal grazed on. Some cheeses can seem daunting – for example, washed rinds can appear more intimidating than they taste – but remember, looks can be deceiving. The more familiar you become with categories of cheese and the more cheese you eat, the more you will start to build your information bank on what looks normal. Inspect the cheese from the outside in and look at the rind and paste.

PASTE COLOURS

White and ivory: A bright-white paste usually means the cheese has been made from goat's or buffalo's milk, as they convert the beta-carotene (a pigment that makes things yellow) into vitamin A, which is colourless. Ivory pastes usually indicate sheep's milk cheese due to the high butterfat content, or cows that have been fed hay or grain.

Orange: This can indicate the cheese has added annatto (see below).

Yellow: A buttery-to-yellow hue suggests the cheese is made with milk from cows that have grazed on grass. Cows absorb carotenoid from the grass, which comes out in their milk.

Blue, grey and green moulds: These show a cheese has been inoculated with *Penicillium roqueforti* or *Penicillium glaucum*. A good cheese will have veins radiating from the centre and an even distribution and patterning of mould.

WHY ARE SOME CHEESES ORANGE?

The short answer is marketing. There is a long history of natural dyes being added to milk to either impersonate high-quality summer cow's milk or make a cheese stand out from the crowd.

Grass-fed cows produce milk that is a deep-yellow hue from the beta-carotene pigment in grass. Throughout history, unscrupulous cheesemakers have added colouring agents, such as carrot juice, turmeric, saffron and annatto, to their cheese to impersonate this yellow and be deceptive about a cheese's quality. Annatto has been the preferred ingredient since the 17th century. It has no flavour or aroma and can achieve varying degrees of yellow, orange and red.

Annatto is still used in cheesemaking today to maintain tradition, create visual interest and differentiate a cheese. Some examples of cheeses that use annatto are Mimolette, Red Leicester, Langres, Cheshire, American cheddar, Shropshire Blue and Colby.

Feel

Run your finger over the rind and paste, even give it a little squeeze. Grab a small morsel of cheese and rub it between your thumb and forefinger (professional cheese judges do this, especially for cheddars and Alpine cheeses, as it helps release the aromas and relaxes the fat so you can taste more flavours). Ask yourself these questions.

- Does the cheese feel elastic, crumbly, oily, squishy or smooth?
- Is it at room temperature?
- Does it feel ripe?

Smell

Give your cheese a good sniff to see what you can smell on the surface. Rub a small section between your fingers and inhale before tasting it. Keep in mind that smell can be deceptive and not translate to what you will taste. Some strong cheeses actually end up being milder once you taste them. Try to identify familiar scents and 'taste of place' in a cheese; for example, wet hay from the fertile lands of Normandy. Sometimes, closing your eyes helps. Can you identify at least three aromas? The more present you are to smell, the more vibrant your experience will be.

Taste

Take your time when tasting. Make sure the cheese comes into contact with your whole tongue and the roof of your mouth to ensure even distribution among your tastebuds. Taste receptors are spread all over your tongue as well as the roof of your mouth and throat, so moving the cheese around your mouth ensures contact and allows the receptors to identify different tastes. Evidence shows that areas of the tongue are sensitive to, rather than solely responsible for, particular tastes. On a primal level, we are very attuned to what is poisonous and what is safe.

Start from the middle of the cheese, then move to the rind. Chew slowly and gently. Chewing begins the process of breaking down flavour compounds, starting with our saliva. It also allows us to pick up on mouthfeel, texture and flavour. To get super pro, put a piece of cheese on your tongue, inhale a breath over it, then exhale through your nose before chewing. Practise some Darth Vader breathing or yoga ujjayi/ocean breaths. This sends the aromas straight to your nasopharynx so that you can pick up on some bonus notes.

While chewing, think of cheese as a journey through layers of flavour, balance and texture. Consider the texture, how it breaks on your teeth and the amount of time it sticks in your mouth. Finally, swallow and remain present.

The six tastes

Our mouths experience each of the tastes as individual notes, as well as in combination. Taste buds are located all over the tongue, soft palate and throat, and receptors allow us to detect each of the tastes: salt, sweet, bitter, acid and umami, the satisfying savoury taste.

There is relatively new evidence pushing for fat to be added as the sixth taste.[6] 'Oleogustus', or the taste of fat, has been pitched as tasting like oxidised oil. It can be pleasant or rancid. You can taste fat in cheese as it ages.

The journey of taste

Different cheeses have different lengths of journey in the mouth, but in general:

- Younger and higher-moisture cheeses usually have a short journey, with flavours vanishing quickly after you swallow.
- Aged cheeses with firm textures and lower-moisture cheeses usually have a longer finish that lingers in your mouth even after you swallow, and will usually be felt by the whole mouth. A sign of a well-made aged hard cheese is one that has a long mouth journey with lingering flavours, rather than ones that disappear quickly. The flavours can also evolve. For example, an English clothbound cheddar might start citrusy, then move to a nutty and buttery finish.
- Highly acidic cheeses often make the sides of your mouth water. The opposite is true for sweet and low-acidic cheeses.
- Feeling like you have a hairy tongue? Usually, this sensation occurs when you pick up on tropical fruit flavours (like when you eat pineapple) in cheeses like cheddar and Gouda.

A good cheese will:

- Have a distinct, unique flavour and personality.
- Express its terroir and tell a story. You can almost tell how happy the animals are, their Alpage and what season the cheese was made in.
- Inspire you to remember it after you've eaten it (long journey plus flavour).
- Be complex, multidimensional and have depth, rather than a one-note journey.
- Have balance – you do not want a cheese that's bitter or overly salty.

THE TASTE JOURNEY

Describe the journey! How does it start in your mouth?
Does the taste linger after you've swallowed? What
is the mouthfeel? What flavours emerge? If it's nutty,
for example, are they roasted or blanched, walnuts or
hazelnuts? Is it complex? Does it fade out? Is it bland?
Does it start small, then crescendo? Do you like to eat it?
Eat it if you like it!

Tip-of-the-tongue tastings

Cheeses that respond particularly well to being placed on the tip of the tongue to maximise flavour are feta and Roquefort. Press feta at the tip of your tongue, then let it melt. Traditional Greek Feta will be creamy from the sheep's milk and have a lemony zing from the goat's milk. If it has been barrel-aged, it will have a crumbly texture. A good Roquefort placed on the tip of the tongue should vanish off it! It should be moist, balanced and salty, with a syrupy sweetness.

Sound

This is a sense that affineurs rely on for cheese assessment (don't worry, you don't have to). It is known as 'cheese tapping' and is used to identify interior issues, such as fissures and cracks, as well as density, in large-format cheeses such as Parmigiano Reggiano, Emmentaler and Comté. Affineurs use a tool called a cheese iron or cheese trier to tap the rind and listen – each cheese has its own distinct sound; for example, Emmentaler will have a slight hollow sound because of its 'eyes'. It is a skill that takes years to learn. If you do want to explore using this sense, one sound to keep your ears peeled for is the crunch of tyrosine crystals (see page 16).

CAN I EAT THE RIND?

This is definitely the top question when we do our cheese masterclasses. Even when we're not asked this question, we usually witness a poor student with their face a centimetre from the cheese, poking the rind with a knife while worriedly looking around at others for guidance to see if it's safe to eat.

Firstly, let's get the Captain Obvious exceptions out of the way. Do not eat bark, cheesecloth, wax, wax coating, paper or foil; for instance, on Gouda, clothbound cheddars or bark-wrapped cheese.

Now, to eat or to not eat the rind? The answer is up to you, but they are safe to eat! Keep in mind, some rinds are more palatable than others. Bloomy rinds, for example, can enhance your cheese-eating experience by adding texture and flavour – brie and camembert rinds are meant to be eaten. Aged cheeses will usually have a harder rind and, therefore, be less approachable and palatable.

Rinds are used to protect a cheese as well as impact the way a cheese matures and, consequently, its overall flavour. When making a cheese, the cheesemaker intentionally thinks through the kind of rind they want to create for that specific cheese. They are also aiming for an even and consistent rind, with no holes.

When you are presented with a cheese with a rind, take a nibble of the rind with the cheese and see if you like it. Trust your tongue. If it's gritty or sandy or hard and you aren't digging it, cut it off. No judgements here. The important thing is to try it, otherwise you'll never know what you're missing out on. Also, by reading our Types of Cheese section (see page 81), you should start to gain confidence in identifying and steering clear of rinds that are slimy, overly wet or have brown spots.

Here is a general guide to what to expect, the types of rind we encourage you to try and what to avoid.

BARK-WRAPPED

Cheeses wrapped in bark were common before plastic, paper and foil were introduced. The bark works in much the same way as leaves do and adds some foresty notes. Dig around the bark for maximum flavour, but don't eat it.

BLOOMY RINDS

Intended to be eaten, bloomy rinds are mould and/or yeasts. They're white to straw-coloured and soft, varying from marshmallowy to wrinkly. White and clean moulds indicate a young cheese, while thicker rinds and a little browning suggest a riper cheese. Bloomy rinds taste of mushrooms, are creamy, tangy, peppery and woody, and can add to the texture of your bite. Cheeses covered with just *Penicillium candidum* (PC), the really white and fluffy mould, look pretty but can taste like wet newspaper and have an unpleasant aftertaste.

CHARCOAL/BLUE-GREY ASH

Ash is usually made from vegetables and, therefore, edible. The ash neutralises acidity, acts as a natural preserve and encourages rind development.

FLOWERS & HERBS

These ingredients can be used to add flavour and encourage rind formation. They are edible.

LEAF-WRAPPED

Wrapping cheese in leaves was also a precursor to plastic, paper and foil, and was used for transportation and to age cheese. The leaves protect the cheese, discouraging mould growth and providing ventilation, and can be a natural preservative and add to the flavour. Leaves can be marinated in alcohol or left dry. Remove before eating.

NATURAL RINDS

Formed naturally by air and humidity, natural rinds vary from mottled, gritty crusts to hard or waxy. Some are rubbed in salt, paprika or olive oil. The rinds vary in taste and can be musty and barnyardy or waxy and chewy/dense. We usually cut these rinds off and leave them to the side. We keep Parmigiano Reggiano rinds in the freezer to add to stocks or soups (see page 148 for more ideas).

WASHED RINDS

These rinds have been washed in brine, alcohol or both. They vary in shades of orange, pink and red, and may look sticky, gritty or have natural white flecks. Most are edible. Expect mineral, funky, beefy, fermented-beer flavours. Washed rinds usually smell worse than they taste and can sometimes be gritty in texture.

HOW TO PAIR CHEESE

(AKA ONLINE DATING)

When it comes to pairing cheese, we find it helpful to compare the process to finding a romantic match through online dating. As with love, there are no rules, only general guidelines for what makes a good union. Sometimes the elements that seem an unlikely pairing are the most harmonious. So don't be scared to step outside the box. At the end of the day, if you like it, then it's a fabulous match! If you're unsure where to start, settle on some classic combinations, then venture out. But don't worry, we're not sending you out there alone. Consider this guide your wingman.

Our pairing philosophy centres on one solid-gold rule: it's all about the cheese. A compatible match should elevate the cheese rather than overwhelm or attack it head on. Pairing is also an opportunity to highlight characteristics in a cheese that may otherwise remain hidden until coaxed out by the right partner. Remember to be flexible: artisan cheese will vary in ripeness and will often taste different throughout the seasons, so you may have to adjust your pairings accordingly.

Before we get down to dating, let's begin with some general principles around finding your match. From there, we'll give you specific elements to help you swipe right for yes and left for no.

1. TASTE BEFORE YOU PAIR

Cheesemakers usually go to great efforts to ensure their product tastes a certain way. To respect this, we encourage you to try the cheese as it is, before smothering it with honey or other accompaniments that hide the true flavour of the cheese.

2. COMPLEMENT & CONTRAST

Cheese is essentially salt, protein and fat. From that you can essentially go two ways. The first is to *complement* the cheese; the second is to *contrast* the cheese.

The complementary relationship

A compatible match should flatter the cheese, allowing it to shine. In an ideal pairing, your cheese will find a delicious harmony of flavour profiles. To achieve this, you need to balance the flavour, intensity and texture of the cheese, like for like. So, acid likes acid, fruitiness loves fruitiness, fat works with fat, nuttiness enjoys nuttiness, strong goes well with strong, and bitter loves bitterness. You get the idea ...

Opposites attract

On the other hand, the feistiness of an opposite pairing is truly exciting. Opposite doesn't mean incompatible, though. In fact, it's a pleasant contrast of flavour or texture that doesn't dominate or attack the natural attributes of the cheese. To contrast the butterfat or funkiness of a cheese, you can add an acidic component to cut through it. That might include pickled veggies, fruit or a sharp chutney. If a cheese is salty, add a touch of sweetness, such as honey, fruit, chocolate, jam or dessert wine. Sweetness also works to bring balance to an acidic cheese. If a cheese has bitter or spicy notes, the perfect foils are sweetness or acidity.

STUDD SIBLINGS
SECRET

Our pairing philosophy centres on one solid-gold rule: it's all about the cheese.

3. FEELING TEXTURAL

Pleasure isn't just about flavour, it's also in texture. Naturally, our mouths love contrasting textures, so adding a juxtaposition creates the ultimate satisfying mouthfeel. This involves playing with the gooiness of a cheese and adding something crispy or crunchy. Crunch balances out the rich, buttery paste of soft cheeses, while hard cheeses enjoy sticky pairings, such as honey.

4. WHAT GROWS TOGETHER GOES TOGETHER

You may have heard this before. It's a truism that makes sense when you consider that the terroir of a region will naturally grow produce that pairs well with a particular cheese made in the same area. These pairings are often steeped in tradition and are known to be a match for a reason. Serving seasonally appropriate produce with a cheese aligns with this principle as they are both tasting at their peak. We've highlighted this rule in our following match selections with 'super likes'.

Is it a match?

So how do you know if your chosen mix of cheese and accompaniment is a true match? It's simple. Put the pairing together in your mouth. Your aim is to fill the taste circle in your mouth with a rounded and pleasurable experience. First, ask yourself these questions.

- **What qualities does the cheese have?** Is it hard, soft, punchy, mild, a bit funky? Once you know what you're dealing with, you can match the cheese accordingly.
- **What flavours and textures could complement or contrast these qualities?** These natural attributes need to be encouraged, not dampened.
- **What dominant flavours are you left with?** If you're no longer tasting the cheese, then you're missing the point and it's time to move on.

Classic pairings are classics for good reason. Let's take a look at why they work and the cheeses with which they find true companionship.

Acid &

crunch

NUTS

Nuts add crunch, of course, but they also have other cheese-enhancing qualities. Candied, smoked, salted, seasoned and toasted, nuts can bring bitterness, sweetness and richness to the fattiness of cheese. They go particularly well with aged cheeses, due to their toasty notes.

♥ IT'S A MATCH

CANDIED NUTS	aged Gouda, Coolea, Mimolette, Cornish Kern, blues
CASHEWS	aged Gouda
HAZELNUTS	ricotta, feta, washed rinds such as Taleggio, Alpines, blues
PISTACHIOS	feta, halloumi, chèvre
ROASTED ALMONDS	sheep's milk cheeses such as Manchego or Ossau-Iraty, aged Gouda
WALNUTS	goat's cheeses, triple creams, camembert, Pecorino, Alpines, blues

FRUIT & VEGGIES

When selecting fruit and veggies to go with cheese, think about their crunchiness, sweetness and acidity. It may not seem obvious, but the acidity of pickles goes particularly well with the funky, meaty profiles of washed rinds. They cut through with their acidic tang and salt, with the added bonus of a crunch factor. Raw veggies can add a vegetal character for cheeses to play off, while acidic fruit can contrast the butterfat of cheese and act as a palate refresher. They also bring a nice juiciness or succulence to your palate. If you are adding fruit, make sure it's in season. You'll do your nice cheese a disservice if you pair it with a lacklustre fruit that's spent three months in a cool room. If you had to choose just two fruits to serve with cheese, you can never really go wrong with apple or pear.

♥ FRUIT: IT'S A MATCH

APPLE	all cheeses
BERRIES	mascarpone, ricotta, crème fraîche, goat's cheeses, triple creams
BLACK OLIVES	feta, goat's cheeses, burrata, Kefalotyri, Pecorino Toscano
CANDIED ORANGE	funky washed rinds such as Taleggio
CHERRIES	ricotta, brie, Vacherin, Gorgonzola
CRANBERRIES	Fromage Blanc, brie, Mimolette
FIGS	chèvre, triple creams, Parmigiano Reggiano, blues
GRAPES	feta, Taleggio, Fontina
GREEN OLIVES	feta, goat's cheeses, Spanish cheeses such as Mahón, Jarlsberg, Gorgonzola Piccante
MEDJOOL DATES	Manchego, blues
MUSCATELS	hard Spanish sheep's milk cheeses
PEARS	feta, Taleggio, Pecorino, blues
POMEGRANATE	halloumi, chèvre, feta
STONE FRUITS	mascarpone, burrata, triple creams, P'tit Basque, washed rinds

♥ VEGGIES: IT'S A MATCH

BREAD AND BUTTER PICKLES	cheddars
CHARGRILLED CAPSICUMS	feta, chèvre
COOKED BEETROOT	feta, goat's cheeses, cheddars, blues
CUCUMBER PICKLES	washed rinds such as Fontina or Raclette, Havarti, Alpines, cheddars
NEW POTATOES	washed rinds such as Raclette or Vacherin, strong bloomies such as camembert
PICKLED GREEN BEANS/CARROTS/BEETROOT	creamy fresh cheeses, funky washed rinds
PICKLED ONIONS	washed rinds such as Taleggio, Alpines
RADISHES TOSSED IN VINEGAR	a hunk of Parmigiano Reggiano, cultured butter
RAW VEGGIES SUCH AS RADISH, CAULIFLOWER, FENNEL, ENDIVE	feta, gooey bloomies, funky washed rinds, creamy blues

✕ SWIPE LEFT

Sweet veggies such as raw red capsicum.

✕ SWIPE LEFT

Olives bring brine and saltiness, so avoid pairing with blue cheese, which is also salty.

Sweet &

sticky

HONEY, MAPLE SYRUP, MOLASSES & BALSAMIC VINEGAR

If you were going to choose just one sweet ingredient to pair with cheese, make it honey. Essentially, cheese is fat and salt, and the sweetness of honey loves both these elements. If a cheese is acidic, honey can balance this out, making it a versatile and often irresistible pairing. It also adds another aromatic layer, which is gorgeous.

Honey often complements younger cheeses, goat's cheese and bloomy cheeses with chalky textures, and can juxtapose funky cheeses. It's also something most people have on hand in their pantry. Honey can vary in strength and texture, so take these things into consideration. But, while honey is a tried-and-true cheese match, don't let it be the only sweet pairing you ever try. There are other viscous syrups that are worth pushing outside your comfort zone to give a go.

CHOCOLATE

Trust us, dark chocolate and cheese is a pairing you must take out for a spin. With its bitter and coffee notes, chocolate can enhance the existing roastiness, fruitiness and milkiness of a cheese. Dark chocolate goes particularly well with cheeses with a high butterfat content. Blue cheese and chocolate have a strange but mesmerising affinity with each other, due to the sweet and earthy flavours of blue.

♥ IT'S A MATCH

CHOCOLATE PIEDRAS	triple creams
DARK CHOCOLATE	ricotta, mascarpone, Alpines such as Gruyère, Appenzeller or aged Gouda
DARK CHOCOLATE SPREAD	whipped ricotta
SHAVED DARK BITTER CHOCOLATE	triple creams, blues such as Rogue River Blue, Roquefort or Cashel Blue, chèvre

♥ IT'S A MATCH

EXTRA-AGED BALSAMIC	creamy blues such as Gorgonzola Dolce, burrata
FLORAL HONEY	ricotta, goat's cheeses, creamy bloomies
HONEY	most cheeses
HONEYCOMB	ricotta, triple creams
MAPLE SYRUP + CRACKED BLACK PEPPER	Gouda
POMEGRANATE MOLASSES	halloumi, Kefalotyri
TRUFFLE HONEY	sheep's milk cheeses such as Pecorino, blues

♥♥♥ SUPER LIKE

A drizzle of northern Italian sticky aged balsamic vinegar + Parmigiano Reggiano chunks – once you try this taste sensation, it'll be a fixture on your cheese plate.

PRESERVES & PASTES

The caramelised, condensed-sugar sweetness of jams and fruit pastes, such as quince, balance salty and acidic cheeses. In general, pastes, jams and compotes pair better with hard, dry or crumbly cheeses rather than soft-textured cheeses. That's because, sometimes, two rights make a wrong and 'soft with soft' can equal a bad mouthfeel. Sweeter pickles and chutneys bring a desirable sweetness and acidity that brighten up earthy cheeses, such as cheddar.

♥ IT'S A MATCH

APRICOT JAM	double and triple creams
BERRY JAM	goat's cheese, brie, double creams
CHUTNEY	clothbound cheddars
FIG JAM	camembert, Manchego, Alpines, Gorgonzola Dolce
KIMCHI OR SAUERKRAUT	cheddars, Alpines, mozzarella
MARMALADE	ricotta, Galotyri, mascarpone, Brillat-Savarin
MUSTARD	firm Swiss cheeses, cheddars, Alpines
ONION JAM	Alpines such as Gruyère, creamy blues such as Cashel Blue
POMEGRANATE MOLASSES	halloumi, Kefalotyri

♥♥♥ SUPER LIKE

BLACK CHERRY JAM	Ossau-Iraty
QUINCE PASTE OR MEMBRILLO	sheep's milk cheeses from Basque Country, such as Ossau-Iraty, or from Spain such as Manchego.

✕ SWIPE LEFT

Pastes and spreadable condiments with gooey, soft cheeses, as the mouthfeel can be too smooshy/similar in the mouth.

OTHER MATCHES (NEVER HAVE I EVER)

Not all good matches make sense straight away. One of our favourite things to do is ask cheesemongers to tell us their best and weirdest pairing. To be fair, this often happens in America, where cheese cults and mongering are a big movement. Some of the strangest, but oddly satisfying, combinations we've heard of and have tested ourselves seem completely outrageous at first. But there's sound logic to them that checks out. Give them a go, if you're game.

♥ IT'S A MATCH

BACON + HONEY	chèvre
BONITO FLAKES	buffalo mozzarella
CAVIAR	Brillat-Savarin
CINNAMON RAISIN BAGEL	blues
COOKIES/ SHORTBREAD	Lancashire, chèvre, Gorgonzola Dolce
FRUIT CAKE	clothbound cheddars
KITKAT OR GINGER SNAPS	Stilton
LEMON CURD + RASPBERRIES	triple creams, mascarpone
MACARONS	Delice de Bourgogne
MATCHA MARSHMALLOW	chèvre
PANETTONE	mascarpone, Delice de Bourgogne
SALT AND VINEGAR CHIPS	feta
VEGGIE CRISPS OR BURNT BRISKET TIPS	Époisses

Bread & crackers

Created using natural fermentation, bread and cheese have long made a delicious union. While both are simple foods in terms of ingredients, it's the quality of these ingredients and the skill of the maker that transforms these products into something incredible. And, of course, they go exceptionally well together, with the crunch of bread crust, soft interior and toasty aroma and flavour a wonderful foil to cheese. Our general rule is to match the strength of the bread with the strength of the cheese, but if ever in doubt, you can't mess it up with a baguette.

Crackers, too, are a classic friend of cheese (despite us being raised as bread purists). They're not just for ferrying the cheese to your mouth: they also bring qualities of crunch, saltiness, sweetness and even bitterness, depending on the type. Crackers work best with spreadable, soft and semi-hard cheeses for textural contrast. Again, reach for a neutral-tasting cracker 95 per cent of the time, so as to not detract from the taste of the cheese.

BAGELS	spreadable rindless cheeses such as Galotyri or marinated feta, creamy bloomies
BAGUETTE	all cheeses
FRUIT BREAD	fresh cheeses, washed rinds, blues
OLIVE BREAD	creamy fresh cheeses
SOURDOUGH BREAD	bloomies, cheddars, Alpines, blues
WALNUT BREAD	cheddars, blues such as Roquefort or Stilton
WHOLEMEAL, PUMPERNICKEL OR RYE BREAD	washed rinds, firm Swiss cheeses such as Emmentaler, blues such as Roquefort

♥ CRACKERS: IT'S A MATCH

CHARCOAL CRACKERS	chèvre
CROSTINI	goat's cheeses
FRUIT OR NUT CRISPBREAD	blues, washed rinds
OATCAKES	blues such as Stilton
PLAIN WATER CRACKERS OR LAVOSH	most cheeses

✖ SWIPE LEFT

Crackers and bread that are overly flavoured.
Only pairing cheese with crackers (no bread).

Cheese with

drinks

Come aperitivo hour, the cheese board is often thrown together with cling-wrapped scraps of cheese from last week's soiree and served with whatever vino is in the cupboard. But you, your palate and your friends deserve better. Not to mention doing justice to those who have produced good wines and cheeses. To kick off this chapter, let's throw out a home truth here: just because a cheese is delicious and a wine is lovely, it can't be assumed they'll get along.

As with food pairings, a well-considered drink match can bring out the personality of your chosen cheese. There are a few guidelines to help smooth out this process and ensure you have a good time, but, of course, if you're into wildly experimental flavours, then feel free to ignore this and go nuts.

For most of us, though, we're looking for a smooth drinking partner to befriend our cheese. To find one, you'll need your drink to harmonise with the texture and flavour of a cheese. This means assessing a drink's favourable attributes, such as texture, effervescence, body, smell, flavour and temperature.

When deciding on a pairing, we suggest tuning into what you feel like drinking, rather than reaching for any alcoholic beverage you find loitering in the fridge or drinks cupboard.

Still unsure? Let's unpack this. Here's how to pair cheese and drinks like a pro in five easy steps.

1. Sip the beverage and allow it to coat your mouth.
2. Take a nibble of the cheese.
3. Sip the beverage again.
4. Now, swirl both around in your mouth together.
5. Breathe out through your nose to encourage the retronasal effects. Side note: if you're wondering what a retronasal effect is, it's a way of tasting via your olfactory system.

IS IT A MATCH?

What flavours come to you? Do the flavours, and thus the pairing, work? If it does, congratulations, you've met your match. If it doesn't feel right, let it go. In life and cheese, always trust your intuition.

Wine

First up, we must, unfortunately, stick an oversized novelty pin in the myth that wine matches easily with cheese. Pop! It doesn't. Like any relationship, there's light and shade. Wine, with its complexity of flavour, is in fact one of the most complex beverages to pair with cheese and can easily clash or be flat-out repulsive.

As with food pairings, the simplest approach is to look for similarities in taste and texture, or contrasts that enhance the character and strength of the cheese. Cheeses that go better with wine usually have a balanced flavour profile – for example, salty and sweet – and aren't going to be bossed around by the wine.

One of the challenges comes from our culture of eating cheese at the end of a meal. By this stage, we have peaked at full-bodied red wine, making it difficult to match with cheese. It's a hard place to come back from.

If you like to play it safe, but are determined to drink wine, go for white wine or sparkling, which both have higher acidity and clean flavours.

WHITE WINE & ROSE

White wine and rose can be more forgiving than red because they have fewer tannins and astringency and are lighter in alcohol. They are also more acidic and sharper in flavour, which provides balance to rich, salty cheeses.

♥ IT'S A MATCH

AROMATIC WHITES SUCH AS GEWÜRZTRAMINER (SWEET, SLIGHTLY SPICY)	washed rinds
DRY WHITES SUCH AS VERDEJO	mild, hard and nutty cheeses such as Beaufort
FRUIT-FORWARD WINES SUCH AS SWEET RIESLING	Alpines – their rich, dense flavours of nuts, toast and grass emphasise riesling's floral, delicate perfume and crisp finish
FULL-BODIED WHITES SUCH AS CHARDONNAY	hard, aged and nutty cheeses such as Gruyère and cheddars, sheep's milk cheeses, creamy and buttery cheeses such as brie and Havarti
LIGHT-BODIED WHITES SUCH AS SAUVIGNON BLANC	young chèvre such as Holy Goat's La Luna, mild and fresh cheeses such as fromage frais and fromage blanc (acidic and bright with a crisp finish)
ROSE AND ORANGE NATURAL WINES	Havarti, fresh cheeses such as buffalo mozzarella and ricotta

♥♥♥ SUPER LIKE

JURA WINE	Comté (what grows together, goes together). This pairing of Switzerland-adjacent products brings cool-climate flavours to the palate.

BUBBLES

Sparkling wines such as Champagne, Cava and Prosecco all have delightfully tongue-tingling bubbles, which add another dimension and sophistication to the palate. They prance around particularly well with creamy cheeses, including blues. This is down to how the butterfat in the cheese initially coats the tongue, before the bubbles wash over and remove that coating, acting as a pleasing palate-cleanser. Bubbles also match with harder and low-moisture cheeses including Alpines and Parmigiano Reggiano.

♥ IT'S A MATCH

AUSTRALIAN SPARKLING WINE	fresh young chèvre
CAVA	young Le Gruyère
CHAMPAGNE AND SPARKLING WINES	Pecorino, aged Gouda and Manchego (perhaps a surprising match to some, but the fizz bounces off the grittiness of the cheese), dreamy creamies such as Delice de Bourgogne (indulgent creamy cheeses coat the mouth and finish with a light, lactic kick before being washed away by bubbles), creamy blues such as Cashel Blue and Gorgonzola
PROSECCO	mascarpone, mozzarella

♥♥♥ SUPER LIKE

CHAMPAGNE	Langres. The concave well on the top of the cheese can cradle Champagne, brandy or Chablis. Simply pour 125 ml (½ cup) on top of the Langres and watch the cheese start to bubble. Serve immediately with chilled Champagne.

RED WINE

Apologies in advance, because what we're about to say will shake a few people's core beliefs. Red wine and cheese are akin to a bad Netflix series with a good promo. They seem to have all the elements for a quality production, but actually, it's a deflating experience. Red wines often contain a lot of tannins, which clash with cheese and overpower it, resulting in bitter, metallic or mousey flavours. As cheese is salty, this amplifies the bitterness. Red wines are an especially bad match for creamy cheeses.

If you *must* drink a red, stick to cleaner, lighter reds and choose cheeses with bold flavour profiles to help mind the gap. Go for blues, washed rinds or firm and aged cheeses such as Parmigiano Reggiano.

♥ IT'S A MATCH

CHILLED REDS	brie and other dreamy creamies with high acidity and brightness
PINOT NOIR	Alpines such as Gruyère, camembert, brie, smoked Gouda. This wine has soft tannins and high acidity, so can pair with some cheeses. It has red fruit and spice flavours.

✗ SWIPE LEFT

Tannic red wines and blue cheese deliver ratty flavours. Arrange a friend to call with a fake emergency, so you can escape this bad match.

DESSERT WINE

The sweet, lip-smacking dessert wine family includes sweet wines, such as Sauternes, as well as varieties of sherry, port and Madeira. Their mostly sweet and viscous attributes are a magnetising force for creamy blues and milky Alpine cheeses, with the wine swirling well with the intensity of blue mould, salt and spice. The opposing flavours and texture balance out to create a velvety journey we are all on board for.

♥ IT'S A MATCH

AMONTILLADO SHERRY	nutty, aged Alpines such as Beaufort and Gruyère – these make a harmonious pairing of toffee-on-toffee as well as nutty-with-nutty
FINO SHERRY	Manchego, feta
MOSCATEL SHERRY	Valedeón, Manchego
MOSCATO	Gorgonzola Dolce with biscotti
TAWNY PORT	hard cheeses such as Manchego, P'tit Basque and cheddars, blue cheeses such as Stilton, Roquefort and Gorgonzola – the port's fruit-and-nut sweetness balances well with the spicy, salty and savoury characteristics of blue cheese
TOKAJI (HUNGARIAN DESSERT WINE)	Roquefort

♥♥♥ SUPER LIKE

SAUTERNES	Roquefort. Both the wine and cheese have high minerality (hello, umami paradise!). Roquefort has an intense blue and salty flavour with a fatty texture, due to the sheep's milk, which is softened by the luscious texture and sweetness of the wine. Serve this tactile, textural pairing to stoke a little romance.

Beer

Beer might not be an obvious romantic counterpart for cheese, but can end up being a date that ends in great mates with its reliable, forgiving and balancing qualities. Matching beer is similar to matching wine, but instead of aiming for a complementary or harmonising flavour, you're looking for balance. You are aiming to balance the acidity, sweetness and/or bitterness of the beer with the cheese. Beer also has the bonus of effervescence with the bubbles creating a sensation on the tongue that, when combined with cheese, elevates the flavours of individual ingredients. Effervescence also helpfully cuts through the fat of cheese to cleanse your palate.

Like wine, beer comes with its own scientific rabbit holes that enthusiasts can merrily disappear down, but the ancient beverage can essentially be separated into two very broad categories: ale and lager.

ALE (STRONGER-TASTING BEER)

♥ IT'S A MATCH

DARK ALES, STOUTS AND PORTERS	aged Gouda, blues such as Roquefort and Stilton – stout's heavy earthiness pairs particularly well with the creamy richness of Stilton
FARMHOUSE ALES	cheddars – the buttery, grassy tang of cheddars partners with the sourness of farmhouse ales
FULL-BODIED ALES	Manchego, Stilton
INDIAN PALE ALES	Taleggio, hard, crumbly cheeses such as cheddars and Parmigiano Reggiano
LIGHT-BODIED ALES	brie or any young cheese
PALE ALES AND HOPPY BEERS	cheddars – their bold, buttery, grassy and acidic flavours go well with hoppy, toasty and strong ales

✕ SWIPE LEFT

Hoppy IPAs and intense stouts with bright, lactic cheeses such as fromage blanc – the flavour of the ales is too overpowering.

LAGER (MILDER-TASTING WITH FRUITY NOTES & LIGHTER MOUTHFEEL)

♥ IT'S A MATCH

CITRUS WHEAT BEERS	soft chèvre
FULL-BODIED LAGERS	Alpines such as Gruyère
PILSNERS AND LIGHT LAGERS	mozzarella, fresh chèvre, bloomies, Monterey Jack
SOURS	Brillat-Savarin, cheddars, mild washed rinds such as Soumaintrain, Stone & Crow Goat's Milk Tomme.

Cider

Sometimes sweet, sometimes scrumpy, always effervescent, ciders bring a new swag of matches to the table. When you think of pairing cheese and cider, consider which cheeses go with apple or pear. In general, reach for ciders that are complex, unfiltered and not overwhelmingly sweet.

Cider has enjoyed a long and mostly happy marriage with washed rind cheeses from Normandy. Its crisp acidity cosies up well with their funk. Similarly, English cheddars pair well with cider, as they romp together in nearby fields, singing the song of what grows together goes together. Ciders may also sip well with bloomies, the butterfat in the cheese creating a joyous juxtaposition with the acidity, contrasting against the richness of the cheese.

♥ IT'S A MATCH

ENGLISH NON-SWEET CIDERS	cheddars (particularly those from Somerset), Stilton
MEDIUM-DRY SPARKLING FARMHOUSE CIDERS	dreamy creamy bloomies such as Délice de Bourgogne – this assertive bloomy, with rich and peppery notes dances off the cider's dry qualities
NORMANDY CIDER	Normandy washed rinds such as Camembert and Pont-l'Évêque – their funk pairs with the cider's acidify

Sake

The union of cheese and sake is a little akin to going to a party you're dreading, only to meet an unexpected guest that turns out to be fabulous. The banter is strong, the conversation is interesting and, to your surprise, you want to do it all again. Not everything needs to be romantic to be fulfilling.

If selected carefully, sake can be the wingman to your cheese board. Its high alcohol content brings a pure and clean match for cheese. There are many types of sake, but our favourites for cheese are Daiginjo, Junmai and Nigori.

♥ IT'S A MATCH

DAIGINJO	Comté, hard sheep's milk cheeses such as Ossau-Iraty – the weight, richness and umami of the sake pair well with these cheeses
JUNMAI	Parmigiano Reggiano, Roquefort – the pure flavour of the sake works with the intense saltiness of these cheeses
NIGORI	Brillat-Savarin, Gorgonzola Dolce – the fruity notes of sake pair well with creamy and blue cheeses
SPARKLING SAKE	dreamy creamy bloomies will play off both sweet and dry sparkling sake

Whiskey

There is a lot to know when it comes to whiskey. But, for the purpose of pairing it with cheese, you have our permission to side-step the intricacies of this spirit and simply take a refresher of the basics.

Essentially, whiskey is a distilled spirit made from grains, such as corn and rye, which is aged in wooden barrels. This particular set of circumstances works rather well with cheese. When pairing, it's best to focus on the finish of your whiskey, rather than its first taste. The butterscotch and spicy notes of whiskey can be harmonised with cheeses that have butterscotch-forward profiles. They also seem to commune really well with flaky, aged-textured cheeses.

Also in the whiskey family is bourbon, a type of whiskey distilled from fermented grains, mostly corn, which impart the spirit's distinct sweetness.

♥ IT'S A MATCH

MELLOW WHISKEY	Alpines, Cashel Blue, cheddars, aged Gouda – the caramel notes in cheddars and aged Gouda work well with whiskey's natural spiciness
SINGLE MALTS	aged salty cheeses such as Isle of Mull cheese, Parmigiano Reggiano and Mahón, washed rinds – the savouriness of malt works with the bold flavours and gritty textures
TWICE-BARRELLED BOURBON	L'Amuse Signature Gouda
WHISKEY-BASED COCKTAILS, SUCH AS AN OLD-FASHIONED OR MANHATTAN	aged Gouda

Tea

Tea and cheese might be a seemingly unconventional pairing, but put down the scone and hear us out, because it's a delightful world to swirl around in. The experience is like a warm, encompassing embrace.

Like coffee and other warm drinks, the heat tea imparts opens up the flavours of cheese and can bring out dormant qualities of earthiness, fruitiness or sweetness. When pairing tea and cheese, remember that tea has tannins and astringency, so look to salty cheeses as well as those high in butterfat, as they both soothe bitterness.

♥ IT'S A MATCH

EARL GREY	Cornish Kern, Coolea, Alpines, aged Gouda – the latter has complex, caramel-hued and dense flavours, which complement the sweet bergamot in the tea
GREEN	chèvre with grassy notes such as Holy Goat's La Luna – the grassy, spring floral qualities of a light, bright green tea share freshness and vegetal aromas with goat's cheeses
LAPSANG (SMOKY)	blues – the smokiness of the tea stands up to the complexity and saltiness of the cheese
ROASTED, AGED CHINESE TEA	Alpines – the roastiness of the tea amplifies the nuttiness of the cheese
ROOIBOS	camembert, cheddars – the earthy flavours of rooibos work well with these cheeses
ROSE	Brillat-Savarin – the creaminess of the cheese benefits from something sweet and floral, although, really, any herbal fruity tea will go with that creamy rind

Coffee

Coffee and cheese may seem like an oddball match but, in fact, they're a wildly compatible duo. They're a bit like that couple who are so good together, it makes you feel slightly awkward to be in their orbit. Actually, this double act is less uncommon than you might think. Many Europeans enjoy cheese with their morning coffee, as do Americans with their love for coffee and cream cheese bagels.

Our favourite way to pair cheese and coffee is with filter coffee. Its clean flavour profile is a true expression of the bean, making it pretty easy to pair with cheese. As with cheese, no two coffees are the same. There are myriad intricacies within a single cup of coffee that change depending on the brewing method, where the beans originate, their age and seasonality, among other variables.

For an entry-level coffee and cheese pairing, begin with Alpine cheeses and filter coffee. The warmth of the coffee awakens the nutty, brown butter flavours of the cheese.

♥ IT'S A MATCH

ANY COFFEE	Gjetost (pronounced YAY-toast) – a caramelised Norwegian cheese made from the whey of goat's cheese
ESPRESSO	lemony chèvre and ricotta – try drizzling them with a little honey or maple syrup and enjoy with biscotti instead of bread
FILTER AND POUR-OVER BLACK COFFEE	aged Gouda, Section28 Monforte Reserve, Mimolette, Alpines with toffee notes – the warmth of coffee awakens the complex nutty and brown-butter flavours of cheeses in this style
MILKY COFFEE	Beaufort

✕ SWIPE LEFT

Blue cheeses and coffee. This deal-breaker may turn you right off coffee and cheese altogether.

Cocktails

Artisanal cheese and cocktails deserve more airtime. Both express creativity, originality and unique flavours. Cocktails can contrast well with cheese in various ways, from sweetness, sourness, creaminess and refreshing acidity. The important thing is to determine the direction and dominant flavours of the cocktail and work from there. Check out more of our favourite cheese and cocktail pairings on pages 154–7.

♥ IT'S A MATCH

COGNAC	aged Gouda, Mimolette
DARK AND STORMY (RUM)	aged Gouda
GIN-BASED	goat's cheese, Gouda, Gruyère – a good gin has a fresh taste with herbal and floral notes, so can match well with similar qualities in the cheese
MARGARITA	chèvre logs, Manchego – this pairing is all about contrast, as Manchego is salty and can have some bite, so balances well with the cocktail's acidity and the vegetal tequila
OLD-FASHIONED (WHISKEY)	Comté
SAKE-BASED	Alpines, Asiago, young Gouda
TEQUILA-BASED	mozzarella, tangy and buttery cheeses like Meredith Dairy marinated goat cheese
VODKA	fresh cheeses like mozzarella, Pecorino Romano, Parmigiano Reggiano, cheddars, blues such as Stilton

THE PERFECT CHEESE BOARD

Personally, we think the cheese board station in any room holds a special and almost spiritual resonance; it is the meeting place where many a good chat and banter occur within a comfortable rubbing shoulder distance of someone new or an old friend. If the cheese is particularly good, one of our favourite things to witness from afar is the pause in conversation, when a guest involuntarily muffles mid-mouthful: 'OMG … this cheese!' Always wide-eyed with expressions of glee, pleasure and delight on their face.

We love and celebrate the fact that cheese brings people together on so many occasions: dates, work drinks, weddings, funerals. Personally, we whip out a cheese board when everything else feels too hard to organise. It's our go-to crutch when we are wigging out that the mains at our dinner party might not be up to scratch, or late … Filling guests up on cheese upon arrival is a fantastic secret weapon to have in your arsenal (not very French, who would be outraged by moving it from the end of a meal, but it works a treat!).

For us, curating a simple cheese board is second nature and a no-brainer. But we are emotionally intelligent enough and have been around enough friends and strangers to know that many people find this a paralysingly daunting task. Some fear being judged on the combination of cheese. Others, the quality and how much to serve. Many feel vulnerable or exposed and lack confidence in their own art direction and curation of putting it all together, like you are being judged on your art (when you are not an artist!).

If reading this is increasing your stress levels and you are nodding in agreement, take a deep breath. It's going to be okay. Relax. We are about to rewire your relationship with the cheese board and help you create and curate like the dreamboat cheese god/goddess you are.

Set the mood

Pop on a playlist and pour yourself a glass of wine or a cup of tea. It's time to let the cheese do the talking and walking. We want this to be a pleasurable experience for you!

Plan your cheese board

If you haven't already done so, read our section on how to buy cheese (see page 20) to help you plan a board that includes a beautiful selection of different cheese textures, styles and flavours. Remember, it's not a competition on the amount or how many types of cheese you can cram on your cheese board. We recommend serving the below quantities, depending on when you're serving the cheese. Next, choose a theme or style of cheese board (see pages 74–9 for ideas). This is your canvas to do whatever the f*ck you want in a classy way.

WHEN	TOTAL CHEESE (PER PERSON)	NUTS (PER PERSON)	CONDIMENTS (PER PERSON)	VEG/FRUIT (PER PERSON)	CHARCUTERIE (PER PERSON)
AT THE START OF A MEAL WITH NIBBLES	50–80 g	1–2 tablespoons	1–2 tablespoons	4–6 pieces	30 g
CHEESE-ONLY DINNER	120–200 g	2–3 tablespoons	3–4 tablespoons	6–10 pieces	30 g
AFTER DINNER	80–150 g	1–2 tablespoons	1–2 tablespoons	4–6 pieces	—

Take your cheese out of the damn fridge!

If you only follow one rule, make it this one. The optimum temperature for serving cheese is 14–16°C. It's the opposite of how you like your Asahi beer or Coca-Cola. You want to give your cheese a chance to fully express its true flavour and texture, and to be at its optimum. Taking your cheese out of the fridge and sitting it at room temperature allows the fats and proteins to relax, so its aromas can be expressed and appreciated in full bloom.

Remove the cheese from its packaging and sit at room temperature for at least one hour before serving, depending on how warm or cool your room is (if you are running short of time, we will forgive a minimum 20 minutes). To be honest, we leave our cheeses out for two or three hours – especially camemberts and washed rinds – for the full reveal and effect. Cover the cheese with a cool damp linen cloth until you are ready to serve it to your guests. This allows the cheese to breathe, not dry out, and slowly rise in temperature. One exception to the out-of-the-fridge rule is blue cheese. Blues often need less time to come to room temperature than harder cheeses, due to their higher moisture content. Remove from the fridge around 30 minutes before serving and cover with a damp linen cloth or tea towel.

Take only the amount you will be serving out of the fridge. Refresh hard cheeses by scraping the exterior with the back of a knife to remove any dried or slightly discoloured surfaces. Washed rinds that appear dry on the rind can also be warmed back up by diluting white wine in water (1 tablespoon of wine to 125 ml (½ cup) of boiled and cooled water) and rubbing it into the rind to make it glisten a little.

We typically start compiling our cheese board an hour ahead of our guests arriving, adding charcuterie and condiments 15 minutes before serving and edible flowers or fresh herbs just moments before.

STUDD SIBLINGS
SECRET

When you f*ck up dinner
for your guests, fill them up
on bread and cheese.

Choose your surface

This is your blank canvas. Get creative and don't be afraid to mix and match different textures, colours and shapes, and use more than one surface. Think wooden boards, round slate, chalkboards, ceramic plates and cake stands, or materials, such as glass, books, tiles, marble, wicker, granite, stone, or even directly on a work surface with butcher's paper underneath for a cheese spread. A nonporous surface is best so that liquid or strong cheese odours are not absorbed.

Think about what base colour and shape will make your cheeses pop. For example, dark colours are great to contrast white bloomies. We lean towards larger plates and boards for aesthetics, and less chaos and risk of overcrowding. If you are doing a full-blown cheese spread on a table, think about varying the heights of boards by using wooden blocks as props to add to the overall aesthetic of the table.

Make it a cheese board, not a mandala

We know that cheese mandalas are trending hard on the 'Gram and with catering companies but, to be perfectly honest, we are not fans of this style of serving cheese, and instead like to channel the OG cheese board. It is frustrating to see cheese boards that make it hard for people to access the cheese because the accompaniments are so jammed in, and the spread looks overwhelmingly cluttered.

Adding fillers to make your board look fuller/emphasise your generosity is shooting yourself in the foot and dilutes the experience for your guests. It can be detracting and distracting. Instead, aim for a cheese board that is flowing and inviting for guests to tuck into. For assembly, we suggest placing the cheese on the board first, then adding your pairings one at a time, and then bread and crackers. This way, the cheese remains the star of the show.

Call us weirdos or perfectionists, but we find an odd number of cheeses looks most attractive on a cheese board. Choose one, three, five or seven cheeses. We suggest following one of the themes listed on pages 74–9, as they offer your guests a balanced experience. If serving multiple cheeses, varying milk type, country and textures is ideal. Alternatively, you can serve the same type of cheese and use vertical comparisons; for example, clothbound cheddars from the US, Australia and England – just make sure you select the right cheese crowd to present this to.

Arrange your cheeses from 'mild to wild' either in a circle (with mild at 12 o'clock) or a line. Let your guests know where to start and encourage them to enjoy each cheese in that order at least once. If you have a wedge, point the triangle nose inwards. Always start with the dreamy creamies and goat's cheeses, then build up to the washed rinds and end with a blue. In terms of milk types, the order should be goat, sheep, then cow. Place complementary pairings near the appropriate cheese so your guests know what goes with what.

Choose a *few* thoughtful pairings that match your cheese rather than going OTT. Some juxtapositions of texture and flavour can create a harmonious experience. Make sure the elements of crunch, acidity or sweetness are considered, as well as how they will play with the overall flavour. Use this as an opportunity to add colour to your board, too. Here are some further tips.

- Try your pairings before serving to see if they work, and make sure there is enough room for guests to access the cheese from any angle.
- Aim for produce to be in season for optimum taste and use complementing colours for effect.

- Cut fruit and veggies into bite-sized pieces so they're easy to snack on and dip with. The same goes for sweet additions such as dark chocolate.
- For accompaniments such as honey, jam and olives, it looks sexier to contain them in small vessels, such as mini glass jars, wooden bowls or ceramic dishes. Always check the size and scale here – a giant accompaniment next to a small cheese is not the aim of the game.
- Bread or crackers can go in a bowl beside your cheese board, so you can easily refill it.
- Add charcuterie sparingly, as it is very salty and can compete with cheeses that are also strong, salty, gamey and fatty.

If you want to skip accompaniments altogether, go for it. Simply serve your cheese on a large board with a knife or spoon and some bread.

Choose your vehicle – bread vs crackers

Before we even go there, let us preface this by saying that we grew up in a cheese-purist household that ate cheese 'as is' 99 per cent of the time ... meaning from the knife to the mouth. Obvious reasons for this are the appreciation of cheese in its purest form, witnessing and experiencing the quality and texture, just as the cheesemaker intended.

In the real world, however, most people prefer to use a vehicle to support the journey of cheese to their mouth. So our next purist answer is to suggest a fresh, crunchy baguette – like the French do. A baguette provides a versatile and neutral vehicle that still showcases the cheese.

In saying this, it is time for another confession ... swirl on by either of our homes on a Friday afternoon, and you will most likely find a stack of Vita-Weats, a jar of pickles and a healthy slice of Comté on the countertop. We get it! Crackers are sometimes a thing, and we agree they can add some sexy texture and crunch, especially to soft cheeses. If crackers make an appearance, the same rules apply as bread – make sure they are as neutral as possible to complement, not distract from, your cheese.

The final touch

The final touch to a cheese board can be a garnish to reinforce your theme and add some festivity. Fresh herbs, such as rosemary, sage and thyme, work well, as do holly, pine needles or native gum leaves. Edible flowers, such as lavender, carnations, daisies and roses, can be a delicate touch to add brightness and colour. Add edible flowers and fresh herbs to your cheese board moments before serving.

STUDD SIBLINGS SECRET

Arrange your cheeses from 'mild to wild', either in a circle (with mild at 12 o'clock) or a line.

HOW TO CUT CHEESE

(AKA 'SUGGESTIVE' CUTTING)

By using the following illustrations as a guide, you will ensure your guests get the best taste in every slice or mouthful of cheese. These guides can also add an important visual element to your cheese board. Cutting your cheeses from the centre to the outside allows your guests to experience the full range of flavour, from the outside, which is stronger and more intense, to the milder centre.

In general, keep soft cheeses in their original shape with a suggestive slice cut out for your guests to copy. For harder cheeses, pre-cut slices or crumbles next to a wedge can look best. If you are cutting slices, do this just before serving to your guests so they don't dry out, wilt or sweat.

The way to cut depends on the cheese type and shape. Here are some general rules to follow. Please do not cut cheese into cubes. You are better than that.

Fresh/oozy cheeses (burrata, ricotta, crème fraîche, mascarpone): Serve these in their own vessel with a spoon for smearing.

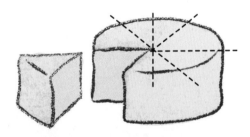

Wheels (camembert, Brillat-Savarin, Soumaintrain): Approach these cheeses like you would a cake by cutting the wheel into equal wedges. Encompass a cross-section of the whole, from the centre to the rind, so each person gets a taste of the different flavours from the outside to the middle. If the cheese is particularly gooey (Époisses), a fork can be used to hold the rind while you cut.

Bark-wrapped wheels (Le Duc Vacherin, Long Paddock Driftwood): Score the rind on top by following where the rind meets the spruce. Cut a half or full circle 'lid' and peel back the spruce like a sardine can. Lick and discard! Plunge a spoon into the cheese, or rip off and drag hunks of bread through it.

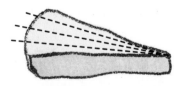

Soft wedge-shaped cheeses (brie): A cheese harp/wire or skeleton knife can assist here. Cut from the centre of the narrow edge outwards. Because the nose of the brie is considered the best part, ideally everyone should have a piece.

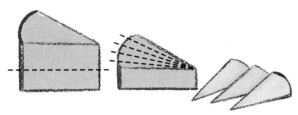

Firm, triangular wedges

Option 1: 'The triangle' (Manchego): If the wedge is thick, consider cutting it into two smaller triangles. Cut into thin triangle slices, keeping the back rind attached for serving so that your guests can use it as a handle. The rind also adds a nice visual and textural element. This is a classic cut for Manchego.

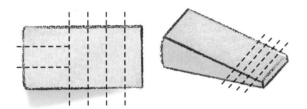

Option 2: 'The matchstick' (Alpines, Gouda): This can be used for larger triangular wedges or rectangular pieces of cheese. Place it horizontally in front of you and cut it into two portions about one-third of the way along the cheese. Cut the two-thirds piece lengthways and one-third piece widthways into 5 mm thick strips. These strips help to release maximum aroma and flavour and even flavour distribution. You can leave the rind on one end for a handle.

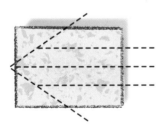

Blue cheeses (Roquefort, Stilton, Fourme d'Ambert, Danish Blue, Gorgonzola): A long, thin knife can help cut sticky blues like Roquefort. If a wedge is possible, aim for guests to access equal blueness. Slice it into points from the centre of the thin edge of the wedge. If the cheese is too crumbly, 'the crumble' can suffice.

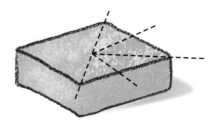

Square cheeses (Pont-l'Évêque, Taleggio): Apply the same philosophy as for wheel cheeses, but cut into cute triangles. Cut from corner to corner to begin.

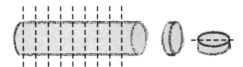

Logs and cylindrical-shaped cheeses (chèvre, Holy Goat's La Luna): Cut into coins/thin rectangles, around 1–2 cm thick. Aim for an even rind-to-paste ratio.

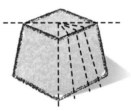

Pyramid-shaped cheeses (Valençay): Cut corner to corner, then smaller, taller diagonal wedges from the top.

'The crumble', for crumbly, hard wedges (Parmigiano Reggiano, clothbound cheddars): Put the tip of the knife in the wedge and wiggle it a little to encourage large crumbles. Leave the knife there so guests can do the same.

WHICH KNIFE TO USE

Always follow the rule of one knife, one cheese. This protects your guests from experiencing shmooshed weird flavours and prevents different moulds from hopping between cheeses. The cheese knife you choose should be based on the texture of the cheese. If you're limited in knives, dipping a knife into boiling water and wiping between cuts can help make your cuts cleaner when preparing a cheese board. If you were to choose two essential cheese knives, we recommend a thin-bladed cheese knife for soft cheeses and a large, long chef's knife for hard (see picture opposite).

Spreader: Sometimes called a dull spreader due to its rounded edge. Perfect for very soft cheeses like ricotta.

Skeleton knife: The large holes prevent the cheese from sticking to the blade. Use for gooey cheeses, such as brie.

Thin blade/offset cheese knife: Skinny blade to decrease surface area. Great for soft cheeses, such as double creams, up to semi hards. The angled handle assists cutting.

Spade knife: Rounded head like a spear. Good for cutting chunks of hard cheese, such as Parmigiano Reggiano.

Forked tip/spear knife: All-purpose knife for soft and semi-hard cheeses. The fork can be used to spear cheese for transfer onto a plate or into your mouth.

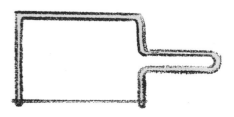

Cheese wire: Good for soft and semi-hard cheeses, such as chèvre. Enables a clean cut.

Cleaver: Wide, rectangular blade like an axe. Perfect for hard and firm cheeses, especially if you are doing the rockstar cheese board on page 74, but not essential.

Cheese plane: Good for shaving semi-hard cheeses, such as Havarti and Fontina, and hard cheeses like Emmentaler. Can leave unattractive marks on the remaining cheese.

Other cheese props

Some people like to add cheese labels. If your cheese comes in a wooden box, you can use it as a prop and put the cheese on top of it. Go with whatever feels the most natural to you.

Other props can be bought online or hired from cheese shops to make a fun addition to a cheese party.

Girolle: This is the cheese turner that makes the flowers of cheese you see on Instagram. It was originally made for Tête de Moine cheese which, to be honest, is an acquired taste. We have used it on other small-wheeled firm cheeses, such as P'tit Basque, with pleasing results. Your cheesemonger will be able to help you choose a suitable cheese.

Fondue pot: What could be cuter than guests dipping into a communal pot of bubbling melted cheese with long, tiny forks?! Some fondue sets can be lit by tea light candles, while others have all the bells and whistles. Fondue pots add some novelty to a party or gathering. Assess your cupboard space to ascertain whether you buy, rent or borrow. If you want a less fancy version, we have been known to make fondue in a ceramic pot on the stove and dip in from there. Baked cheese in its box is also a great alternative (see pages 180–1 for recipes).

Raclette grill: This grill turns cheese into a golden melted centrepiece, which is then scraped onto potatoes, charcuterie and pickles. It's fabulous for large events and parties, and totally worth it for all the oohs and aahs you will receive from your guests as you scrape the cheese from the grill. You can rent a large grill for half wheels of Raclette or buy smaller individual raclette trays (very on trend at the moment) online. Our top cheeses to melt on a raclette grill are Raclette (in particular, Heidi Farm Raclette) and Emmentaler.

THREE WAYS TO PUT TOGETHER AN EXCEPTIONAL CHEESE BOARD

Anyone can throw together a cheese board, but to really land that lactose-laden snack plate with style, you'll need some (board) game. Consider this your guide to serving up an impressive collection of cheese with perfectly matched accompaniments.

1. THE ROCKSTAR CHEESE BOARD

This involves choosing one rockstar cheese to steal the show. It is a deliberate and intentional attempt to make your guests do a doubletake, be present for the one-star show, and be wowed. Because you are presenting just one cheese, you can pool your money into something more expensive, in optimum condition. We choose this approach for small gatherings (two to six people). For larger get-togethers, we serve a sizeable chunk or wheel with a knife stuck into it for guests to gather a nugget for themselves. If accompaniments are added, they should be classic, flawless and kept to a minimum for an all-round show-stopping performance. Here are some examples.

- Brillat-Savarin, served with a spoon and a chilled bottle of Champagne. Optional additions: bread, honeycomb or dark chocolate.
- Hunk of quality Parmigiano Reggiano, served with a knife stabbed into it to encourage guests to nibble and crumble it themselves, with some aged balsamic to drizzle on top of a bite-sized nugget of cheese.
- Langres, with Champagne poured over the dip in the cheese.
- Hunk of farmhouse cheddar with a knife stabbed in. Or, if you need to make a plate of it, make a ploughman's board with sourdough, ham, pickles, slices of apple, a spicy relish and mustard.

- Stilton, served with glasses of port.
- Rogue River Blue Cheese Special Reserve, served with walnut bread.
- 1 kg wheel of Le Duc Vacherin or artisan brie, baked with wine and garlic and served with a crusty baguette.
- Homemade ricotta, served with honey, thyme, figs, pistachios, crunchy salt, toasted bread and a chilled bottle of Prosecco.
- Fresh mozzarella, served with freshly shaved truffle.

PICTURED

1. Brillat-Savarin, Will Studd

2. THE CEREMONIAL CHEESE BOARD

'Something old, something new, something stinky, something blue.'

For this cheese board, one cheese is chosen from each of these categories. Feel free to ditch a category if you want to make a simpler spread, but the saying is a good one to remember all the same. Pair each cheese with a contrasting accompaniment. Within this rule, think of mixing up different textures of cheese and arranging them from mild to wild. You can add a couple from one category if you are obeying our odd number of cheeses on a cheese board rule.

Old: Choose one cheese from our firm section (see page 128). Examples include: clothbound cheddar, Comté, Manchego, Pecorino Romano, Ossau-Iraty, Parmigiano Reggiano, aged Gouda. For cheeses such as Manchego and Pecorino Romano that will probably come in wedges, cut them into thin triangle slices with the back rind attached so your guests can use it as a handle to pick it up. It also adds a visual and textural element. For blocks, such as cheddar and Parmigiano Reggiano, keep the cheese as a larger wedge and crumble it.

New: Choose a cheese from the rindless (see page 84) or bloomy sections (see page 96) for their soft, creamy texture. Examples include: Brillat-Savarin, burrata, ricotta, crème fraîche, mascarpone, fresh chèvre, feta. These cheeses match well with something sweet, like honey. Oozy cheeses will need their own vessel.

Stinky: Select a cheese from our washed rind section (see page 118). These cheeses will usually be semi-soft and add some funk to your cheese board. Examples include: Raclette, Taleggio, Pont-l'Évêque, King River Gold; camembert also works. They go well with something moist and crunchy, like a pickle, so put some nearby.

Blue: This is for the blue lovers out there. Examples include: Roquefort, Stilton, Berrys Creek Riverine Blue, Gorgonzola. See our blue cheese section on page 106 for more ideas. Blue cheese is usually stronger and bolder in taste, so you don't need to serve as much. Blue cheese pairs really well with the sweet things in life, like fruit and honey. Serve crumbled or in wedges.

PICTURED

1. Quicke's Clothbound Cheddar
2. Ossau-Iraty, Agour
3. Mothais sur Feuille
4. Monte Rosso, Section28
5. Cashel Blue

3. CHOOSE YOUR OWN ADVENTURE

Pick a theme and run with it. Think about the golden rules of diversifying the textures within your chosen adventure. Here are some ideas for themes to get you started.

- Different countries: Cheese from Spain, England, France, Italy.
- Same country, different styles.
- Different milk types: Cow, goat, sheep, buffalo.
- Same milk type.
- Seasonal spread: An autumn cheese board with washed rinds; light and fresh cheeses for summer; goat's cheeses for spring; and baked and Alpine cheeses for winter. Serve with in-season fruits and veggies.

PICTURED: AUSTRALIAN THEMED BOARD

1. Raw Milk C2, Bruny Island
2. Driftwood, Long Paddock
3. La Luna Barrel, Holy Goat

TYPES OF CHEESE

CATEGORISING CHEESE

Truth be told, cheese doesn't want to be put in a box. There's no mystical, unifying system for adequately categorising cheese. The world of cheese is near infinite and incredibly nuanced, so any attempt to square cheese away in a Dewey Decimal System–style classification is inevitably flawed. In researching this book, this was the hardest chapter to nut out, with every single cheese book having a vastly different take on categorisation.

Traditional systems have categorised cheese by milk type and country. Cheesemakers and those who work in cheese often use microbiological or technical classifications based on how a cheese is made. Recently, there have been some new-age systems, which pragmatically guide consumers to loose categories with gateway cheeses.

The problem with categorising cheese by country and milk type is the limitation on the inclusion of new-age cheeses. Many countries have broadened their variety of artisan cheeses, extending beyond the traditional catalogue they've been known for excelling at for centuries.

Still, it's helpful to take a broad look at what a few countries are traditionally recognised for when it comes to artisan cheesemaking.

BRITAIN: The Brits make excellent clothbound cheddars, as well as English territorials such as Cheshire, Wensleydale and Lancashire cheeses.

FRANCE: Of course, this cheese-loving country takes the (cheese) cake for many cheeses, but the French are especially good at bloomies and washed rinds.

GREECE: As we all know, this country is synonymous with traditional barrel-aged Feta.

ITALY: From the Italians we have been bequeathed Pecorino, Parmigiano Reggiano and fresh cheeses such as ricotta and burrata.

SPAIN: Manchego and other hard sheep's milk cheeses are produced here.

SWITZERLAND: Rolling meadows populated by Swiss cows produce fine Alpine cheeses such as Gruyère and Emmentaler.

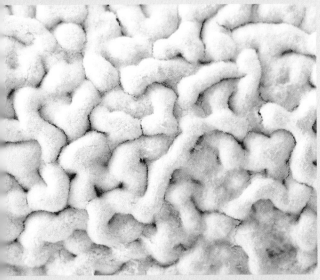

If you adopt a technical systems approach, it can be handy to understand the characteristics of what makes a certain cheese based on its microbiology and cheese-making techniques. The challenge is that a cheese will often fit into multiple categories. Take, for example, the French Reblochon, which is primarily a washed rind, while also being a washed curd cheese that's bloomy; or there's Cambozola, which is a bloomy and blue.

Because you are not a microbiologist who specialises in cheese, but rather, an ordinary cheese-loving human looking for a bit more knowledge on how to choose damn good cheese, we've whittled down our classification process to be as streamlined as possible. We've organised cheese into five categories or broad types, loosely based on their techniques and characteristics. Some cheeses will overlap and fit into a couple of categories, which we have noted in the individual cheese ID. Some of the categories have been further broken down into subcategories, which, although not ideal, speaks to the reality of the complexities of cheese. It's an intricate web that will probably never be solved. Sigh.

If it all gets too much with the subcategories, go back to the basic five. At the end of the day, it's about slowly piecing together clues about a cheese type when you see it in a cheese shop or on a cheese board. After reading this chapter, you will be able to make declarations about a cheese's character with relative confidence. 'Oh, I think this is a bloomy, because it's white and fluffy.' Or 'This smells and is orange, so it's a washed rind, and, do I detect some meatiness?' Just a warning, though, please use your newfound knowledge responsibly and don't bore other partygoers with unnecessary cheese chat.

Our intention in this section is to guide you in becoming familiar with the unique qualities of a cheese. And, most importantly, help you eat cheese that you enjoy. This section will provide you with some landmark flags to orientate you in the world of cheese and empower you to wade through the endless sea of cheese types. It is to be used in conjunction with the Cheese Essentials chapter, where we share insights into buying and storing cheese, and how to be a curious investigator of a cheese's rind, interior texture and flavour, as well as what to pair it with. This chapter is by no means an encyclopedia of all the cheeses out there, more just our top picks.

RINDLESS

'Cheese is born of a miracle.'
CLIFTON FADIMAN

Turning milk into cheese is primordial. We personally feel it is one of the human race's most outstanding culinary achievements. However, the knowledge of cheesemaking didn't simply manifest like some mystical gift bestowed upon us mortals by higher beings. As with many of humanity's most notable triumphs, cheese came into this world through the ever-prosperous alchemy of survival and sustenance. In other words, necessity. The jury is out as to when exactly the miracle of cheese occurred, but historians and archaeologists suggest it was at least 8000 years ago in the Fertile Crescent, often called the 'cradle of civilisation', which you'd know as modern-day Turkestan and Iran.[2] Cheese was most likely discovered by a fortunate accident and, initially, took the form of a rindless cheese.

The nomadic people who inhabited this area travelled relentlessly between pastures, with their goats and sheep in tow. Milk was considered an important, yet rare, nutrient source that was only available during the lactation period in the warmer months. The creationist theory of how cheese was discovered teaches that excess milk was stored in bags made from the stomachs and skins of livestock animals for transportation. A mixture of heat, acidification and rennet (enzymes present in ruminant guts) was the ideal environment to kick off the process of cheesemaking and separate the curds and whey. These nomadic people soon realised that turning milk into cheese was a fantastic and delicious way to extend the life of this precious sustenance. The whey made an excellent nutritional drink or could be fermented into alcohol (bonus!), while the curd could be eaten fresh or dried, strained, shaped and kept for a later date. This is how cheese was born and provided humans with the rudimentary building blocks of cheesemaking, which, although much evolved, continue to be used to this day.

What is a rindless cheese?

The one and only defining characteristic of this category is that none of these cheeses have any rind development. They are the purest and most simple expressions of cheese and, when made well, you'll find your face turns to the heavens to thank God for their existence. The rindless cheese category covers more than you might expect, and includes cheeses ranging from delicate, creamy fresh curds and oozy mozzarella, to crumbly Greek barrel-ripened Feta. To help navigate this broad category, we've separated it into three parts: fresh, stretched and brined. Rindless cheeses often sit within multiple subcategories. For example, mozzarella is both stretched curd and fresh.

As with all cheese, the personality of rindless cheese depends on the type of milk and starters used and how the curds are handled. Rindless cheeses are generally made with large, juicy, delicate curds and require a lot of care when handling. These curds retain their moisture and are naturally high in fats, proteins, minerals and milk sugars (lactose), giving this cheese type its distinctive sweet and milky characteristics.

Unlike other types of cheese, rindless cheese doesn't rely on its rind for maturation or to develop a flavour profile. Hence, these cheeses are really all about the quality of the milk, the season and what the animals have been grazing on, as well as the intricacies of the cheesemaking process, for their flavour.

Making these cheeses is relatively simple and requires minimal equipment. The milk is curdled by acidifying bacteria (starters), which help to convert the lactose into lactic acid. A coagulant is added to knit the milk proteins together and turns the milk into curds.

Some rindless cheeses, such as chèvre, undergo a long, slow acidification process with a small amount of rennet, resulting in a fragile and delicate texture. Mozzarella, on the other hand, undergoes a shorter acidification process and the curds are heated, resulting in a stretchy and meltable texture. As you can see, the rindless category covers a lot of ground and a surprising array of different cheeses, but remains one of the most fundamental types of cheese.

Types of rindless cheese

FRESH

Fresh cheese is exactly what it sounds like. It can be defined as cheese that is typically only a few days old, does not always contain rennet and should always be eaten fresh. They are easy to recognise as they have no rind, a high moisture content, uniform texture and are wet to the touch. They can be enjoyed on their own and are characterised by a light, bright milky flavour. This subcategory includes, but is not limited to: cottage cheese, ricotta, fromage frais, mascarpone, cream cheese, quark, paneer and fresh chèvre. A general rule of thumb for this subcategory is the higher the moisture content, the shorter the shelf life.

Cultures around the world who practise traditional cheesemaking all have their own signature fresh rindless cheese, and it will often be the star of their traditional dishes. Examples include chèvre from France, ricotta from Italy and paneer from India. Today, many industrial giants make poor imitations of these traditional cheeses, so when talking about buying local cheeses, it is never more important than in this category.

STRETCHED

Stretched curd cheeses or 'pasta filata', Italian for 'spun paste', are aptly named because the curd undergoes a stretching process. This creates their desirable and characteristically stringy, squidgy, elastic and stretchy qualities – perfect for cooking. The process begins with milk being curdled; the curds are cut into pieces and the whey is drained off. The curds are then steeped in hot whey or water, and when they begin to float, the liquid is drained off and the curds are stretched until smooth and elastic. Finally, the cheese is divided and chopped into the desired size and shape.

This process aligns the protein structure of the curds into strands, allowing the cheese to have better stretchability. Temperature is critical in this process and it relies heavily on the skill, intuition and judgement of the cheesemaker. The longer the curds spend in the hot whey or water, the more resistant they will be to heat.

The most famous stretched curd cheese is mozzarella, but this cheese type also includes a broad range of other cheeses, such as bocconcini, caciocavallo and provolone. Theses cheeses have varying shelf lives, depending on how they are stored or packaged. For example, provolone is dipped in wax to protect it from the atmosphere and can last months or even years. It is also a brined cheese and, therefore, belongs in both subcategories.

BRINED & OILED

Humans have been pickling and brining fresh food to prevent decay for an exceedingly long time. Cheese is no different, and the process of placing cheese in brine or oil can be traced back centuries. The longevity of these cheeses relies on removing oxygen and preserving the fresh cheese by secreting it away from the atmosphere through a sort of mummification process. As you can imagine, in a time before refrigeration, mould growth, spoilage and cracking were problematic. There was no nipping to the shop for a replacement, and you'd have to wait months for the lactation period of your flock to roll around again. Hence people came up with the solution of lovingly drowning cheese in brine or oil. By submerging fresh cheese this way, a previously perishable and fragile rindless cheese, with a life expectancy similar to a butterfly, suddenly became near indestructible.

This process can also add flavour complexity to a cheese, through salt or aromatics that have been added to the brine solution or oil. Examples include feta, halloumi and goat's curd in oil.

Look

Because rindless cheeses do not have a rind there should be no distinction between the interior and exterior. Unfortunately, the absence of a rind makes these naked gems quite prone to spoilage, unless they are brined, waxed or oiled. Once opened and exposed to air, even brined cheeses will also succumb to a particularly short shelf life. But it's this fragility of youth that makes them so delicious. Keep your eyes peeled for handmade varieties of rindless cheese – fragile curds are sensitive and affected by human touch, so will often be better in quality and have more integrity when hand made.

A defining characteristic of fresh rindless cheeses is that they are usually bright-white in colour, which should remain intact up until consumption. If these cheeses don't have a uniform texture and colour, it's a sure sign they've begun their descent into a sad and unstoppable decay. They may be ivory, ecru or golden if they have been preserved.

Texture

The texture of rindless cheeses varies a lot depending on style. It can range from spreadable to oozy to bouncy. Avoid cheeses with grainy textures and splotches of discolouration throughout.

Taste & aroma

Rindless cheese should smell light, delightfully fresh, milky and almost of nothing (similar to a smell test for fresh fish). Flavour derived from maturation, which comes with multiple ripening bacteria and enzymes, combined with time (months or even years), isn't an option for fresh cheese. As such, these cheeses tend to taste like the milk from which they're made, augmented by salt or oil, but should never be boring. Cow's milk and buffalo's milk are usually reserved for fresh rindless cheeses, and generally have an approachable, clean flavour. Other milk types, such as sheep's and goat's milk, are usually turned into brined cheeses and will hold stronger flavours as a result. Relish their transience and youthful flavours that include sweet, mild, milky, buttery, creamy, delicate, salty, acidic, tart, tangy, lemony and yeasty.

Top global rindless cheeses

TRADITIONAL MOZZARELLA

Made: Italy (and the rest of the world)
Milk: Cow, buffalo

Mozzarella can be one of the most delectable and cosmic of cheese-eating experiences, but it depends on what sort of mozzarella you are chewing on. The name is used to describe a whole variety of different cheeses that range from industrial rubbery blocks and the dry shredded stuff you find at the supermarket, to the mouth-watering velvety parcel of stretched curd that swims in a light brine at your local deli. The latter is, in essence, what rindless cheeses are: fresh, with high moisture and a sweet, milky taste.

The word 'mozzarella' derives from the Italian verb 'mozzare', meaning 'to cut off', referring to the method of stretching and pulling the warm curd, then cutting it and forming it into various shapes. This process can be done by hand or machines, especially as the cheesemaker needs to withstand high temperatures and can easily scald their hands. The length of time the curd is stretched and heated impacts the texture and flavour.

Mozzarella originates from Campania in Southern Italy. Its existence can be traced as far back as the 3rd century, with one myth suggesting it was discovered by accident when some curds fell into a bucket of hot water in a cheese vat in Naples. It was probably first made with sheep's milk, until buffalo were introduced to the region from Southern Asia and became 'the cow of Campania'. Today, mozzarella is one of the most popular cheeses in the world, with most examples now made using cow's milk due to cost. In Italy, the fresh cow's milk version is called fior di latte.

Buy handmade and locally made fresh mozzarella if you can. Handmade mozzarella will be oval in shape and have a rough seam formed by the cheesemaker's hands. Industrial versions will have a rubbery texture, with no seam.

Mozzarella is best eaten as close to fresh as possible before its tenuous connection to the physical realm dissolves. Make sure to store it in brine, whether from the deli counter or pre-packaged. Once the seal is broken, consume rapidly, and keep for no more than three days.

Mozzarella is a bit of a chameleon. It comes in many different shapes, sizes and degrees of quality. Here are the basic groups of mozzarella and the extended pasta filata family.

BOCCONCINI

Meaning 'small mouthfuls', bocconcini are adorable, bite-sized forms of mozzarella. They're perfect for adding to salads or enjoying in a single bite with fresh basil and tomato on an antipasti plate. Due to their smaller size, they are firmer in texture.

BUFFALO MOZZARELLA

Mozzarella di Bufala Campana PDO is the name-protected cheese from Campania. Made from water buffalo's milk, it is technically the only 'authentic mozzarella'. You will have to add this cheese to your bucket list for when you are in Italy, as eating it will likely result in an out-of-body experience, with its rich, succulent texture and taste. Local versions of mozzarella made from buffalo's and cow's milk are available in Australia. Any 'authentic' Mozzarella di Bufala imported from Campania, Italy, will most likely have been frozen and defrosted.

The main difference between cow's and buffalo's milk mozzarella is that mozzarella made with buffalo's milk will have a more succulent texture, whiter colour and pronounced richer taste, with grassy notes and a balanced tang. Cow's milk mozzarella has a tighter texture, buttery aroma and will taste mild, milky and sweet.

LOOK: Porcelain white and firm. Fresh stretched curd cheeses should have a glistening, glossy skin without any interior holes.

TEXTURE: Variable, depending on the size of the ball. Fior di latte and mozzarella balls should shred in a similar way to poached chicken, rather than be tough or claggy.

TASTE & AROMA: Fresh, milky, creamy and grassy with floral notes and a hint of tang.

EAT WITH: Best celebrated in a Caprese salad or on a pizza, but also slips very well into a lasagne or eggplant parmigiana. Fresh mozzarella and tomatoes are an exquisite union of perfection. Go all in and find beautiful heirloom tomatoes and top with basil leaves and good-quality extra-virgin olive oil, finishing with a good crack of black pepper. Mozzarella also tastes great with roasted capsicums and grilled zucchini, or a lightly toasted baguette rubbed with garlic and your choice of olive oil.

DRINK WITH: Rose, sauvignon blanc or pinot grigio; Prosecco; low-tannin beer.

BURRATA

This orb of creamy decadence makes any meal special! The name 'burrata' translates to 'buttery' in Italian. The concept of adding cream and mozzarella strips to fresh stretched cheese was born in the 1920s out of the desire to reduce cheese scraps and waste.

The technique used to make burrata is similar to that of mozzarella, with the hot curds hand-stretched. The cream and rags are then added to the mozzarella skin, which is said to require both skill and intuition by the cheesemaker. The top is then twisted at the neck. Traditionally, the cheese was wrapped in green asphodel leaves, a relative of the leek. It should be buttery, milky and herbaceous in taste.

CACIOCAVALLO

Made using cow's or sheep's milk, 'caciocavallo' translates to 'horse cheese', referring to the way it is traditionally cured by tying two cheeses together over a wooden beam, similar to saddling bags over a horse's back. This is another snowman/pear-shaped pasta filata–style cheese. It can be grilled, fried or served fresh as a table cheese.

FIOR DI LATTE MOZZARELLA

If you want to sound like you know what you are talking about, mozzarella made from cow's milk is called 'fior di latte', meaning 'flower of the milk'. This is your classic and most accessible type of mozzarella and probably what first comes to mind when you think of fresh mozzarella. Made with fresh, whole cow's milk, it has a sweet, light and milky flavour, with an elastic texture. It usually comes in a plastic tub or small plastic bag filled with brine.

NODINI

This cheese is basically mozzarella dressed in drag and is formed by knotting the curds together. The elegant shape of the little knots makes it a great cheese to serve during festive occasions or to show off to your mates. It has a chewy, spongy texture.

PROVOLONE

This is more or less hard mozzarella that has been brined. It has a smooth 'rind' with a mild, mellow taste when young and bitey and metallic when aged. As well as age, provolone varies in shape and size, from round cantaloupes and salami logs to pears. It is hung from a rope or twine to age, which creates the cheese's dense yet pliable texture. This is one of the biggest culprits you see hanging above the counters of traditional delis (the other is caciocavallo).

SCAMORZA

Scamorza is a pasta filata cow's milk cheese that has been further stretched than mozzarella, so is a little firmer. Pear-shaped and with a semi-soft texture, scamorza is eaten fresh or aged for around two weeks by hanging from a string. You will often find it smoked, which can add sweetness and acidity to the flavour.

STRACCIATELLA

This cheese is the underrated cousin of burrata and is often cheaper, but just as tasty. Soft, dreamy and oh-so creamy! Deriving its name from the Italian word 'straccia', meaning 'rag' or 'shred', stracciatella is created with shreds of mozzarella curds and fresh cream. It is lusciously spoonable and perfect for spreading atop bread or even stirring through pasta.

MASS-PRODUCED MOZZARELLA

Sold pre-shredded or in dry bulbus blocks tightly wrapped in plastic, processed mozzarella is firm, low in moisture and rubbery. The flavour is very mild and a little salty. It is used in cooking (such as pizza), as it produces the perfect melt with satisfying cheese pull, without becoming watery. However, don't be fooled by its low price tag; it is an inferior imposter to fresh mozzarella. Having said this, there is a time and place for this type of cheese, but if you want to try the real deal (fresh mozzarella) in a recipe, splash out and buy the traditional – you'll be surprised at how much better your dish tastes. When cooking with fresh mozzarella on things like pizza, to avoid sogginess, pat it dry with paper towel before using and withhold adding salt until just before serving.

HALLOUMI PDO

Made: Cyprus
Milk: Goat, sheep

Halloumi originates from the small Mediterranean island of Cyprus. The origins of this cheese date back thousands of years when shepherds working in the mountains would make it out of the seasonal flush of sheep's and goat's milk. The name derives from the Greek word 'almi', meaning 'salty water'. While men tended to the animals, the cheesemaking process was often undertaken by women and supervised by a 'galatarka', or the most experienced 'cheese woman'. Today, however, most examples available on the market are industrially produced, bulked up with cow's milk, and a far cry from what real PDO Halloumi should taste and look like. Cow's milk makes it much cheaper to produce, but this usually results in less flavour and a squeaky cheese that sweats when cooked. No doubt the galatarkas of old would churn with fury in their graves.

To avoid invoking the ire of the ghosts of galatarkas past, try to buy traditional Halloumi made from a mixture of sheep's and goat's milk from Cyprus. The goat's milk adds a lemony tang, while the sheep's milk allows for a beautiful, crispy golden crust to form when fried. Artisan hand-folded examples are well worth looking for – once you taste them, there is no going back.

LOOK: White and rindless when uncooked, turning to a golden brown when fried. The best examples are random in weight and you will see a seam, which shows they're handmade. They sometimes have a sprinkle of dried mint added.

TEXTURE: Firm when uncooked, good Halloumi should be crisp yet elastic when cooked.

TASTE & AROMA: Simple, salty goodness that is rich and lemony.

EAT WITH: Watermelon, peaches, figs, mint and smoked ham; drizzle with honey or pomegranate molasses. Grill or pan-fry in thick slices until golden brown, or cook on a gas or coal barbecue and serve simply with a good squeeze of lemon. Can be grated and melted on top of dishes like mac 'n' cheese (for our recipe, see page 186).

DRINK WITH: Pinot noir or whiskey; also try authentic Cypriot Commandaria (a sweet dessert wine) or Zivania (a Cypriot pomace brandy).

HOT TIP: When making a dish with real Halloumi, make sure it is the last ingredient to be cooked so it remains hot. Make sure your guests are ready to eat immediately! This is more of an order than a hot tip!

FETA PDO

Made: Greece
Milk: Goat, sheep

'Feta' means 'sliced' in Greek and it was traditionally matured and transported in barrels made from beechwood. Feta is rindless brined cheese made with a blend of sheep's and goat's milk. History suggests that this style of cheese has been made in Greece for at least 5000 years, and is widely considered the oldest and most distinguished of all European benchmark cheeses. The poetic genius, Homer, even waxed lyrical about this delicious cheese in *The Odyssey* (well worth a read if you haven't come across it).

Despite its long history, Feta remains one of the most misrepresented cheeses in the Australia. Most examples are mass-produced knock-offs made from cow's milk or sold under cleverly worded synonyms (i.e. fetta). While similar cheeses exist worldwide, and some of these taste fine, they are sold on price and are not regulated by the PDO system. We recommend trying PDO-certified Feta, which is the OG and guaranteed to be made following specific guidelines. If this is not available, be sure that it is at least made with sheep's and goat's milk.

If you're thinking, 'why is one animal's milk better than another's?', let us shed some science-illuminated light. Cows produce a lot more milk than sheep or goats do, thus cow's milk feta will always be cheaper. But in the case of feta made only from cow's milk, it does not have the same depth or complexity of flavour, because non-bovine milks contain more short-chain fatty acids than cow's milk. This means they're far more pungent and defined in flavour. The composition of sheep's milk provides a rich, milky flavour and creamy, soft texture that balances with the salty flavours in Feta, while the goat's milk provides a lingering acidity and tang, and contributes to a chalky crumble.

LOOK: White and rindless, sometimes in brine.

TEXTURE: Feta has a firm, crumbly-yet-creamy texture.

TASTE & AROMA: Feta will vary depending on the milk quality and ageing methods, but expect a briny saltiness and a citrusy tang, with herbal notes. In contrast to feta imitations, PDO Feta yields greater complexity and rich creaminess, thanks to the sheep's milk, and a lingering lemony finish due to the goat's milk.

EAT WITH: Feta can be paired with an endless range of ingredients, from olive oil to octopus. It goes exceptionally well with cucumber, tomatoes or blanched greens. Great crumbled over a salad, baked in a tart, drizzled with honey, fried with honey and sesame seeds, or served with extra-virgin olive oil and a sprinkle of fresh oregano.

DRINK WITH: Chardonnay or merlot; pilsner or draught beer.

BARREL-AGED FETA

Much industrially made feta is matured in tins and shock-ripened (matured quickly in high salt), which adds a metallic flavour. True barrel-aged Feta will be a triangular wedge, as it's cut from the circular barrel. It is best brined, rather than vacuum-packed. If you come across barrel-aged Feta, grab it! It is the Rolls Royce of Feta, a labour of love and an involved process. Each barrel is made by hand, stave-by-stave, by skilled coopers. The cheese is usually matured in the barrel between three months and a year. This enables it to develop a crumbly, milky texture, balanced, salty flavour and seriously creamy, complex finish. The barrel's flavour influences the taste of the cheese through the cultures and natural flora of the wood grain.

FETA-LIKE CHEESES

Overwhelmed by or curious about all the other feta-like cheeses staring at you, and wondering what they are? Here is an explanation of some of the most common types.

French feta: Often made with 100 per cent sheep's milk, it is typically mild, creamy and the least salty of all the fetas. It's good for spreading on a baguette with some olive oil.

Bulgarian feta: Mostly made from cow's milk, it has a firm but creamy texture, and is the saltiest of all varieties. A lack of regulations often means that Bulgarian feta has a slight grassy or 'sheepy' flavour. It can also taste quite lemony. It's best used in cooking.

Danish feta: Made from cow's milk, with a mild, creamy and smooth texture, as opposed to crumby. It can serve a purpose, but it's a mass-produced facsimile of the real deal.

Australian feta: Often made with cow's milk, the predominant flavours are usually tangy and salty, and the texture is less creamy and more crumbly.

GALOTYRI PDO

Made: Greece
Milk: Goat, sheep

We first came across Galotyri quite by accident while on a work trip in Northern Greece. We were at a lunch meeting with Feta producers and, as is typical in our industry, the tabletop was crowded with local produce. We didn't even notice the soft white cheese sitting inconspicuously in a bowl at the end of the table, until our hosts offered it as a post-meal digestif. A couple of spoons were dipped into the white curd and handed to us. All of a sudden, we stumbled into cheese utopia. Our tastebuds began to vibrate at a higher level, with the flavour and texture of this creamy, smooth cheese, with its fabulously clean finish. There was no going back to life before Galotyri.

Galotyri, which translates to 'milk cheese', was once a seasonal treat produced in summer by shepherds who roamed the hillside pastures of the Epirus and Thessaly regions of ancient Greece. At that time of year, the late-lactation milk they collected from their flocks of sheep and goats was slammed with milk solids. The traditional making of this cheese is both basic and fascinating. After natural acidification and salting, the curds were slowly drained in a cloth and cooled in a running stream in clay pots, creating a cheese full of probiotics, which was perfect for aiding digestion. The shepherds kept the cheese all to themselves and ate it after their large meat-heavy meals. Today, Galotyri remains relatively unknown outside of the country … we sense this will change, though, because it's lip-smackingly good.

LOOK: Pristine white, softly gelatinous, almost like pot-set yoghurt in appearance.

TEXTURE: Smooth, soft, creamy and infinitely spreadable.

TASTE & AROMA: Savoury flavours, refreshing acidity and a creamy, milky finish.

EAT WITH: Very versatile. Enjoy by the spoonful or as a simple dip with crackers. It's perfect for cutting through the richness of meats such as roasted lamb or smoked meats. Serve a dollop on slow-roasted tomatoes or vegetables. It's also lovely as a dessert with berry compote or marmalade, or in place of crème fraîche or sour cream.

DRINK WITH: White wine or vodka.

PANEER

Made: South Asia
Milk: Cow, buffalo

Paneer is a fresh, rindless cheese with a spongy texture and clean taste, often used in cooking. The exact origins of paneer are uncertain; however, we know that it developed in South Asia (India, Iran, Pakistan and Nepal). Interestingly, India is the world's largest producer of milk and milk products, but makes relatively few cheeses. Paneer's popularity in this region rose with Portuguese settlers during 18th-century colonial rule, as they encouraged cheesemaking in a culture that traditionally viewed cheese as taboo. As cows are sacred in Hindu Indian culture, cheeses made with traditional animal rennet are not allowed to be consumed. Luckily, paneer is not made with rennet and is very easy to make. Cow's or buffalo's milk is heated, then acidified with lemon or vinegar. The curds are then drained in muslin cloth, pressed and cooled in water baths for several hours.

There is also a sweet, softer version of paneer called 'chana', which is used to make Indian sweets. Paneer can usually be found next to halloumi in the supermarket. Or, have a go at making it yourself (see page 260 in recipes).

LOOK: Marble white, often homogenous in appearance.

TEXTURE: Squidgy, dense and moist.

TASTE & AROMA: Mild acidity with a creamy, milky finish.

EAT WITH: Pickles and mango or tomato chutney, or pineapple ginger jam. Paneer is a non-melter, so use it to its advantage and cook in a spinach curry or with grilled veggies.

DRINK WITH: Sauvignon blanc.

Top Australian rindless cheeses

DREAMING GOAT CHÈVRE, DREAMING GOAT DAIRY

Made: Macedon Ranges, Victoria
Milk: Goat

Dreaming Goat Dairy in Victoria is a small-scale artisan producer of stunning farmstead fresh cheeses, halloumi-style grilled cheese and yoghurt. Sarah Ajzner and her husband Daniel run a small herd of 30 dairy goats on their 50-acre farm in the hilly and rocky Macedon Ranges, on Wurundjeri Woi Wurrung country. Their story is both romantic and humbling, involving a solid life pivot from Melbourne-based lawyer and engineer, to full-time goat wranglers and cheesemakers.

Sarah and Daniel learned their trade from local cheesemaking legends Ann-Marie Monda and Carla Meurs from Holy Goat, and Ivan Larcher from the Castlemaine Cheese School. After a challenging start to trading in 2019, coinciding with the pandemic, the couple relied on farmers' markets for distribution and support. Today, gentle animal husbandry remains a core value for Sarah and Daniel, who say the secret to the flavour of their cheese is down to their 'happy goats'.

Our favourite Dreaming Goat cheese is the chèvre, a fresh goat's curd that has been lightly salted. The small jar contains a brilliant bright-white curd, with a smooth, spreadable texture. The flavour is pleasantly 'non goaty', with fresh pasture notes, rich and creamy with a clean, mouth-watering finish. This cheese is not easy to unearth, so when you see it, savour this gem.

LOOK: Snow-white curd in a jar.

TEXTURE: Ethereally light, smooth and spreadable.

TASTE & AROMA: Creamy curd, lightly salted with fresh acidity and a sweet, milky finish. Fresh pasture notes hum pleasantly in the background.

EAT WITH: On its own, slathered on bread or a bagel, or with smoked salmon. Dollop on soup or smear over a plate of roasted veggies. For sweet, drizzle with a strong-flavoured honey.

DRINK WITH: Sauvignon blanc, Prosecco or a dry rose.

MARINATED GOAT CHEESE, MEREDITH DAIRY

Made: Meredith, Victoria
Milk: Goat

Set up by Sandy and Julie Cameron back in 1991, Meredith Dairy produces an array of yoghurts as well as fresh and marinated curd cheeses. It is now the second largest goat dairy in Australia, with about 12,000 goats and 3500 sheep grazing on their land, located 90 minutes from Melbourne's CBD on Wadawurrung country. Meredith remains a family business, with Sandy and Julie as directors and their son, Angus, on the team. Sustainable farming practices are a high priority: they use solar panels and rely on their animals to fertilise the land.

Meredith Dairy is best known for its cult product, Marinated Goat Cheese, which is arguably the most recognised Australian cheese, described by some as 'cheese crack'. The cheese dates back to the '90s, when legendary Aussie cheesemaker Richard Thomas helped Sandy and Julie develop a fresh curd cheese emulsified with oil, garlic, black peppercorns and thyme. Richard was inspired by a trip to Iran, where he was taught how to make Persian-style feta in clay pots by a local shaman. Today, you would be hard-pressed to find an Australian cheese lover's fridge without a jar (or what's left of it).

LOOK: White, soft, immersed in oil in a jar.

TEXTURE: Fine-textured but dense curd that is smooth and spreadable.

TASTE & AROMA: Subtle creamy and clean salt and citrus flavours, balanced with oil and garlic.

EAT WITH: Spooned straight out of the jar; with toast (with or without avo), eggs, ocean trout or salmon; and in beetroot salads.

DRINK WITH: Pinot grigio or riesling; pilsner.

OTHER FAVE AUSSIE RINDLESS

Honourable mentions to: Vannella's Buffalo Mozzarella; Holy Goat's Fromage Frais; Prom Country Cheese's Inspiration (cow's curd marinated in lemon myrtle and native pepperberries); and Butterfly Factory's Chamela, an understated but elegant fresh lactic cow's milk cheese. WA residents should enjoy Cambray Cheese's Marinated Sheep's Milk Fetta, which is rich and perfectly salted.

BLOOMIES

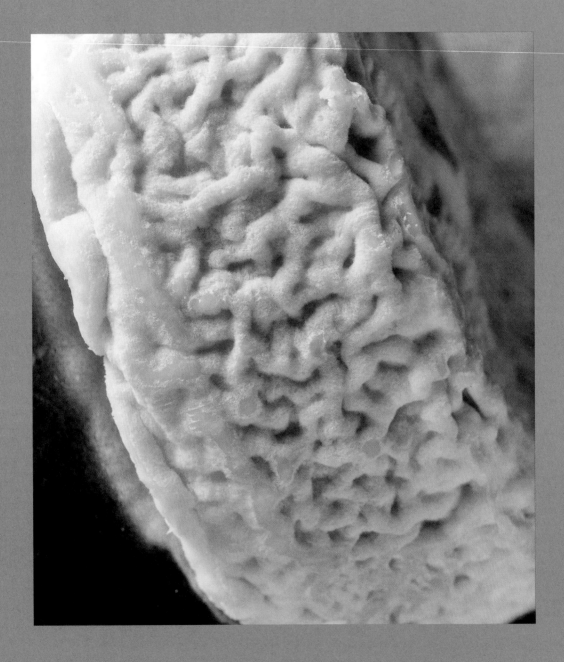

'I have just discovered one
of the most delicious things.'
CHARLEMAGNE'S RESPONSE TO HIS FIRST TASTE OF BRIE IN 774

We visited Normandy with our father, Will, in November 2019, just before the pandemic. Blissfully unaware the world was about to change forever, our biggest problem was trying to capture a photo for our socials next to Norman cows (Sammy's favourite), who were grazing under apple blossoms in the orchards. Every time we snuck under a fence, the cows sauntered away with what seemed like total apathy, or perhaps it was derision, at our quest. In any case, the photo was never captured. The cows won.

Uncooperative bovines aside, the trip was still a wonderful success. We have memories of the lush, fertile grass beneath our feet and the smell of the fallen end-of-season apples fermenting, solidly reminding us of the link between terroir and cheese. We were lucky enough to see traditional Camembert in production. The maturation room smelt of a mixture of freshly baked bread and button mushrooms, and there were rows upon rows of budding Camemberts with ridiculously fluffy white mould growing on them. They looked a bit like a litter of white kittens and just as cute, if you ask us. The cheesemaker grabbed a young Camembert from the rack and opened it, inviting us over to take a look. The characteristic creamline we're used to seeing in camembert hadn't yet formed; however, it did have the tell-tale five layers of hand-ladled curd. Will looked pleased that we were receiving a full induction into this particular type of cheesemaking, and forming an understanding of what's involved in the production of traditional bloomy rind cheese.

What is a bloomy cheese?

If you put a bloomy cheese under a microscope, you would likely see some impressive and cute fluffballs in full bloom. These are actually the moulds and yeasts that have been intentionally added during the cheesemaking process to produce (as the name suggests) a cheese with a fluffy white rind that has 'bloomed'. The helpful moulds and yeasts essentially break down the cheese's fats and proteins, adding to the overall flavour and texture, and softening the cheese as it ages.

Textures on the interior of the cheese vary vastly, from oozy to chalky centres, as do the flavours and intensity, which range from milky and buttery to fungal and barnyardy. The cheeses in this category could be described as the teenagers of cheese, due to their shorter, temperamental shelf life and the fact they're a little touchy and need to be handled with care. In technical cheese land, they are called 'soft surface mould-ripened cheeses' or 'mould-ripened cheeses' (both a bit of a mouthful, but logical names, nonetheless), because it's the surface mould that ripens the cheese, which softens with age. These cheeses are made using all milk types, but you'll see them most often made from cow's milk.

The cheesemaker will decide on the desired moisture of a bloomy by playing with the cheese's acidity and starter culture, and the careful handling and cutting of the curd. Typically, the fragile curds are cut large and kept moist. They are salted, moulded to hold the moisture, and drained overnight. After moulding, they are dry-salted or put in a brine bath with the intention of providing the right environment for the moulds or yeasts to attach and grow.

Sometimes the moulds and yeasts are added to the milk at the start of cheesemaking, and sometimes they are sprayed on at the start of affinage (maturation). They may also be picked up in the cheesemaking environment. The moulds and yeasts bloom after a few days in maturation rooms that are temperature controlled with high humidity for optimal cheese development. The maturation rooms need to be closed environments to prevent the contamination of other moulds taking over the cheese.

Historically, bloomies were a breakthrough in cheesemaking, as they extended the life of fresh milk by preserving it and reducing moisture loss. When bloomies were first made in France by 11th-century monks in monasteries, moulds would have been naturally collected from the cave walls and cellars where they matured, and they would have been blue, grey and even black. These days, they are more friendly looking with yellow or white hues, and are safely lab-grown with single strains isolated. Here are the main strains of moulds and yeasts in bloomies.

Penicillium camemberti: Mould. White, turning grey/brown after several days. Fluffy, but can be patted down if wrapped in cheese paper. Smells like fermented apples. Cheese example: Normandy Camembert.

Penicillium candidum: Mould. White, fluffy, silky, looks like soft snow. Smells and can taste like wet cardboard, slightly bitter. This is a variant of the mould *P. camemberti* (above). Cheese example: Délice de Bourgogne.

Geotrichum candidum: Yeast. Ivory/yellow, wrinkled and looks like a brain or coral. It's a complex yeast that behaves like a mould and reduces bitterness. It's hard to grow, with sensitivities to salt, some moulds and humidity. It smells yeasty and buttery, and tastes more yeasty and bready compared to moulds. Often called 'geo' for short. Cheese example: La Luna by Holy Goat.

Types of bloomies

TRADITIONAL

Traditional bloomies mature from the outside in, which you can see in action at the creamline (the area between the rind and paste) where it's translucent, as well as a chalky centre in young cheeses. They take more time to mature than modern bloomies and often won't have a perfectly white rind. Some cheesemakers use rennet for coagulation, which creates a buttery, dense texture, such as in traditional Camembert. Others use little-to-no rennet and the milk is coagulated using acid and heat. These are called 'lactic bloomies' or 'lactic-set bloomies'. Examples of this are French goat's milk cheeses from the Loire Valley, or Holy Goat cheeses from Australia.

Unfortunately, traditional bloomies are endangered due to lack of demand and customer education around their appearance, as well as retailers finding it hard to care for them properly. They can smell earthy or yeasty and sometimes a little ammoniated, if older. A quality traditional bloomy has a rich, full and sophisticated flavour.

MODERN/STABILISED

You will find these bloomies sold as pre-wrapped wedges at most supermarkets. These cheeses have the unfortunate industrial 'perfect apple' vibe, whereby supermarkets expect producers to create cheeses with pretty, white moulds for the fast-paced, grab-and-go customer. To achieve this perceived perfection, the cheesemaker doesn't allow the cheese to acidify, and the temperature is very regulated to make the cheese shelf-stable for longer. These cheeses have very little smell and a pleasant, creamy taste, which translates to bland, boring and predictable. They're no party starter. As they've been pre-ripened, you won't spot a creamline or chalky centre, but rather a consistent, creamy paste. Cheesemakers often add cream to make up for a lack of character in the cheese.

DOUBLE & TRIPLE CREAMS

When you see 'double cream' or 'triple cream' on a bloomy, it essentially means that cream has been added during the cheesemaking process to give the cheese a velvety texture, rich and buttery taste, and luscious mouthfeel. Many people worry that double and triple creams are higher in fat, but due to their high moisture content, the amount of fat is, in fact, quite similar to what is found in a hard cheese.

Look

Traditional bloomies will usually be wrapped in wax paper, which enables the cheese to breathe. Triple creams and traditional goat's cheeses will usually only be partly wrapped and in wooden boxes.

The most distinguishing feature of a bloomy is the rind. Yeasts will have a wrinkly and brain-like appearance. Moulds on the rind can be fluffy, marshmallowy, velvety, felt-like and soft to touch. A mould that is perfectly white and clean is usually an indication that the cheese is quite young or just a stabilised bloomy. The colour of the rind will vary: white, off-white, linen, straw, pale pink or ash grey (if vegetable ash has been added). A traditional bloomy can have a little browning on the outside or some red patches, which can indicate that the cheese is riper and/or other cultures have been added. It's cheeses like these that need support and education – to move us away from the expectation that they will always be a pristine-white colour. Bloomies are diverse in shape and size. You won't often find larger-format bloomy cheeses (above 1 kg or 2 kg), as the soft curds are too fragile to hold that weight, and the moulds and yeasts find it hard to stick. Paste colour is variable from white, off-white and ivory to yellow.

Texture

Bloomies are high-moisture cheeses, and their texture goes through a transformation from when they are young to mature. Young traditional bloomies will have a dry, chalky centre and may be flaky; mature cheeses will generally be soft, creamy, smooth, oozing and fudgy in the centre. Other textures include buttery, light, airy, velvety, slippery, wet, moist, gooey, supple and cloud-like.

Taste & aroma

A bloomy rind should smell clean with yeasty and fungal aromas. The rind is usually edible and intentionally made by the cheesemaker for you to eat, so have a nibble. The rind will usually taste mushroomy or yeasty in flavour. Other possible flavours you may encounter include milky, crème fraîche, buttery, earthy, meaty, citrusy or herbal. The strength of the bloomy will depend on the moulds used, how long it has been matured and the specific cheese. If the bloomy is young, it may taste acidic.

How to serve

Balance the creaminess of bloomies with sweet accompaniments such as jams, chocolate and berries or stone fruit. Gooey bloomies can benefit from the textural juxtaposition of radishes, celery or even a salty pop with a spoonful of caviar. Double creams and triple creams pair very well with Champagne and sparkling wines, with their richness contrasting superbly with the beverage's effervescence.

Top global bloomy cheeses

BRIE

Made: France
Milk: Cow

'One only has to press it with one's fingers, for it to split its sides with laughter, and run over with fat.' – Marc-Antoine Girard de Saint-Amant, 17th-century French poet.

Travel to France and you'll discover that Brie holds cultural, economic and historical significance, and means something very particular and specific. Only two Bries are name-protected: Brie de Melun and Brie de Meaux hold official PDO status and set the benchmark of what soft cheese is. The former is the grandmother of all bries, while the latter is an impressive 35 cm-wide disc, weighing 3 kg. Brie de Melun is a lactic-set cheese, whereas Brie de Meaux is rennet-set. They are two of the world's oldest cheeses, made using raw milk, which unfortunately means they are not available in Australia, due to our regulations.

Even though you see many cheeses labelled 'brie' on the market, the lack of name protection means the cheese can be produced anywhere, from any milk type. Many of these cheeses are, unfortunately, cheap industrial impersonations of traditional Brie, with bland flavours. Often, the moulds used on these versions are fast-growing industrial moulds, which taste cardboardy and bitter. Pasteurised traditional brie styles available in Australia include Fromage de Meaux, Le Marquis Brie de Ramboulliet Farmstead Brie, Dongé Brie and Brie de Nangis.

LOOK: Variable white bloomy rind, with possible mottled brown spots. The creamline just under the rind can be seen, especially if ripe.

TEXTURE: Pillowy, soft, plump and ideally smooth, consistent texture throughout, rather than runny. A cut piece should have a visual sheen. It can be chalky when young.

TASTE & AROMA: Rounded, with the smell and taste of mushrooms. Some have faint ammonia on the rind and taste variable: fruity, sweet, earthy, buttery, rich and nutty, with notes of hay. It should not be bitter or have a chemical aftertaste.

EAT WITH: You can't go wrong with a simple baguette and fresh pear.

DRINK WITH: Enjoy with a glass of buttery unoaked chardonnay.

CAMEMBERT

Made: France
Milk: Cow

The best Camembert available in Australia comes from the cool and wet pastures of Normandy, France. It is a benchmark cheese, with its fungal and barnyard funk mirroring the terroir in which it is made.

Camembert's creation can be attributed to Marie Harel, who hid a monk in her farmer's cottage in the small village of Camembert and saved him from beheading during the French Revolution. Originally from the region of Brie, the monk showed Marie how to make the disc-shaped cheese using special moulds. Camembert, however, did not get its fame until 60 years later, when the development of the railroads allowed transport of the cheese from Normandy to Paris. It was presented to Napoleon III by Marie's great granddaughter. 'Where is this delicious cheese from?' he asked, with a mouth full of it. 'Camembert' she announced … or something of that nature.

Camembert's success can be partly attributed to the development of the poplar box for transporting the cheese. The box (still to this day), acts as a microclimate for the cheese to mature in. It also provided some of the first advertising opportunities for producers to communicate where the cheese was made and who made it.

If you ever get the chance to try genuine Camembert de Normandie PDO, take it. It's a hand-ladled, raw milk Camembert and its existence is under threat by campaigns for it to be pasteurised by industrial giants pushing to change regulation.

LOOK: Good-quality Camembert from Normandy is wrapped in wax paper in a traditional poplar box.

TEXTURE: Fudgy and springy, with a chalky centre when young. Do the squeeze and bounce test to make sure it's ready: make a fist with one hand and press between your thumb and index finger with the other hand, similar to how you test a steak. Take it out of the box and press the centre and pinch around it. If it feels like your hand, then it's ready.

TASTE & AROMA: Good-quality Camembert should be whiffy! It should smell and taste like cooked cauliflower, porcini mushrooms, apples and wet hay.

EAT WITH: Apples, chutney, walnuts and a fresh baguette. For something a little wilder, slice in half horizontally and add a fresh nori sheet in between – umami paradise!

DRINK WITH: Best enjoyed with a Normandy or other dry cider, or Calvados.

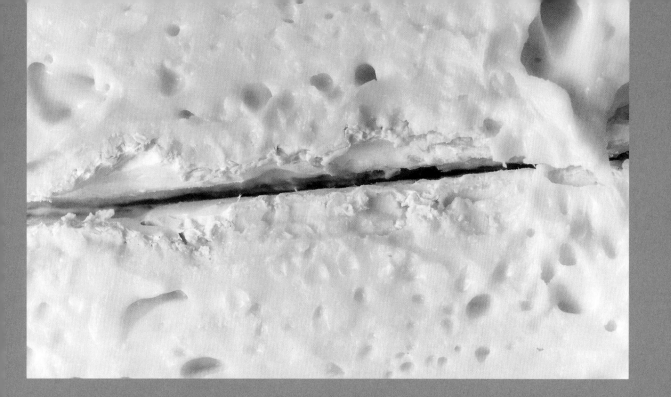

WHAT'S THE DIFFERENCE BETWEEN BRIE & CAMEMBERT?

Everyone seems to have an opinion on what Brie and Camembert are ... or are not. Many are too quick to point to any old wedge on a cheese board with a white fluffy mould and shout out 'that's Brie' or 'this is Camembert'. Not helping the frequent case of mistaken identity is that the words 'Camembert' and 'Brie' are not name protected. This means you will find them in many different shapes, from many different countries and often misrepresented. It also makes it difficult for people to grasp the historical significance of these cheeses, as well as how they should taste and how they are made. After reading about these two cheeses, we encourage you to embrace the cheese geek you are becoming and point to your next cheese board and say 'this is a brie-style cheese'. It also, in our opinion, highlights the need to create new cheese names, rather than rely on European place names.

NAME

Official Brie PDO is called Brie de Meaux or Brie de Melun. Genuine Camembert is called Camembert de Normandie PDO. These are not available in Australia as both are made with raw milk. You can buy pasteurised versions in Australia.

LOCATION/TERROIR

Brie can only be made in the Île-de-France region of France (northeast of Paris); Camembert is made in Normandy. The terroir/climate also affects the flavour of each cheese.

AGE

Brie was first created in the 7th century, whereas Camembert was recognised in the 18th century.

SIZE

Traditional Brie comes in much larger formats than Camembert – a Brie de Meaux wheel is around 35 cm and weighs about 3 kg. Camembert's traditional size is 10 cm and 250 g (and it matures faster than Brie as a result). You will find impersonator brie and camembert styles in all sorts of sizes and from various countries.

PACKAGING

Brie was traditionally matured on straw; Camembert in wooden poplar boxes (from the 1890s onwards), which added important protection when it was transported from Normandy to the Parisian markets. The box also adds a microclimate for ripening.

TASTE

Traditional Brie has a mild fungal smell, buttery texture and milky/savoury flavour. Camembert is more stinky and smells like cooked brassicas, has a fudgy texture and a longer, fuller flavour. In general (unless you're in France, where they eat Camembert young), Camembert is stronger in taste.

BRILLAT-SAVARIN PGI

Made: France
Milk: Cow

'Tell me what you eat, and I will tell you what you are.'
– Jean Anthelme Brillat-Savarin, 18th-century food writer

If you had to choose one cheese for a party, this would be it. By our calculation, the record for this cheese disappearing at a gathering with just a spoon left in the centre is 3 minutes, 59 seconds. It takes its name from the famous 18th-century French food writer Jean Anthelme Brillat-Savarin. A relatively modern cheese, Brillat-Savarin was first commercially produced in the 1950s by Parisian affineur, Pierre Androuët, after cream became a commodity and was seen as a symbol of opulence and luxury, a reputation that is maintained today.

Prepare to experience a sophisticated buttercream that coats your palate with velvet and fills your mouth with a rich, creamy taste. The journey will continue and leave you with gentle, yeasty undertones, finishing with a zesty sour cream bite, thanks to the long lactic cheesemaking. We personally call her 'brilliant salvation'.

Brillat-Savarin is classified as a triple cream cheese, meaning it has added cream. Many Brillats on the market will have *Penicillium candidum* mould added instead of geo as it looks prettier and is easier to grow, but the hunt for a geo rind is well worth the effort, as the taste is less peppery and the texture more delectable. We recommend selecting cheese close to its use-by date, when the geo has broken down some of the chalky paste.

LOOK: Geo Brillats will have a 'brainy look' and be ivory on the outside. *P. candidum* versions will be white and fluffy. This is a cheese that is known to particularly grow 'bunny tails', a fluffy mould on top of the cheese. Don't be alarmed by these furry additions, simply pat them down.

TEXTURE: Chalky when young, buttercream and fudgy when eaten close to its use-by date. It has a silky, velvety, creamy and indulgent mouthfeel.

TASTE & AROMA: Expect a rich, buttery flavour (like buttered popcorn), with yeasty undertones and a lingering sour cream finish.

EAT WITH: Plunge a spoon into it and serve straight out of the box. Okay, if you need something a little more civilised, enjoy with crispy baguette, fresh berries, a drizzle of honey, caviar, orange marmalade, muscatels, dates, prosciutto, chocolate, cherries and grilled stone fruits.

DRINK WITH: Incredible with Champagne or Prosecco, the effervescence of the bubbles cuts through the fat of the cheese, creating an immeasurably pleasurable mouthfeel.

LA TUR

Made: Italy
Milk: Cow, goat, sheep

Literally the most delightful mini cheese cupcake you will ever eat, La Tur brings a complex and bold flavour with its unique combination of goat's, sheep's and cow's milk. It's creamy, sweet, earthy and tangy all at once. Made in the Piemonte region of Italy, La Tur has a wrinkled yellow geo rind, with yeasty undertones and a tangy finish. The interior is cloud-like and silky, with flavours ranging from honeycomb to moss and butter. It's the perfect cheese for a sexy date, or enjoyed solo with nothing but a spoon.

LOOK: A cupcake-sized cheese with a soft geo pale-yellow rind and straw-coloured interior paste.

TEXTURE: Creamy, cloud-like, buttery and smooth.

TASTE & AROMA: Complicated in the best kind of way with buttery, honeycomb, mossy, rich, tangy and yeasty flavours all contributing to a full-bodied beauty. It can be quite piquant in flavour with the addition of sheep's milk.

EAT WITH: Wonderful with berries, honey and fruit toast.

DRINK WITH: Pop it with some bubbles.

LES SECRET DES LYS

Made: France
Milk: Cow

This bloomy is super cute, staring up at you from an adorable little terracotta pot (where it has been maturing for six weeks). Based on the raw milk Saint-Marcellin, it is made by the Perrin family in the mountains of Franche-Comté, France. It has a joyous silky and delicate mouthfeel and shows off flavours similar to that of a brie with cream.

LOOK: You can pick out this petite 80 g cheese by its collectable terracotta pot.

TEXTURE: Lush and plush, like a cake batter.

TASTE & AROMA: This cutie is earthy and melt-in-your-mouth, with mushroom, cream and butter flavours, and a balanced tang.

EAT WITH: Scoop from the pot with crusty bread or, if you desire, heat in the pot and drizzle with honey.

DRINK WITH: Sparkling wine.

Top Australian bloomy cheeses

LA LUNA RING & PETITE BARREL, HOLY GOAT

Made: Sutton Grange, Victoria
Milk: Goat

The Holy Grail of Australian goat's cheese is Holy Goat in Sutton Grange, Victoria, on the land of the Dja Dja Wurrung people. Here, Carla Meurs, Ann-Marie Monda and their team make a spectacular range of organic goat's cheeses. The single herd of well-pampered and individually named Saanen and British Alpine goats happily nibble on native and perennial grasses, herbs, flowers and shrubs.

Hands-down the best goat's cheese in Australia, La Luna Ring, if you are lucky enough to see it in a full wheel, looks like a giant Life Saver lolly. Covered in geo, it delivers everything you want in a goat's cheese. This exemplary cheese is a true reflection of fine farmhouse cheesemaking skills that tell the story of the Australian bush. Enjoy it on the patio in the fading afternoon sun, with a glass of crisp white wine and your mum or mother figure.

LOOK: La Luna Ring weighs 1.4 kg and is cut to order; Petite La Luna Barrel comes in 110 g or 50 g cylinders. All have geo wrinkles on the outside, but the cut to order ring is our favourite for the complexity and depth of flavour.

TEXTURE: Lusciously velvety and dense.

TASTE & AROMA: Tangy and elegantly herbaceous, with an icing-bite finish. The La Luna Barrel is a less mature version of the ring, with a milder taste.

EAT WITH: A baguette is the only addition you really need; honey, if you desire.

DRINK WITH: Sauvignon blanc, riesling or a dry rose.

PECORA BLOOMY ASHED, PECORA DAIRY

Made: Robertson, NSW
Milk: Sheep

Pecora Dairy was founded by Michael and Cressida Cains in 2011, and produces some of Australia's best sheep's milk cheese. Picture 200 acres of lush, regenerative pastoral land, in NSW's Southern Highlands on Tharawal country, populated by happy East Friesian sheep that drink from crystal-clear springs at the edge of the Kangaroo Valley. Idyllic, yes? This farm embraces biodiversity, preserving native ecosystems, while taking a gentle approach to animal husbandry, milking and cheesemaking. Michael and Cressida are also helping to revolutionise the cheese industry with the creation of Australia's first non-cooked raw milk cheese, called Yarrawa.

Our favourite Pecora Dairy cheese is called Bloomy. It's made from new-season sheep's milk that has been long lactic-set and has a pillowy texture. It can make a handsome-looking addition to your cheese board, with its small disc shape lightly dusted with vegetable ash. Spring is the best time to take Bloomy out for a spin.

LOOK: Weighing 120 g, this cheese has an ashed, geo-wrinkled rind with an ivory-white interior.

TEXTURE: Pillowy and chalky when young; gooey as it develops.

TASTE & AROMA: Gentle lemony tang, buttery and sweet. As it ages, Bloomy becomes earthier and more intense, but the flavour changes seasonally.

EAT WITH: Nosh this cheese on some bread with slices of apple and pear on the side, or serve with black cherry preserve or muscatels.

DRINK WITH: Riesling. Michael recommends a sherry cask–matured whiskey.

OTHER FAVE AUSSIE BLOOMIES

Honourable mentions to: the oh-so snackable Silver Wattle by Long Paddock, along with their Flannel Flower brie-style cheese; Stone & Crow's Amiel, a divine-looking and gentle-tasting geo goat's cheese; the lovely Holy Goat's Brigid's Well, with its ash-coated ring and fresh hazelnut taste; Butterfly Factory's crave-worthy Monkery; and Cambray Cheese's Friesette, a delicate but rich sheep's milk bloomy that's a real winner for those residing in WA.

BLUES

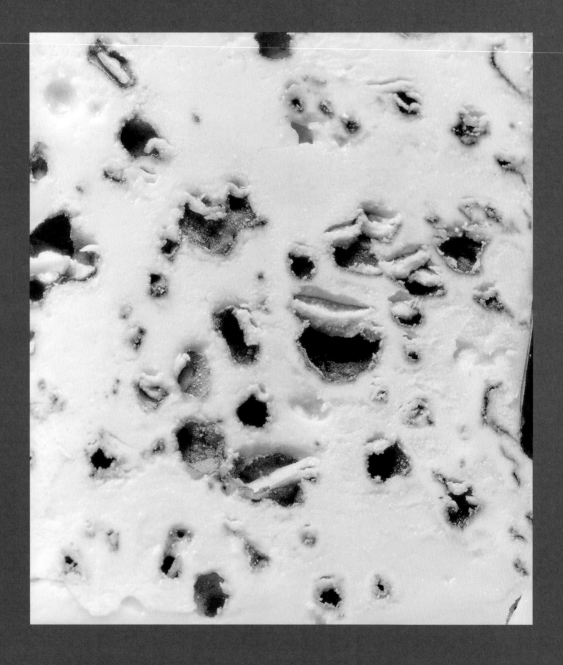

'*Roquefort should be eaten
on one's knees.*'
18TH-CENTURY GASTRONOME GRIMOD DE LA REYNIÈRE

One of the most memorable moments of our collective cheese journey was watching our father clamber up the damp limestone cave wall in Roquefort-sur-Soulzon in France, returning to us with a thick layer of *Penicillium roqueforti* mould on his pointer finger. Breathless with excitement, eyes wide, he exclaimed, 'Kids, this is where all blue cheese comes from!'.

Our father told a true story. *P. roqueforti* is the mother mould for most blue cheeses in the world, and it is responsible for their defining characteristics and signature punch. The story of the mould's discovery is also one of our favourite cheese legends, and it happens to involve a lovesick shepherd.

A thousand or so years ago, a shepherd was watching his flock in the mouth of the Roquefort caves. Munching a cheese sandwich, he suddenly spotted a shepherdess in the fields who happened to be a complete babe. He dropped his cheese sandwich in excitement and went after her in hot pursuit. The pair actually had mad chemistry and an autumn romance of field-romping and star-gazing followed, but it wasn't meant to be. Ultimately, she just wasn't that into him.

Heartbroken, the poor shepherd returned to his cave. His eyes were full of tears, and he collapsed in a heap next to his now mouldy-blue cheese sandwich, took a nibble in despair, and then his tears vanished. He nibbled some more. 'This is the best cheese I have *ever* eaten!', he announced in pure excitement, and then sprinted back to his village to tell everyone about his new discovery. The romantic dalliance may have been fleeting, but this alchemy of cheese and fungus developed into an enduring love for the ages.

Look, we may have hammed up this famous fable, but there is a nugget of truth in it. *P. roqueforti* is found in the soil and on the walls of the Roquefort-sur-Soulzon caves and, historically, this mould was cultivated on bread for blue cheesemaking. Some producers of Roquefort still cultivate it this way today. So, long live romance, happy-ever-afters, and the incredible flavour and texture of a high-quality blue cheese.

What is blue cheese?

Blue cheese is made by introducing a mould (usually *P. roqueforti* or a sub-species) into the milk or curds, giving the cheese its signature flavour or bite. The blue, green or grey mould grows from the centre of the cheese to the rind. Ripening from the inside out makes blue cheese special and distinct, compared to other types of cheese that ripen from the outside in. The mould breaks down the fat in the cheese, a process called 'lipolysis', and creates a diverse range of flavours that might be spicy, nutty, chocolatey or minerally. This process also breaks down the structure of the cheese to create a soft and creamy paste.

As in the folklore, originally, blue moulds were cultivated on bread and then dried and ground into a powder and scattered into the milk or curd. These days, most *P. roqueforti* moulds, although related to the ones from Roquefort-sur-Soulzon, are grown in a lab. They come in powdered or liquid form, and cheesemakers can choose very specific strains to create a unique cheese identity. Lab-grown strains are used for their predictability, as cultivating the mould by hand can lead to inconsistent results. Sub-species, such as *P. glaucum*, are less commonly used, but you will find it in cheeses, such as Bleu d'Auvergne and Gorgonzola Dolce, which usually have a milder flavour profile. Only a small amount is needed per vat to make the cheese blue – about 1 teaspoon of mould per 550 litres of milk.

People who are gluten free may need to avoid blue cheese, as there could be traces of gluten on the moulds, if the cheese was propagated on bread, as with Roquefort.

How do blues get blued?

A common misconception is that blue mould is injected into cheese wheels to create the veining. In fact, cheeses are inoculated with mould at the *beginning* of the cheesemaking process, either into the milk or the formed curd. The blueing itself does not occur until a few weeks into maturation, when cheese wheels are pierced with long metal or wooden needles that oxygenate the cheese and activate the growth of mould spores, a process known as 'needling'. You can sometimes spot these holes on the outside of blue cheeses, or you can see the trail inside the cheese where the mould grew along the spike lines. Without this process of piercing and oxygenating the cheese, blue mould would not grow. To encourage ongoing blue mould development, blue cheeses are never pressed and are often loosely packed.

Look

A sign of a good blue cheese is when the veins begin at the centre and radiate out to the rind, with even distribution and patterning. Cheesemongers will often cut blue cheeses in half when displaying them for this reason. If there are just a few blue streaks visible, this may mean the cheese will be milder in taste. Stronger and saltier cheeses will have more prevalent blue streaks and pockets, and smell more pungent. There's a spectrum of mould colour in blues, including light blue, blue, dark blue, grey, greenish-grey, dark grey and aqua green. Blue cheeses are often wrapped in foil and cooled to shut out oxygen and prevent further spreading of the mould or maturation of the cheese.

Texture

The texture of blue cheeses varies wildly, from crumbly, flaky, grainy and lumpy to buttery, supple, wet and velvety.

Taste & aroma

The jury is still out as to why some people have a strong aversion to blues, but if you don't have a closed palate, the blue cheese galaxy is worth exploring. It is diverse in strength and intensity – from relaxed and mild to blow-your-pants-off wild. Some blues will be melt-in-the-mouth, rich and buttery; others will ambush your tastebuds like a stampede of wild horses. Some may be complex or spicy or nutty. But the flavour of the blue should be balanced and not overpowering, so you can still detect some of the other characteristics of the milk and terroir. You don't want your tongue being held at ransom by too much blue flavour.

In general, blue cheeses are saltier than other cheeses, so expect the sides of your tongue to be activated as you eat it. This is because blues often require more salt in production to support the mould and decrease any microflora that could adversely affect it. Blue cheese also loses moisture as it ages, so it becomes saltier per square inch. All these factors put blues at risk of being too salty.

We also find umami (or savoury) quite activated in blue cheese. Again, this should not overwhelm, but rather enhance the existing flavours in the cheese. Overall, the taste of blues will often linger in the mouth.

If you're a new member of the blue cheese fan club, it's probably a good idea to start with a creamier iteration that will allow your tastebuds to adjust. You could even add some butter to the bread like French school kids do, to ease you in. Once you've acclimatised, move your way up to bolder expressions. It's a similar theory to training your palate to enjoy coffee in your tween years, by bombarding it with sugar, chocolate and milk, then slowly stripping back those safety nets. There's a veritable kaleidoscope of flavour to unravel. Some you're likely to encounter are:

- Milky, crème fraîche, buttery.
- Fruity, fermented fruits, berries.
- Earthy, mushroomy.
- Chocolatey, dark chocolate, white chocolate.
- Nutty, caramel, coffee.
- Meaty, beefy, bacon.
- Herbaceous, black pepper, liquorice, white pepper, anise.
- Citrusy, yeasty, strong, acidic, herbal.
- Minerally.
- Metallic (default).

How to serve

Balance the saltiness of blues with sweet accompaniments such as honey, figs, grapes and compotes. They're known for having wild chemistry with bitter dark chocolate, as the bitterness beautifully cuts through the fat. Blues often pair well with nuts, such as walnuts and hazelnuts, and more interesting breads than just a baguette, such as a dark rye, walnut bread, raisin and walnut bagel or cinnamon bagel. They also almost always are seduced by a sweet sticky wine.

Top global blue cheeses

On the milder side (beginner blues)

STILTON PDO

Made: England
Milk: Cow

First up, a little clarification. Stilton is not made in Stilton. Rather, it is named after the village of Stilton in Cambridgeshire, where travellers on horseback used to stop and rest on route to London, and snack on this delicious cheese while their horses were changed over.

The actual origin of Stilton is a topic that, perhaps unsurprisingly, conjures hot debate between the French and English. The French claim it's a replica of Fourme d'Ambert, while the English argue a different tale. Their version dates back to the 1700s and the city of Leicester, where the recipe came into existence via a housekeeper called Lady Beaumont. She, apparently, sold her cheese to the Bell Inn in Stilton and was responsible for standardising the recipe.

Stilton is a total princess to make. It demands regular turning, and correct temperature and humidity are vital for ripening. This sensitivity is where the practice of pouring port into the centre of bad cheeses to mask the taste originated. To be fair, port and Stilton do, in fact, go together, just not in the same mouthful.

A sub-species of *P. roqueforti* is responsible for the blue moulds in Stilton, which were originally cultivated on bread or, according to some accounts, straps of mouldy leather, which were dragged through the vats. If that makes you feel slightly queasy, you'll be happy to learn that, today, it is lab-grown. Curds are packed quite loosely and not pressed, which creates an open-textured cheese.

Stilton is a PDO cheese, meaning the region and recipe are protected, with just six dairies left in production. Compared to other PDOs, however, regulations are fairly vague in detail, which does not ensure quality. Thus, many Stiltons on the market are quite industrially made and price-driven, leading to an overall variance in quality. If possible, avoid pre-cut, vacuum-packed, frozen, potted, port-soaked or waxed Stilton. Potted Stilton looks pretty, but is often lower quality and made from off-cuts.

Age does matter when it comes to Stilton. Many pre-wrapped wedges at the supermarket have only been aged for eight weeks, which can mean the cheese is dry and highly acidic. We enjoy a profile of 12 weeks, as the mould has had time to break down the cheese, and is creamier and more buttery in texture and taste.

The best Stilton producers are Colston Basset and Cropwell Bishop. Both produce excellent-quality cheeses and use handmade techniques, such as hand-ladling and hand-salting.

LOOK: A full wheel of Stilton is an 8 kg drum with a natural dusty pink–spotted and brown rind. The rind should be even and not too moist. The paste varies from ivory to light creamed corn. It will have minimum to moderate green-blue marbled moulds that run from the centre to the rind. Cheese shops will often cut Stilton horizontally to display optimal, even veining.

TEXTURE: A buttery, soft, crumbly and smooth interior, with a biscuity rind.

TASTE & AROMA: Not all Stiltons are created equal, with quality varying according to the season, scale of production and age of the cheese. A good Stilton will have a mellow, earthy and fruity aroma, a long flavour that melts in the mouth and a satisfying spice to it. It shouldn't be overpowering, sharp or too acidic. Stilton may taste buttery, rich, nutty, salty, syrupy and of fresh hay and buttercups.

EAT WITH: Throw some walnuts, honey or dark chocolate on the cheese board. Stilton is also a fab cooking cheese and goes well with many soups as a replacement for cream. It makes good friends with veggies, such as leek and broccoli. We sneak a crumble of it on top of mince pies at Christmas too – don't judge until you try it.

DRINK WITH: The rumours are true, port does pair well with Stilton. You can also try stout and fortified wines.

HOT TIP: According to artisan Stilton producers, it is a near-criminal offence to cut the nose off the Stilton and enjoy it yourself. It's considered the best part of the cheese with the most moisture, and should be shared with your guests.

Stilton often steals the limelight at Christmas, and for good reason. The cheese at this time has been made from late-summer milk, which is the best milk for Stilton. The cows have been out on the pasture for a number of months and the milk is rich, with a higher fat and protein content. By the time the cheese is matured, it's Christmas. This is a great time to buy a large wedge of it (and employ the rockstar cheese board principle – see page 74), as not only will it make a statement centrepiece, but it will also hold its form and last longer than other cheeses. If you're ever in Europe, keep your eyes out for the raw milk version of Stilton, called Stichelton.

GORGONZOLA PDO

Made: Italy
Milk: Cow

What is it about cheese and romance? Turns out that Gorgonzola involves another lovesick human swayed by lusty distractions. Rumour has it that a young cheesemaker left his curds in a vat while he rushed off to a hot date. When he returned, the beginnings of blue mould from the cellar walls were forming on top of the milk. Worried about the repercussions, or perhaps just lazy, he covered his mistake by adding the next morning's milkings to the cheese. In true curious cheesemaker style, when this batch of cheese was ready, he took a nibble and was surprised and delighted by the taste bequeathed by those tasty spores.

Gorgonzola is quite the old fella, dating back to the 9th century, and takes its name from the village of Gorgonzola in the Lombardy region in Northern Italy. Originally, it was made only in autumn, when cows, who had spent the summer grazing in the mountains, were resting in the village just below the snow line. At this time, the cows were at the end of their lactation cycle, meaning their milk had more fat but less volume. With less milk to make cheese, the cows were milked twice – once in the evening and then the following morning – to make one batch of cheese. This is considered an unusual practice in cheesemaking as it affects the cheese's acidity, but it also provides an opportunity for the creation of crevices, where the blue-green veins can form. These are called 'erborinato' in Italian, meaning 'parsley', which the veins kind of resemble.

Only a few producers still mature their Gorgonzola in the mountain caves of the Valsassina Valley, with most now using the giant underground cellar complex in the city of Novara. These days, Gorgonzola is quite an industrial and modernised cheese, so it can be disappointing at times. Unlike its ancestor, it's matured year-round and made from just one milking. There are two types of Gorgonzola.

GORGONZOLA DOLCE PDO

This sweet Gorgonzola used to be hand-ladled with a single milking, but is now an industrial product. It is matured for only 60 days, with less blue and less salt added, compared to Gorgonzola Piccante. Gorgonzola Dolce accounts for 90 per cent of Gorgonzola production.

Gorgonzola Dolce degrades on its trip to Australia, so must be handled carefully or it can become sour and very strong, especially if it's been open for a few days. It's best enjoyed straight from the wheel, but you will see it mainly cut into quarters. Mauri is one of the best Italian producers available in Australia.

Look for cheeses with evenly spaced veining, as these have the best flavour and won't be bitter, salty or spicy. The best cheese is made in autumn, as per the fable of the cows being tired and the milk having more fat.

LOOK: A full wheel of Gorgonzola Dolce weighs 10–12 kg. This is the largest blue cheese you will see in a traditional deli or cheese shop, usually with a big spoon dug in for scooping. You can also buy it in prepacked portions.

TEXTURE: Soft, luscious, sticky and spoonable, and gooey when mature. This velvety cheese has all the makings of a great date-night cheese.

TASTE & AROMA: Sweet, mild, creamy, mellow, rich and yeasty, with a slightly spicy finish. It could pass for a spicy ice cream cake and be eaten with a spoon. If you're after a milder Gorgonzola, reach for this one. It can also be used in cooking – try dolloping it on top of pasta or risotto.

EAT WITH: Honey, fig jam, dark rye bread and juicy pear. Add a drizzle of extra-aged balsamic vinegar.

DRINK WITH: Sparkling wines, including red, contrast the creaminess beautifully.

GORGONZOLA PICCANTE PDO

Sometimes known as Gorgonzola Naturale or Mountain Gorgonzola, the traditional method of two separate milkings is still used to make this cheese; however, it is now mostly made in one day, rather than two. Due to a longer maturation time (three to four months) than Gorgonzola Dolce, the flavours are more complex and sophisticated, giving the cheese a greater depth of character.

LOOK: A full wheel of Gorgonzola Piccante is a 6–12 kg drum, with a natural crusty rind and wrapped in its signature aluminium foil printed with a gold 'G'. You'll usually see it in cheese cabinets cut into quarters. The paste is straw white with moulds of steely blue and dark blue-green. Gorgonzola Piccante has more prevalent blue veins than Dolce.

TEXTURE: Firm, condensed and crumbly.

TASTE & AROMA: This is a feistier version of Gorgonzola, with flavours that are piquant, spicy, sharp and strong.

EAT WITH: Honey, fig jam, dark rye bread, juicy pear and dark chocolate. Add a drizzle of extra-aged balsamic vinegar. You could also stir it through spaghetti, or, for a colour contrast, squid-ink spaghetti.

DRINK WITH: Sweet fortified wines, including sherry; Moscato.

HOT TIP: If you're looking for an Australian approximation, go for Gippsland Blue.

CASHEL BLUE

Made: Ireland
Milk: Cow

There was no history of blue cheesemaking in Ireland until the Grubb family decided to have a go in the 1980s. Louis Grubb and his wife, Jane, moved home to take over the family's 100-year-old farm after his father's death, and bought some enterprising Friesian cows to kick-start the venture. They decided to make blue cheese as a point of difference to the other cheeses available in Ireland, and add value to the milk.

Made for a local market with a palate unaccustomed to blue cheese, the Grubbs' blue was designed to be lusciously creamy, to encourage the Irish to take it out for a spin. With its rich, buttery texture and gentle tang, Cashel remains one of Ireland's finest blue cheeses and is a wonderful starting point for those just embarking on their discovery of blue cheese. The family continues production as a second-generation farm on 200 acres, populated by 110 happy Friesian cows.

This semi-soft cow's milk cheese is hand-washed in brine, pierced at around day four, then wrapped in foil to stop the blueing.

LOOK: A 1.5 kg cylindrical wheel with gold foil. It has a blue-grey to pink rind, with a white paste when young, changing to buttery yellow as it matures. This cheese has dense, marbled veins.

TEXTURE: Smooth, soft, creamy, moist and crumbly.

TASTE & AROMA: Acidic when young. Creamy, buttery and tangy with subtle minerality, it becomes gently spicy when older and saltier near the rind.

EAT WITH: Fresh figs, pears, dates, apples, walnuts, onion jam, honey and dark chocolate. It goes well in a burger, too, or with coleslaw.

DRINK WITH: Stout; whiskies with caramel notes; gin.

HOT TIP: The Grubb family also make a sheep's milk blue cheese called Crozier Blue that is definitely worth a nibble.

Blues that make you walk on the wild side

ROGUE RIVER SPECIAL RESERVE, ROGUE CREAMERY

Made: USA
Milk: Cow

Crowned 'Best Cheese in the World' two years in a row (2019–20) at the World Cheese Awards, Rogue River Special Reserve is the perfect pin-up for good artisan cheese. Before ageing, each wheel is cloaked in Syrah grape leaves that have been soaked in organic pear spirits, lending the cheese some vanilla sweetness. It's made on the autumn equinox in Oregon by our dear family friend and mentor David Gremmels and his team.

Animal husbandry is a high priority for Rogue Creamery. The single herd of Brown Swiss and Holstein cows are milked up to three times a day by robots (one called Matilda), when they feel like it, and have back scratches on tap. They also graze on pasture for 10 months of the year, eating native organic grasses, organic hay and non-GMO grain. It's not just the cows that are pampered; the curds, too, are played tunes by passionate cheesemakers, who are convinced that every element and sense impacts the end product of a cheese. Wheels are tucked in to be cosily cave-aged for 9–10 months.

Every year and every wheel of Rogue River Blue tastes different, which we find to be a celebration of seasonality. Flavours include a spicy, complex blue due to the *P. roqueforti*. There's also a strong fruity aftertaste, thanks to the pear spirit–soaked leaves. Plan to buy it around Christmas, when Australia gets a very limited supply.

It may be one of the world's most expensive cheeses, but it's definitely worth stumping up the cash for its uniqueness, artisan practices at every stage of production, and abundance of stories to tell your guests.

LOOK: Glistening, leaf-wrapped beauty with an ivory interior and blue-green veins.

TEXTURE: Fudgy, buttery, syrupy and moist.

TASTE & AROMA: Something akin to Christmas pudding, candied bacon and vanilla.

EAT WITH: The sweetness in the cheese matches with pear, hazelnuts, walnuts and milk and dark chocolate.

DRINK WITH: Champagne, viognier, dessert wine, Syrah, pinot noir and Sancerre; stout.

HOT TIP: Rogue's Caveman Blue is our other absolute fave.

ROQUEFORT PDO

Made: France
Milk: Sheep

We bet even the lactose intolerant have heard of this regal stalwart. The French call this cheese the 'King of Blue' and, needless to say, it's the most popular raw milk blue cheese in the country. It's also the oldest and most famous. We think eating a good Roquefort is similar to a slippery villain in a play, grabbing you by the balls with an assertive yet balanced salty kick of *P. roqueforti*, while seductively vanishing off your tongue in a syrupy, salty manoeuvre.

Roquefort is a benchmark raw milk blue we are allowed to savour in Australia, thanks to our father (see page 116). Under Australian laws, it's difficult for any soft, raw milk blue to meet standards, but Roquefort is an exception. Made exclusively from the milk of a single breed of sheep, called Lacaune, in the Massif Central region of France, Roquefort has a unique maturing environment. The cheeses age, tenderly tucked into deep limestone caves and fleurines that stretch for 2 km. The 'fleurines' are chimney-shaped flutes that essentially breathe in cool, fresh air and exhale stale air, which allows for the correct humidity and consistency in temperature throughout the year. This natural geological formation exists thanks to a series of landslides and earthquakes millions of years ago and is essential for the maturation of the cheese. Some say any modern cheesemonger or affineur cave aims to replicate these exact conditions as they are so perfect.

Cheese shops often sell Roquefort in 'half moons'/half wheels. This is a good thing as it allows the cheese to hold a consistent maturation. The best Roquefort is made at the end of milking season in May and June, when sheep are grazing on fresh pasture. All Roquefort will have been matured for a minimum of 90 days in the caves, which means they are released just in time for Christmas. With only seven producers left, this artisan cheese needs to be protected to ensure it can continue to be made from raw milk. Our favourite artisan Roquefort is by Carles.

LOOK: Ivory in colour with a soft, moist and crumbly texture that glistens. The mould is usually a blue-green hue that forms in pockets. Packaging will have the red Roquefort stamp with a sheep on it, as well as the PDO/AOP symbol. A wheel ranges in weight from 2.5 to 2.9 kg.

TEXTURE: This heritage cheese will be soft, moist, rich, creamy, craggy and open. A young Roquefort will be firm in texture, but as it matures it becomes creamier and the veins extend to the edge.

TASTE & AROMA: As a seasonal cheese, the taste will vary, but is often rich, fatty, creamy, salty and briny like the seaside; mellow with notes of black pepper, green herbs, mushrooms and flowers. It has umami, minerality and a pervasive funk. Roquefort shouldn't be gamey; rather, it should harmonise salt and syrupy sweetness and almost vanish off your tongue.

EAT WITH: Dark rye bread – you're welcome to add butter to the bread, as the French do, to soften the blow. Also match with walnuts, ripe pear, a fruity sourdough loaf, floral honey or dark chocolate, or crumble on a salad of gem lettuce and apple. It makes a rockstar addition to a beef burger or steak.

DRINK WITH: Sauternes is the perfect match as the sweetness of the wine balances the salt. Out-of-the-box pairings include Tokaji, a Hungarian dessert wine, or Junmai sake. It also goes well with stout or port.

HOT TIP: Like Stilton, the creamy, blue point of the wedge is considered the best bit, so don't serve it to yourself. Cut triangular slices from the centre to the rind, otherwise guests will be given the saltiest bits.

WILL STUDD, THE ROQUEFORT REBEL

Once upon a time, about 20 years ago, Australian authorities announced a new national food code that banned the production and sale of *all* raw milk cheese. However, the code was quickly amended to create special exemptions once they realised they had outlawed cheeses such as Parmigiano Reggiano, Grana Padano and Swiss Gruyère. The ban remained for production of similar local raw milk cheeses.

To highlight the inequity of these regulations – imported special exemptions vs local production – our father, Will, formed the Australian Specialist Cheesemakers' Association to lobby for a fair go.

The Food Standards Australia New Zealand (FSANZ) regulations required all cheese produced in Australia to be made from 'pasteurised milk or the equivalent in bacteria reduction'. When FSANZ frustratingly refused to review this, Will took a different tack. He ordered a special consignment of 80 kg of pre-tested French Roquefort that met the equivalent bacteria standards to be airfreighted to Melbourne. On arrival, the offending cheese was seized by the imported food police and Will's requests to test it for equivalence by a recognised government laboratory was denied. Cue legal proceedings and an expensive appeal to overturn the government's ruling.

The Roquefort would spend more than a year in a special cage at a warehouse as authorities prepared for the case. We can still remember being at the family dinner table when Mum interrogated our father's sanity, given he was being threatened with either 10 years in jail or a $100,000 fine if he sold the cheese. Will lost his appeal and was ordered to destroy the Roquefort by deep burial.

Now was his time to let loose with the mischief and ruffle some feathers. A few days later, under the supervision of authorities, the Roquefort in question was placed in a hearse draped with the French flag and slowly driven to the public tip. There it was 'deep buried', as required by the original directive, to the sounds of the French national anthem. The story and pictures of the burial went viral. This in turn triggered diplomatic talks between Australia's trade office and their counterparts in the French government. Two years and millions of dollars later, the Australian food authorities published a 168-page report on why Roquefort (the oldest and most popular raw milk blue cheese in France) was safe for sale in Australia and agreed to grant it a special exemption under the code. Will Studd, the Roquefort Rebel, was victorious and his legend solidified.

The Roquefort funeral procession is well worth a look on YouTube, should you have a minute to pay your respects and mourn the untimely death of 80 kg of Roquefort.

Top Australian blue cheeses

GIPPSLAND BLUE, TARAGO RIVER CHEESE COMPANY

Made: Gippsland, Victoria
Milk: Cow

Handcrafted by the Tarago River Cheese Company, Gippsland Blue is the Australian rendition of Gorgonzola Dolce, but showcasing true Gippsland provenance. This is Australia's first farmhouse blue cheese, developed in the 1980s with help from Richard Thomas and our father, Will. It's now a joint venture by the Jensens and Johnsons, two neighbouring farming families.

Housed in a natural rind, this cheese has a pudding-like consistency and is mild and creamy in flavour, with a hint of sweetness and yeast from the natural blue moulds. Each wheel is hand-salted and pierced and matured in underground cellars. It's a well-balanced cheese.

LOOK: A natural rind with blue-grey streaks and a clotted cream–coloured paste.

TEXTURE: Creamy, smooth and buttery when young.

TASTE & AROMA: A good introduction to blues, it's mild and buttery with a hint of sweetness; older profiles can be spicy.

EAT WITH: Pairs well with pears, dates, figs, honey, walnuts, rye bread, fruit and nut breads, and mushroom pasta.

DRINK WITH: Dessert wines and porter team up well.

RIVERINE BLUE, BERRYS CREEK GOURMET CHEESE

Made: South Gippsland, Victoria
Milk: Buffalo

Barry Charlton from Berrys Creek Gourmet Cheese has been in the industry for 44 years and makes Australia's only buffalo blue cheese using milk from his neighbour's Riverine water buffalo. Known as the 'Master of Blue' in Australian cheese circles, Barry has been making cheese on his farm, tucked between Gunaikurnai and Boonwurrung lands in the Gippsland area, since 2007.

Riverine Blue is a multi-award-winning cheese – and for good reason! Sweet, bright and creamy flavours meet on your palate in the most enchanting manner, lingering with a mineral savouriness that will have you reaching for more before you've finished your first mouthful. It's matured for 8–12 weeks in a purpose-built maturation room on Wilsons Promontory.

A visually striking cheese for your cheese board, its light linen-coloured interior is streaked with the most fabulous and piercing blue-and-green moulds – a bit like the Northern Lights. Riverine Blue is unique, moreish and a true crowd-pleaser. Enjoy it young, served with a white wine, preferably on a leisurely Sunday afternoon.

LOOK: The 150 g portions have an ivory paste with even blue and green moulds.

TEXTURE: Buttery, rich and dense.

TASTE & AROMA: A happy union of sweet, bright, creamy, savoury and minerally flavours, with complexity.

EAT WITH: Spread atop crisp pear slices and oatcakes. Crumble on top of cauliflower soup or cos lettuce salad.

DRINK WITH: Pinot gris and sweet or dry riesling are good friends.

HOT TIP: Another favourite Berrys Creek cheese is the cow's milk Mossvale Blue, which is super creamy and sweet.

OTHER FAVE AUSSIE BLUES

Honourable mentions to: Pecora Dairy's Jamberoo Mountain Blue and Long Paddock's Bluestone; King Island Roaring Forties Blue is a worthy mention – we know that it's waxed, but we love how moist, bold and sweet it is, plus it's easily available.

STINKERS
(AKA WASHED RINDS)

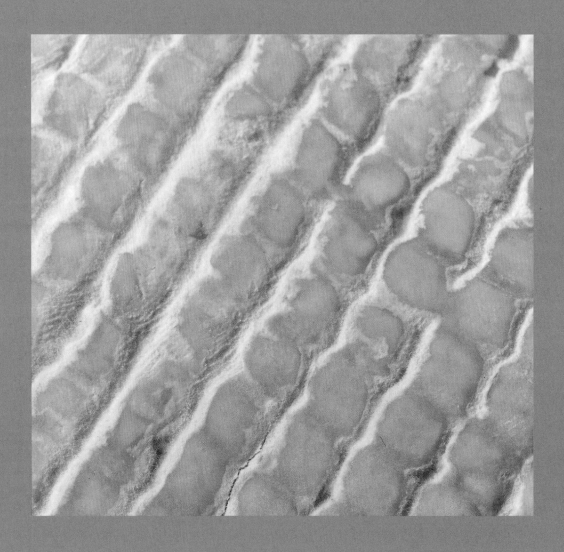

'Their bark is worse than their bite.'
16TH-CENTURY PROVERB

As the name implies, washed rind cheeses are, quite literally, 'washed'. They are one of the most recognisable types of cheese with their signature orange rind and punchy stank. They fill a room with aroma and leave people pointing accusatory fingers at each other, with some so smelly they are supposedly banned on public transport in France. But if you're willing to overlook their polarising perfume and delve a little deeper into these misunderstood beauties, you'll discover cheeses that are balanced, with smooth, milky and cured-meat flavours that are very persuasive on the palate. Like all good things in life, you need to work at it. The word 'Époisses', the name of one of the most infamous stinkers, literally means 'worth the effort' in French. And, indeed, it is.

Stating historical facts as concrete can be problematic. However, the story goes that sometime in the vicinity of the 7th century, a Benedictine monk living in a cool, damp environment noticed some unwanted mould growing on a wheel of cheese. He tried to rub it off with sanitising liquid (most likely saltwater or beer) and when the mould kept appearing, he kept 'washing it'. Eventually, by what the monk could only assume was an act of God, it turned orange. Although it was pungent and a colour not usually associated with edibility, the monk put his divine faith to the test and tasted the mysterious specimen. Hallelujah! A delicious, albeit stinky, washed rind miracle was born.

By washing away surface mould, the monk unknowingly created an ideal environment for *Brevibacterium linens* (a bacteria more succinctly known as *B. linens*) and natural yeasts to grow and help develop their unique, stinky characteristics. Thankfully, since that divine discovery, folk have adopted this method of washing and bathing cheeses in beer, brandy, wine, spirits and brine for all of us to enjoy.

Although the exact origin story of washed rind cheese is up for debate, it's generally accepted that it emerged in Europe during medieval times. Most cheeses are a product of circumstance and, for washed rinds, it came down to the unique conditions of monastic living. Monasteries often had large herds and strict routines, and could transform milk into cheese on a daily basis. The result was fresh milk that was quickly coagulated with slow acidification and high moisture, creating an ideal environment for yeasts and coryneform bacteria. It's said monks originally enjoyed washed rinds as a substitute for meat during religious fasting, calling them 'white meat'. So next time you taste a washed rind, pay attention to its distinct savoury qualities. Even the rind's fleshy-pink colour looks slightly meat like, if you squint.

What is a washed rind cheese?

Washed rind cheeses cover a lot of varieties and can be hard to pigeonhole. The basic definition is a cheese that has been washed, smeared or dunked in some form of liquid to encourage the growth of bacteria and yeasts.

Washed rind cheeses are another type of surface-ripened cheese that mature from the outside in, as bloomy rind cheeses do. But rather than relying on mould to mature the cheese, coryneform bacteria and yeasts on the rind help break down fats and proteins in the cheese for ripening. This microbial breakdown is responsible for the distinctive smell, colour and texture of the cheese.

To encourage the surface-ripening flora to hang around, washed rind cheeses are placed in cool, high-humidity environments such as purpose-built affinage facilities or damp cheese caves.

Typically, the higher the moisture level in the cheese, the greater the stink, and the more orange the rind is, the more funk it will possess. Lower moisture, hard varieties (such as Gruyère or Beaufort) barely register in whiff, and although they technically enter the washed rind category because they are brine-washed, for this book, we've kept them firmly in the firm category. Instead, our focus here will be on the soft to semi-firm monastery-style cheeses with higher moisture content. So, follow your nose.

What do you wash the cheese in?

Many washed rind cheeses are washed in alcohol, including beer, brandy, wine and spirits. Some are simply washed in a saltwater brine, while others are bathed in herbs and spices or annatto. The process is usually as straightforward as dipping a cloth into a small amount of chosen washing liquid, then wiping the whole surface of the cheese with it.

What the cheese is washed in will affect its taste and appearance. For example, cheeses that are washed in alcohol often take on a deep-reddish hue. The frequency of washing adds moisture and attracts microflora. If not for the carefully planned washing of these cheeses, they may become too sticky, overpowering or slimy, a bit like partied-out punters at a Burning Man decompression party.

Why do you wash the cheese?

Cheesemakers wash the rinds with a desired outcome in mind. Washing affects the colour and appearance of the cheese, as well as the texture and taste. Adding moisture encourages good bacteria, yeasts and fungi to flourish and attach to the surface of the cheese as it matures, and supress unwanted moulds. Some cheesemakers wash their cheeses for aesthetic reasons, so their cheeses have striking orange, red or pink hues.

Look

The rinds of washed rind cheeses vary in colour from soft peachy oranges, to neons, dark pinks, deep reds, bronzes and browns. As a general rule of thumb, the brighter terracotta colours and stickier rinds indicate a stronger stink and pungency. Some rinds can look sticky and gritty, and some have natural white flecks (which is normal). Young, soft washed rinds will have a chalky centre. The interior colour will vary.

Texture

The texture of washed rinds will vary depending on the style. The good yeasts and bacteria change the texture of the cheese by 'eating' the cheese from the surface, inwards. This in turn breaks down fats and proteins in the paste, making it squidgy and soft. This texture can be witnessed with the naked eye near the rind. The inside paste can be chalky, buttery, creamy, spoonable and fudgy, yielding through to a runny, sticky mass. In larger-format washed rinds, the paste can be anything from firm to elastic.

You will also notice that a lot of the more intense washed rinds come in a cute little wooden box. This is not just an attempt to style these beastly cheeses into beauties, but done out of necessity, because as they start getting on, they'll become a runny, gooey, hot mess. If you like them in this state, then by all means, you do you, but you may need to employ a spoon to ferry it into your mouth.

Taste & aroma

Washed rind cheeses may smell leathery, barnyardy or even 'unshowered', but give way to a mellow, savoury and milky flavour when eaten. Many are described as tasting like cured meat or leek and onion soup. As many washed rinds have been brine washed, they will usually be saltier compared to other cheeses.

If you are just starting out on your washed rind journey and find yourself scrunching up your nose – you can still employ the 'mild to wild' rule by asking your cheesemonger for a starter washed rind. Beginner washed rinds, such as Taleggio, Fontina, Raclette or Soumaintrain, are approachable for most.

If you decide to eat the rind, it will often taste minerally, savoury and beefy; however, some in this category can be gritty (an acquired taste). Have a nibble and cut it off if it's not your thing.

How to serve

Given their bold personalities, the best way to enjoy washed rinds is simply. We often pull them out in autumn, as these cheeses will have been made at the end of a cow's natural lactation cycle, when their milk is richer and fattier, plus we can say to our guests the cheese board was inspired by the autumn leaves outside! For drinks, these are one of the only cheeses that can take the brunt of your uncle's full-bodied white plonk, a non-sweet cider to cut through the meatiness or an Indian pale ale.

Pair with some pickles, tomato jam or pickled veggies for acidity, to cut through the cheese's funk and meat. Raw veggie sticks also stand up to the wild side of washed rinds, and stone fruits are becoming an increasingly popular match to contrast these stinkers.

Top global washed rind cheeses

TALEGGIO PDO

Made: Italy
Milk: Cow

Taleggio is your gateway washed rind. It still has plenty of funk in the trunk, but it won't send you running home whimpering. Plus, it's great on pizza, which everybody loves. So consider a Taleggio-topped pizza your equivalent of washed-rind training wheels.

This ancient soft cheese began its life in the mountainous regions of Lombardy, around the 11th century. Traditionally only produced in the autumn months, it was called 'stracchino', meaning 'tired', in the local dialect, a reference to the traditional seasonality of this cheese, which was made when exhausted cows returned from their long and arduous descent from the Alpine regions.

The finest examples of Taleggio are matured in the Italian Alps, in granite caves cooled by melting snow. The caves provide a perfect maturing environment with their cool temperature (5°C) and high humidity (95 per cent), which enable the cheese to develop a rich, buttery texture.

In its prime, Taleggio should have a soft, supple texture that melts in your mouth, with a yeasty, slightly salty, finish. The rind adds to its interesting character, and we reckon it should be enjoyed, so be brave and bite down. There are many different Taleggios on the market but, without a doubt, our favourite Taleggio is made and matured by the Mauri family.

LOOK: A soft, square cheese with a slightly pink, yeasty-orange and white-speckled rind, and a smooth, ivory paste. Sometimes you'll see grey mould patches on the rind too – these are okay. Three of the four purposely stamped circles bear a capital T at their centre. Buy a wedge with no rind cracks, as it's a sign that the cheese is reaching the end of its life.

TEXTURE: Moist, smooth, squishy and tempting to poke. The paste has a delicate grain.

TASTE & AROMA: An enigma, Taleggio makes its presence known with a pungent, meaty aroma but, in fact, has a pleasantly mild, buttery, yeasty and elegant flavour. It is fruity and salty, with a slight tang that intensifies with age. If it's a quality Taleggio, the rind should be enjoyed!

EAT WITH: A great melter that levels up risotto, pizza, pasta and polenta. It marries perfectly with cooked mushrooms or roast vegetables. Serve with muscatels, quince paste and crusty bread on a cheese board.

DRINK WITH: Sangiovese, sparkling shiraz and dessert wines; pilsner.

THE VACHERIN FAMILY

Made: France and Switzerland
Milk: Cow

Not many things are sexier than these cold-season spruce bark–bound cheeses. The Vacherin family are not just one trick ponies either; they can be peeled back like a sardine can and eaten with a spoon plunged in, or baked in their boxes for an instant fondue. Hailing from the border between France and Switzerland, the official name-protected Vacherins are known by two names: Mont d'Or AOP (by the Swiss) and Vacherin Mont d'Or or Vacherin du Haut-Doubs PDO (by the French). We appreciate this is highly confusing, but a long-standing argument about the name remains between the two countries. The Swiss version is made from heat-treated milk and washed more frequently, while the French is made from raw milk.

Produced since the Middle Ages, Vacherins were made in winter, when cows returned from high-altitude pastures and there wasn't enough milk to make wheels of Comté and Gruyère. As the cows were at the end of their lactation period, their milk was fattier, resulting in a rich, creamy cheese. Each cheese was hand-wrapped in spruce bark from the Jura Forest, to act as a girdle and prevent oozing. The bark also adds a woody aroma and foresty flavours.

Unfortunately, in Australia, we don't currently have access to these gems, but we have a few bark-wrapped renditions that give you a hint of what you're missing out on. These include Le Duc Vacherin or locally made Long Paddock Driftwood, which are available all year round!

LOOK: Golden, pinky-peach and orange rind, mixed with white-speckled mould. The bark often has white mould, too (this is normal). Straw-to-ivory paste, depending on season.

TEXTURE: Depending on the ripeness and when you eat it, Vacherin and vacherin-style cheeses vary from runny, silky and fudgy, to spoonable cake batter.

TASTE & AROMA: You'll find forest aromas of earth, spruce and bacon, mixed with a little funk and animal. The French Mont d'Or is rich and creamy in taste, with some hints of hay, caramelised onion and pine forest.

EAT WITH: Traditionally served with just a spoon! Or serve with crusty bread, cornichons, pickled veg, boiled potatoes and cured meats. Great for instant fondue (see page 181). We encourage you to eat the rind, but do not eat the bark! See page 70 for how to cut spruce-wrapped cheese.

DRINK WITH: White wine from the Jura, chardonnay; wheat beer or IPAs.

RACLETTE

Made: Switzerland, France and other countries
Milk: Cow

If you had to choose the cheese most likely to star in a sexy foreign film, Raclette would be it. Outrageously sensual and voluptuous, Raclette is best known for the fondue parties of the '60s and '70s. But it also delivers a spectacular performance as a large wedge of golden, bubbling cheese under a hot grill, thanks to its gorgeous meltability. Perhaps the most fetishised cheese, Raclette's molten mess is deliciously scraped off with a knife to ooze promiscuously over boiled potatoes, charcuterie and pickles ... OUSH. Excuse us while we take a moment to compose ourselves.

'Raclette' translates to 'scrape' in French, referencing this ceremonial way to eat it, originally over a coal fire. It also describes the type of cheese. Its origins lie in the Alpine regions of France and Switzerland and date back to the 16th century. Surprisingly, it remained a well-kept secret to the rest of the world until the 1960s.

There are just two name-protected Raclettes: Raclette de Savoie PGI in France and Raclette du Valasis AOP in Switzerland, both made from raw milk under very strict regulations. French Raclette is meatier, whereas Swiss Raclette is often stronger with oniony notes. There are many other Raclette-style cheeses from around the world available on the market also.

If you're looking to host an epic cheese party, hire a raclette scraper or buy paddle grills. It's a great opportunity to go hard and invest in a large hunk of cheese (say a quarter or half a wheel) to feed many mouths. It's a particularly good time in winter – ski gear or Fair Isle knits optional.

LOOK: Wheels weigh 6–8 kg and are 35 cm in diameter and 8 cm heigh. The rind is orange/gold and can be sticky to the touch. Raclette has a butter-coloured paste.

TEXTURE: Semi-firm, supple and lusciously creamy.

TASTE & AROMA: Variable, depending on where it's made and the breed of cows. It ranges from sweet, nutty, meaty, toasty, fruity and buttery, with notes of green pastures. Be prepared for it to be a little smelly in your fridge.

EAT WITH: This is a silky melter with or without a cheese grill. Good-quality versions also stand up to being eaten as a table cheese without heat. If grilling, when it's blistering and golden on top, it's ready to scrape over potatoes, charcuterie and pickles.

DRINK WITH: Riesling with body and spice.

HOT TIP: Try Heidi Farm's Australian Raclette-style cheese.

FONTINA

Made: Italy
Milk: Cow

While Raclette is the star of a late-night foreign film, Fontina is the lead in a more PG-rated rom-com. It has similar vibes to Raclette, with its supple, smooth texture and meltability, but it's easier on the nasal passages and often flies under the radar for consumers.

Fontina originated in Italy, but fontina styles can be found throughout the world, with many iterations made in Denmark, the USA, Sweden, France and Quebec. It is brine-washed and matured in natural caves for about four months, before being inspected for perfect texture. This technique involves extracting a plug of cheese, which is then bent and assessed to see if the ends meet. If they meet, happy days, the texture is deemed perfect and it's ready for consumption.

Fontina PDO (also called Fontina Valle d'Aosta DOP) is the only name-protected version of this cheese. It is regulated by the Consortium of Fontina Producers and can only be made in the Alps of Aosta Valley in Italy, using whole raw milk from Valdostana cows. The cows graze in the lower mountains most of the year due to the cold climate, but come spring, the cheesemakers, herders, dairy farmers and cows all make their way to higher pastures, to take full advantage of the unique flowers, herbs and water, which add earthy and grassy flavours and aromas to the cheese. Fontina is classified as a washed rind cheese, as the rinds are lightly washed and rubbed in brine, but it also falls into the firm category.

LOOK: Flattened, cylindrical wheels weigh 7–12 kg and are 43 cm in diameter and 7–10 cm high. The rind is firm, thin and orange-brown in colour; the paste varies from ivory to straw-yellow, with small eyes.

TEXTURE: Chewy, dense, elastic and smooth.

TASTE & AROMA: Look for flavours that are fruity, nutty, grassy, earthy, buttery, sweet and creamy. Fontina should smell nutty and herbaceous.

EAT WITH: Silky and smooth, this cheese is an exceptional melter. Try it in polenta, rice, fondue, pasta, toasties and salads. Fonduta is an Italian-style fondue melted with fontina, milk and egg yolks, all stirred into a creamy dish.

DRINK WITH: Dry and light whites that complement the earthiness and sweetness of the cheese.

HOT TIP: The most accessible good-quality fontina available in Australia is Mauri Fontina.

ÉPOISSES PDO

Made: France
Milk: Cow

This slippery, stinky and dank little sucker is not for the faint-hearted. If you're just beginning your foray into washed rinds, you might want to retreat from this guy until you're a little more prepared and save him for the finale.

Hailing from the rolling hills of Auxois, northwest of Dijon, Époisses takes its name from its town of origin, where it was first made by Cistercian monks in the 16th century. It later featured at the court of Louis XIV, and was titled the 'King of all Cheeses' by gastronome Jean Brillat-Savarin in the 19th century. Its ubiquity was temporary, however, as Époisses nearly made it to the extinct list after the Second World War, due to industrialisation, changing tastes and, ultimately, a decline in rural manpower. It only made a comeback in the 1950s, thanks to Robert and Simone Berthaut, who did a little CPR, and Époisses was rebirthed yet again.

Époisses is one of the last remaining washed rind cheeses to use the traditional slow lactic ferment that develops over 16 hours and requires very little rennet to set. This results in a fragile curd that breaks down and gives the cheese its oozy paste. Époisses is washed in Marc du Bourgogne (a spirit distilled from grapes) for about four weeks.

The irony of this cheese is that once it reaches the best version of itself, it will start to go downhill fast. So be sure to get this guy on the way up, because it's unforgettable if you time it right.

LOOK: A glistening, almost sticky, ivory-orange to red-brick wrinkly rind that darkens with age, and a white-ivory paste. Avoid buying Époisses that is dark orange or brown, as it is a sign it is past its use-by date. Keep your eyes peeled for close relative L'Ami du Chambertin, an equally delicious and unique stinker.

TEXTURE: Unctuous, creamy, melting, smooth and oozy.

TASTE & AROMA: A serious funk that smells stronger than it tastes. Expect to sniff garlicky, fruity, mushroomy and barnyard notes, layered with a good amount of animal. The taste is similar to what you smell, with some salt, fruitiness and lactic notes, and a hint of alcohol.

EAT WITH: Dried fruits, crusty baguette, rye bread, spiced or chilli jams, honey, crisp apple and dark chocolate. Spoon onto hot potatoes.

DRINK WITH: Red or white wine from Burgundy, Champagne; Trappist beers, such as Orval or Chimay. Also try Calvados or a nice clean gin.

SOUMAINTRAIN PGI

Made: France
Milk: Cow

Like most traditional European washed rinds, enterprising monks were instrumental in Soumaintrain's origin story. It shone bright in the 19th century with the connected railroad network, but then became almost extinct for 30 years when milk prices were low. A few enthusiasts revived its existence in the '70s. Thank God, as in our humble opinion, this is one of the most underrated washed rinds cruising the shelves.

Soumaintrain is produced under PGI regulations and hails from Burgundy. Produced from cow's milk collected from a strictly designated region, the curds are set using traditional, slow overnight lactic fermentation techniques. The young cheeses are then matured in humid cellars for a minimum of 21 days, where they're diligently bathed with a brine solution.

At its peak, Soumaintrain will be mild and creamy with a sweet aroma. The smooth rind gradually develops wrinkles that become more pronounced, along with the aroma, as it ages. We like ours strong on the nose and gentle on the palate. But you'll find no judgment here if you prefer a more dialled down example.

LOOK: Ivory-yellow to white-apricot wrinkled rind with occasional grit, and a yellow-to-ivory paste.

TEXTURE: Soft and pudding-like consistency when ripe; chalky when young.

TASTE & AROMA: Mild, sweet, floral aromas and a milky and acidic taste when young; as it ages, it will develop a funky-sweet aroma with creamy, floral and umami undertones.

EAT WITH: Dried peaches, peanuts, caramelised onion jam and fennel seed crusty bread; melt over vegetables such as asparagus.

DRINK WITH: Chablis or rose; Marc de Bourgogne; lager.

Top Australian washed rind cheeses

KING RIVER GOLD, MILAWA CHEESE COMPANY

Made: Milawa, Victoria
Milk: Cow

Milawa Cheese Company, located in the fertile plains of North East Victoria on Yorta Yorta country, is one of Australia's pioneers of artisan cheese. Started by the Brown family, Milawa is a family-focused business, run by second-generation cheesemaker, Ceridwen Brown. Our favourite Milawa cheese is their righteous but mild little stinker King River Gold, one of the first cheeses off the rank when production started in 1988. The milk is sourced exclusively from a single herd of Australian dairy shorthorn cows. The rounds are washed weekly in brine and develop a peach-coloured rind around their soft interior. The cheese has an enchantingly earthy, fresh milk and delicate smoky aroma, with a lingering savouriness on the palate. It reminds us of an Australian version of Pont-l'Évêque, but it is iconic in its own right.

LOOK: Orange-peach coloured dry rind, with a pale-straw soft paste.

TEXTURE: Gritty rind with a slight tackiness, and a soft, plump and fudgy interior.

TASTE & AROMA: Funky scent and full-flavoured tastes of smoke, earth, nuts and yeast.

EAT WITH: Crusty bread, baked potatoes, pickled onions, cured meats, tomato relish. Melt it over roasted vegetables.

DRINK WITH: Dessert wines; creamy stout; chilled white tea.

MONTE ROSSO, SECTION28 ARTISAN CHEESES

Made: Adelaide Hills, South Australia
Milk: Cow

Monte Rosso is Adelaide Hills' version of Taleggio and a delicious entry-level stinker. It is made by Section28's Kym Masters, a small artisan producer who spent many years working overseas in France and Italy, and loved how the cheese represented the terroir of where it was made, the village and the people. Kym is passionate about capturing the essence of the Adelaide Hills (Peramangk and Kaurna country). He employs traditional techniques to highlight the quality of the milk and matures the cheese in shipping containers repurposed as 'cheese caves'. Monte Rosso offers up a somewhat intense aroma and a savoury flavour, complemented by a slightly sweet and milky finish. Section28 is named after Kym's family farm.

LOOK: Square shape, a yeasty-orange-to-tan rind with brown and green flecks, and a butter-coloured paste.

TEXTURE: Fudgy and almost squishy; small eyes.

TASTE & AROMA: Savoury, fruity and buttery, with a tangy sweet finish; nutty aroma that gets more pungent with age.

EAT WITH: Exceptional melter for risotto, fondue or pizza. Pair with charcuterie, pickles, tomato relish and sourdough.

DRINK WITH: Textural white wine or a light fruity red.

MOUNTAIN MAN, L'ARTISAN

Made: Mortlake, Victoria
Milk: Cow

L'Artisan cheese is made in a small, purpose-built facility located in Mortlake, on Eastern Marr country in Western Victoria. Matthieu Megard is a third-generation French cheesemaker who has adapted traditional French recipes to create his organic, handmade Australian cheese range. The Mountain Man is a delicate washed rind cheese made from organic milk and takes inspiration from the French Reblochon. Washed every second day and matured for up to four weeks, this gem oozes satisfying umami with bacon flavours, and is deliciously complex and balanced.

LOOK: Ivory and nectarine rind with an off-white paste.

TEXTURE: Fudgy, gooey and lusciously oozy when ripe.

TASTE & AROMA: Mildly pungent aroma with umami yeasty flavours that can be fruity, too.

EAT WITH: Crackers and dried fruits. Use as a melting cheese in tartiflette, or melt seductively over roasted potatoes.

DRINK WITH: Dry white wine or a light pinot noir; stout.

OTHER FAVE AUSSIE STINKERS

Honourable mentions to: Stone & Crow's Night Walker, a meaty, creamy washed rind that makes us cooee and howl; L'Artisan's Marcel, Australia's nod to Saint-Marcellin, which is a fab addition to an all-Australian cheese board; and Halls Family Dairy's Suzette in WA, a smoky and nutty washed rind, made with the milk of Normande cows.

FIRM

'Age doesn't matter,
unless you are a cheese.'
ANONYMOUS

Firm cheeses are often the most affable and approachable cheeses on the board. They're not the type to mount a hostile takeover of your palate with robust funk like a blue or washed rind might, and they won't drape their luscious fat content suggestively over your cracker as a sultry bloomy would. Although they're less likely to intimidate and overpower, firms come with their own intensity and complexity, and will linger on your palate like a dream from a pleasant afternoon nap.

The sugar daddies of the cheese world, firm cheeses are irresistibly rich and quite happy to lavish others with gifts until they eventually expire. They're characterised by low moisture content, slow maturation, robust rinds and firm-to-hard textures that include rubbery, pliable, smooth, flaky, firm, hard, chalky, grainy, toothsome, dense, crumbly and granular. This is the biggest (literally), broadest and most diverse cheese category, making it a slippery one to pin down.

Traditionally, firm cheeses reflected their environment and were made in the spring and summer when there was a seasonal flush of milk. They were then stored away to be enjoyed later and provide sustenance for the rest of the year. Today, however, firm cheeses are produced year-round and have been adopted by cheesemakers worldwide.

Firm cheeses can not only survive for months or even years, but they also mature and develop flavours and complexities over time. Unlike their softer brothers and sisters, these guys are built to last. As they ripen, they rely on their protective rind to keep intruders from their inner sanctum, allowing them to focus inwardly on developing flavour and depth.

Long affinage often requires cheeses to be regularly brushed and flipped, labour that adds to the end price tag, but once you taste the kaleidoscope of flavours present in many firm varieties, you'll agree they're worth every cent.

Many firm cheeses also moonlight as other cheese types, so while they may be hard, they may also side hustle as washed rinds. Essentially, hard cheeses defiantly elude neat labels, making this section a motley crew. Still, they can be defined by a few loose characteristics: firm to hard in texture; a lowish moisture content; and housed in a sturdy and protective rind. The alchemy of firm cheese shares one common objective: removing moisture from the curd to extend the life of the cheese. Looking at how cheesemakers achieve this, as well as a few important definitions, can help us understand this broad category. Let's dive in.

Firstly, the curds are often cut quite small in order to release moisture – this is ingeniously called 'cutting'. As removing moisture is pretty imperative to the whole process, all firm cheeses are also pressed, either under their own weight or mechanically. It can help to think of curds as a sponge – the harder you press, the more moisture or liquid will come out. As a rule of thumb, the longer and harder the pressing, the lower the moisture content and the drier and crumblier the cheese.

But we're not done expelling moisture yet. Cooking or scalding curds works to shrink them and, you guessed it, remove moisture. Cut curds are heated in the whey, forcing them to contract. This also caramelises the remaining lactose and leaves a characteristic sweetness. Adding salt to the curd or rind further aids moisture extraction and the higher the salt content, the firmer the cheese will be.

The controlled storage of cheese, known as 'maturing' or 'affinage', ultimately affects its firmness. This is a real science and there are countless books on the subject, but, essentially, the higher the air flow, the lower the moisture and the harder the cheese. Rind, too, plays a role in how firm a cheese will become. If the skin is porous, it will dry out more quickly. If the rind is sealed, it will act as a protective shell and slow maturation.

Types of firm cheeses

Within the firm category, there are some families or styles that are often herded together under one banner. You may find these family groups at your local cheese counter or see them written about in a recipe and wonder what they mean, so here is an explainer. Although, do remember, there are many firm cheeses that don't belong to a particular style.

ALPINE & ALPINE-STYLE

Alpine is a term used to describe cheeses made in the Alps, usually from Switzerland, Jura, France and Northern Italy. Large wheels (usually 40 kg or more) are most often made from raw cow's milk. Cheesemakers still use the term 'Alpine' as a way to describe the style of cheesemaking, whereby milk is slowly heated (often in copper vats), the curd is cut very small, and then drained and heavily pressed. Alpines often have a condensed, firm texture with a caramel, cooked milk and nutty taste. Many are also brine-washed, giving an additional pleasantly savoury and meaty flavour.

To understand Alpine cheeses, you have to look at the tough landscape where they evolved (circa the 12th century). High-altitude, snow-capped mountains – you guessed it, the Alps! Herds were taken up the mountain in summer and spring, a practice called transhumance, to graze on the mountain meadows blossoming with wildflowers. It was an idyllic life for a simple bovine. The animals would munch on biodiverse pastures, which would be vividly captured in the milk and, in turn, expressed in the cheese. The downside, however, came via the tough, steep landscape, which was not logistically friendly for the transportation of cheese. So the cheese had to be efficient, nutritionally dense, durable and stable for long periods.

To combat these challenges, farmers would pool their milk to yield a larger volume. The cheeses were made to preserve this milk, which was packed into each wheel and kept for long periods. This meant making low-moisture, nutritionally dense cheeses, much like an olden-day energy bar. Huts were built for cheesemaking along the grazing route, and larger cheese wheels were made for easier transportation. Interestingly, some cheeses, such as Beaufort, evolved to have concave sides to assist with being strapped to a donkey.

Alpine cheeses include Emmentaler, Gruyère, Beaufort, Appenzeller, Fontina PDO and Comté, and they all make magnificent 'melters'. You will also see cheeses labelled 'Alpine-style' or 'mountain' cheeses. This means the cheese may not be made in the Alps, but has been made using a similar cheesemaking process.

GRANULAR OR GRANA-STYLE

Granular cheese or 'grana' is a style of cheese from Italy with a firm, flaky and grainy texture. They're usually brine-soaked to encourage the development of a natural rind, which is rubbed with the fat that seeps out as the cheese matures. 'Grana' ('grain' in Italian) refers to the curd being cut very small (the size of a rice grain) to achieve the characteristic texture. Examples include: Parmigiano Reggiano, Grana Padano, Pecorino Romano and Pecorino Sardo.

TOMME OR 'TOMM'

'Tomme' is an umbrella term used to describe cheeses that are thick, round and flat, with natural rinds that are usually grey or brown in colour and aged over several months. There are no official rules in what makes a Tomme, although they are usually named after the place in which they are made. They usually have a pliable texture, some creaminess and vary in taste depending on the type of milk used. Their natural rind imparts an earthy quality and many are matured in cellars, which can lead to wet-stone aromas. You will find many Tommes made all over France and Italy (called Toma), but the style is gaining traction globally. The most famous example is Tomme De Savoie PGI.

WASHED CURD

The defining characteristic of washed curd cheeses is that the curds are washed in hot water and the whey is diluted before moulding and pressing. This results in a sweeter, smoother and more mellow cheese, as washing removes the sugar (lactose) and thus stops it from producing lactic acid, which, in turn, reduces the cheese's acidity. Washed curd cheeses tend to be mild with a creamy flavour when young, and take on caramel or butterscotch notes as they age. The process also affects the texture and mineral content, resulting in a more pliable and supple texture when young that becomes hard and flaky when aged. Doesn't that just sound like a very human condition! An example of this is young Gouda compared to aged Gouda.

The amount of water used and the temperature varies with each cheese, as does the type of maturation and rind formation. Many washed curd cheeses are hard Dutch or Dutch-style, but, just to keep you on your toes, there are some semi-firm 'melters' that are washed curds, such as Raclette, Reblochon and Morbier. Some people get confused by washed curd and washed rind cheeses. Washing curds is a process that happens *during* cheesemaking and it's the curds that are washed, as opposed to washed rinds, where the rind is washed *after* the cheese is made.

holzhofer

Testun di vacca

Malga Zebio stravecchio

Bagoss d'alpeggio

Giulin
ACORNERO

Tometta Valdossola

Robiola di Eros

Robiola in foglie di castagno

La Robiola di Eros
LA CA SE RA

CHEDDAR

Cheddar is the world's most popular style of cheese, including in Australia, where it represents 70 per cent of all cheese eaten. Cheddar is both the name of the cheese and a cheesemaking technique called 'cheddaring'. It has also evolved into a generic term to describe a particular flavour and texture of any cheese. Only a small amount of 'cheddar' can actually claim to authentically represent traditional cheddar. All too often, though, the name is borrowed to refer to industrially made, processed bricks of cheese aged in plastic and with descriptors of 'sharp' or 'tasty' on the packaging. Yes, you know the type. There's a whole section dedicated to these pseudo-cheddars in every supermarket. Genuine, artisanal clothbound cheddar originated in the fertile pastures of South West England.

Cheddar – the name

The cheese came to be known as cheddar due to its association with the small village of Cheddar in Somerset, where tourists would come to picnic at Cheddar Gorge. These frolicking day-trippers loved snacking on local cheeses, which they dubbed 'cheeses from Cheddar', but, oddly enough, none of these cheeses were actually what we would call cheddar today.

Cheddar – the technique

Authentic cheddar is made using the time-honoured technique of cheddaring, which involves hand-stacking blocks of formed curd into small towers to force out the whey and encourage acidification. The whey is drained from the curd, which is allowed and encouraged to knit into a mat at the base of the cheese vat. The mat is cut into strips or blocks and stacked on top of one another, then unstacked and, rather laboriously, restacked. This is the defining feature of cheddaring. The weight of the curd helps to squeeze out moisture and gives authentic cheddar its characteristic crumble and sharpness. The cheeses are then milled into small pieces, salted and pressed, then wrapped in breathable muslin or cloth, sealed with lard and matured for a minimum of a year.

Top global firm cheeses

PECORINO

Made: Italy
Milk: Sheep

Pecorino is the grand-daddy of Italian cheese and can be traced back to Roman times, predating all the cow's milk cheeses in Italy. Its name comes from the Italian word 'pecora', meaning 'sheep', an umbrella term used to describe the hundreds of different shapes, sizes, flavours and styles of cheese made from sheep's milk. Think of Pecorino as the chameleon of Italian sheep's milk cheese.

Most Pecorino made in Italy is consumed locally, but the latter part of the name will give clues about the region that the cheese is made in. For example, Pecorino Romano PDO was initially made on the outskirts of Rome and used to feed Roman legions (a daily ration of 25–30 g was allotted). As demand increased, farmers looked towards Sardinia to expand production, and the name Pecorino Romano was born as a means of differentiating.

Pecorinos vary in size and taste, but are often described as a saltier and more intense version of Parmigiano Reggiano. Look for the DOP/PDO symbols, as impersonations with the name 'pecorino' can be made from cow's milk, and will lead to disappointment. Here are a few of our favourites:

- **Pecorino Toscano PDO:** From Tuscany; milder and less bitey than other types; can be cured in olive oil or tomato paste.
- **Pecorino Siciliano PDO:** From Sicily; identifiable by its wicker basket imprint; has a shiny rind and gritty interior.
- **Pecorino Sardo PDO:** From Sardinia; smaller (about 4 kg); tastes slightly sweet.
- **Pecorino Romano PDO:** The original; easily recognisable by the embossed sheep's head on its pale-yellow rind; now made in Sardinia.

LOOK: These fellas are shape-shifters, but will typically have a brown or blackish rind, with a white-ivory paste.

TEXTURE: Dense, moist, flaky and pleasantly granular.

TASTE & AROMA: Soft spices, lactic notes.

EAT WITH: Goes well with honey, fruit preserves, pears, walnuts, carpaccio or bresaola. The high fat content of the sheep's milk means it melts like a dream, and a salty assertive finish can add a good punch of seasoning to your Italian cooking. Great in cacio e pepe (see page 222).

DRINK WITH: Dry or sweet white wines; reds, such as Brunello di Montalcino or Sangiovese; port, sherry or a martini.

OSSAU-IRATY PDO

Made: Basque Country
Milk: Sheep

The Basque region in the Pyrenees has a long history of cheesemaking. Trying Ossau-Iraty is a fabulous way to familiarise yourself with Basque sheep's milk cheeses. A seasonal cheese, as a result of many shepherds still practising transhumance, the shepherds live in stone huts while their flocks graze on lush pastures, then, come the cooler months, man and sheep make their way back down the mountain. The mountain pastures provide the sheep with a diet that is diverse in grass, aromatic plants and mountain flora, which translates into the final taste of the cheese. The challenge these days is to keep the tradition of transhumance alive, as younger shepherds tend not to find this somewhat isolating lifestyle appealing. To be fair, there's probably not a lot of phone reception up in the mountains.

Around 350 producers make farmstead Ossau-Iraty, but there are also nine large industrial markets that use co-operative milk.

LOOK: Wheels vary in size from 1.8 kg to 6 kg, with a variable rind colour from orangey-yellow to brown-grey, and an ivory-white interior. There are many types of Ossau-Iraty, the most prized is called 'estive' and is made with raw milk, but it can be a challenge to find. Raw milk Ossau-Iraty is legal in Australia.

TEXTURE: Smooth, semi-firm paste that is both oily and flowery. Older cheeses will have a more granular texture.

TASTE & AROMA: Variable, from gentle to refined, and with notes of biscuit, toasted almond, brown butter, grass, hay, meat, olives, earth and hazelnut. It can have a slight animal aroma.

EAT WITH: Cherry preserves are a must to serve with Ossau-Iraty, a local specialty that contrasts the cheese's saltiness. It also matches well with ripe tomatoes, olive oil and black pepper. Finely slice the cheese to release the aromas.

DRINK WITH: A traditional sweet Basque wine called Jurançon; Trappist beers; lapsang black tea.

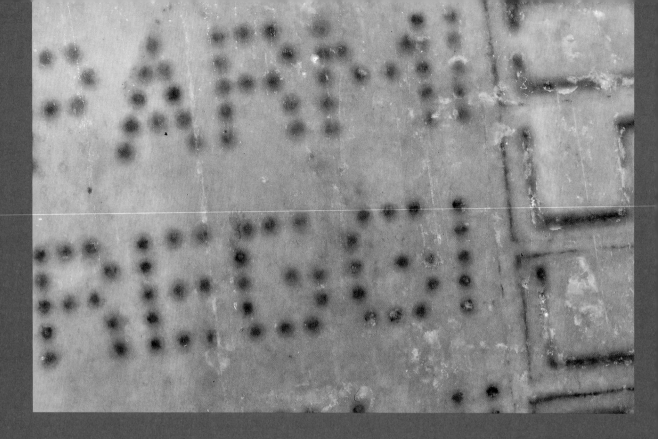

WHAT'S THE DIFFERENCE BETWEEN GRANA PADANO PDO & PARMIGIANO REGGIANO PDO?

LOOK

Every genuine Parmigiano Reggiano has the distinctive dotting of its name imprinted on the rind with the date of production and the code number of the manufacturer. Grana Padano carries the familiar clover-shaped mark, with alternating 'grana' and 'padano' inside a dashed diamond shape. They are similar in size and shape, and both have grainy textures with oily rinds.

LOCATION/TERROIR

Grana Padano is made with milk from a much larger geographical area. Parmigiano Reggiano must be made with raw milk from five specified provinces: Parma, Reggio Emilia, Modena, Bologna and Mantua. Milk quality from these regions varies, and the very best cheese is considered to come from Reggio Emilia and Parma.

FARMING & CHEESEMAKING

Grana Padano is made on a larger, more industrial scale, so its quality is harder to guarantee. It also allows cows to be fed silage and the use of a preserving agent called lysozyme. For Parmigiano Reggiano, cows are only allowed to graze on locally grown grass or hay to ensure milk quality. It is not mass produced, with the average dairy producing around 10 wheels of cheese per day.

Both cheeses are made from raw milk that is partially skimmed, and they use animal rennet. They're also both controlled by consortiums, which grade each cheese before they leave the maturing rooms. The grading is done with a hammer that checks for cracks and holes, and a needle, known as a spoletta, which is used to monitor flavour and texture. First-grade cheeses are the best, while third-grade cheeses are reserved for pre-cutting into quarters, or for prepacked supermarket wedges.

AGE

Grana Padano is often sold as young as nine months old, while Parmigiano Reggiano cannot be sold until it has been aged for 12 months. In both cases, the best cheeses are sold when they are between 18 and 24 months old. Cheeses that are aged for more than 24 months are often sold off at a lower price, because they are considered to have passed their peak in terms of sweetness and moisture content.

TASTE

Grana Padano has a slightly less robust flavour, is fruitier as well as drier in the mouth and more crumbly than Parmigiano Reggiano. Some Grana Padano can be on par with Parmigiano Reggiano, but when the price is lower, so is the quality.

PARMIGIANO REGGIANO PDO

Made: Italy
Milk: Cow

Parmigiano Reggiano PDO is the king of Italian cheese. It is produced by fewer than 500 small dairies, known as Castelli, in a strictly designated area of Northern Italy. Guarded like true Italian royalty, to bear the name Parmigiano Reggiano PDO the cheese must adhere to some of the strictest guidelines around, with grading systems monitored by a consortium before they can earn the official burnt brand stamp. A blend of raw, full-cream and skimmed milk from designated provinces, where cows are fed a diet of hay or grass; a minimum of 12-month maturation; and rigorous inspections, including tapping each cheese with a hammer to identify cracks, are just a few of the stringent requirements to qualify as a legit Parmi.

We've been lucky enough to see Parmigiano Reggiano PDO being made in Reggio Emilia. Commonly referred to as 'witnessing the birthing of twins' in cheese circles, this is considered a crescendo moment in any curd nerd's career. Around 1000 litres of milk is poured into each deep copper cauldron and worked by two masterful and strong cheesemakers to create just two 45 kg wheels of cheese per cauldron. The cheesemakers roll the heavy, molten curds that form at the base of each cauldron into a cheesecloth sling, before they are lifted to drain. After brining, the cheeses are moved to huge cooperative maturation facilities, where they are stacked in towers up to five metres high. The cheese is matured in warm, humid conditions that encourage natural oil to weep through the tough rind. They're turned and brushed regularly to prevent the growth of unwanted surface moulds.

LOOK: Hard, pale-golden, leathery rind with a straw-coloured interior. A full wheel will have the traditional dotted name markings and a seal. Parmigiano's different stages of maturity are recognised by ageing seals given at 18 months, 24 months and 30 months.

TEXTURE: The cheese should have a firm texture that is a little succulent and even moist. Younger wheels will usually be fudgier, while older wheels will be drier, more granular and perhaps studded with crunchy amino-acid crystals.

TASTE & AROMA: A good Parmigiano Reggiano will have a delicate, buttery, sweet aroma and complex nutty taste. If you're lucky, you may crunch down on some sweet-salty crystals that melt in your mouth and leave you with a smile. Due to the number of dairies producing this cheese, taste and aroma varies depending on season and location. A summer cheese is usually grassier and more herbaceous; other seasons yield cheese that is more lactic, buttery or nutty. Age will concentrate the flavour and aroma of Parmigiano Reggiano's umami characteristics.

EAT WITH: Shaving over some quality Parmigiano Reggiano will elevate many a dish, but it can also hold its own on a cheese board. Serve bite-sized chunks with a drop of extra-aged balsamic vinegar as an appetiser or dessert – the nuttiness and crunch of the cheese swoons with the syrupy sweetness of the balsamic; grate over fresh vegetables, dressed with a drizzle of extra-virgin olive oil; or pair with fresh fruit such as apples, pears, grapes, green olives or strawberries. It is also delightful with dried fruits such as apricots, figs or raisins.

DRINK WITH: There's an exquisite affinity between the tingling feel of bubbles in Champagne or Prosecco and the crunchy little crystals of calcium lactate embedded within the dense richness of a good, old Parmigiano Reggiano. Other matches include grappa, riesling, sherry or lager.

HOT TIP: If a cheese is labelled 'parmesan', this means you're buying a cheese that has been made in the style of Parmigiano Reggiano, so make sure you are buying the real deal. Despite popular belief, flavour and texture trump the age of Parmigiano, so don't be sucked into a 24- or 36-month-old cheese being sold as more premium. The optimum age is between 18 and 24 months, and skilled maturation is what impacts the cheese's overall taste, not how old it is. Our favourite is from the Giorgio Cravero family, who have been maturing Parmigiano with in-built storerooms in Bra since 1855. If possible, buy a wedge that has been freshly 'cracked' from a full wheel, or from a store with a high turnover of product. This is a cheese we buy in a large wedge and store in the vegetable drawer of the fridge, to cut off smaller pieces and use as needed. Always freshly grate it from the wedge just before cooking or serving to make it shine.

MANCHEGO PDO

Made: Spain
Milk: Sheep

Manchego is Spain's most famous cheese. It's made from the whole milk of Manchega sheep, a breed well-adapted to the arid but fertile plateau of La Mancha, which, incidentally, is derived from the Arab word meaning 'dry land'. Manchego is a PDO cheese, so each 3 kg wheel must be entirely produced and processed within this region. As a result, all authentic Manchego contains the unique properties of this special terroir. You can identify a wheel by looking for the beautiful braided zig-zag patterns in the rind, which pay homage to the esparto grass belts traditionally used to mould the cheese. These days, it's achieved using plastic moulds. Archaeologists date Manchego cheesemaking as far back as the Bronze Age.

Unfortunately, many examples of Manchego cheese are cheap, mass-produced versions that lack any real reflection of place. Raw milk Manchego is labelled as 'artesano', but it's not legal to buy in Australia. Quality Manchego will also have a natural rind (many industrial versions have plastic-coated rinds), an ivory-coloured interior and a distinctive sweet, moist and nutty finish, with just a hint of the grasses and wild shrubs of the region. As Manchego ages, the flavours become more piquant and peppery, and the texture more granular. We love a six to nine month profile. We do not recommend eating the rind.

The three main types of Manchego you will see outside of Spain are:

- **Semi Curdo:** Aged for around three months; soft, supple texture; grassy, with a tangy finish.
- **Curdo:** Aged for three to six months; greater complexity of flavour, with more nutty and caramel notes.
- **Queso Viejo:** Aged for one to two years; rather intense flavour that's sharp and peppery.

LOOK: Many cheeses on the market will present the similar markings of Manchego, but the real-deal has the rectangular Queso Manchego stamp and is worth the purchase. It comes in 2.5–5 kg wheels, and the best Manchego will have a light-coloured natural rind or be rubbed in olive oil. Its interior, depending on its degree of maturity, varies between white and yellow.

TEXTURE: Semi hard. The interior paste becomes more granulated and drier with age.

TASTE & AROMA: Depending on its age and quality, generally Manchego will taste sweet, complex, grassy, delicate, woolly and piquant. The more mature it is, the more woolly and piquant it will taste.

EAT WITH: Serve with quince for a delightful contrast to the Manchego's salty bite. Also pairs well with grapes, Marcona almonds, membrillo, cured chorizo, toasted pumpkin seeds, Spanish olives, fresh or grilled figs and jamón. Use as you would Parmigiano Reggiano, but expect a little more kick.

DRINK WITH: Fino or Manzanilla sherry to meet the cheese's saltiness; or medium-dry sherry.

HOT TIP: Cut from the wedge into thin triangles, leaving the rind on as a handle. Manchego has a tendency to sweat on a cheese board, due to the high fat content of the sheep's milk. It needs less time to warm up, so don't bring it out of the fridge too early.

SAN SIMÓN PDO

Made: Spain
Milk: Cow

We call this 'smoky boob cheese' for reasons that become obvious when you glimpse its voluptuous teardrop shape. It's a traditional cow's milk cheese from Galicia, Spain, or 'Green Spain', appropriately named for its lush pastures, rivers and maritime landscape. Galicia is home to more than one million cows and is also famous for Tetilla, another cow's milk cheese that looks like a boob. So, from these two cheeses, we can ascertain the Spaniards of this area have an affinity for cows, boobs and cheese, not necessarily in that order.

San Simón cheeses are brined, then cold-smoked over native birchwood for two weeks, giving them a gorgeous smoky and woody flavour and an ochre-tan rind. Some say this cheese dates back to Celtic times and was originally made only by women. There are no official historical recordings of how the cheese's shape came to fruition, only a rumour mill of wonderous stories, including the suggestions that it was based on the Madonna's breast or shaped from a drinking goblet.

LOOK: Ochre-tan rind with a light yellow to gold paste, about 900 g.

TEXTURE: This is a semi-firm cheese that is pliable and with small eyes.

TASTE & AROMA: Nutty, sweet, buttery, earthy and smoky on the nose and the palate.

EAT WITH: Delicious in toasties and goes really well with ham and apple.

DRINK WITH: Pour a dry sherry or rose to swill with this cheese.

COMTÉ PDO

Made: France
Milk: Cow

Comté is a French Alpine cheese produced in the picturesque Jura mountains in Eastern France. This benchmark cheese's outstanding reputation is upheld by some of the strictest regulations of the French appellation system and is the epitome of a symbiotic relationship between farmers, cooperative dairies and affineurs.

Each year, more than a million wheels (that's a huge 40,000 tonnes) of Comté are produced, yet there's no such thing as a large producer. The average farm milks less than 50 Montbéliarde and/or Simmental cows, which require a minimum of 2.5 acres of natural pasture each. The milk from the numerous small dairies is collected daily, delivered to the cooperatives and transformed into cheese. Each wheel of Comté is made to a specific recipe in gigantic copper cauldrons and takes a whopping 500 litres of milk to make a 45 kg wheel. The wheels are then taken to the caves de affinage, which is a fancy name for where they mature the cheese. These are usually large cavernous cellars, where each cheese is meticulously washed, ripened and matured by highly engaged and skilled affineurs, until it is ready to be eaten.

Although Comté was first created in the 13th century, the game changer in Comté's story came in 1960, when affineur Marcel Petite selected cheese to mature in the damp vaults of Fort Saint-Antoine in the high mountains of the Jura. The fort was cooler than traditional caves at lower altitudes, which resulted in the cheese being matured much more slowly. The granite walls of the fort were also home to flora, referred to as the 'spirit of the fort', which further impacted flavour.

What is truly fascinating about Comté is that every stage of the process affects how the cheese tastes. We encourage you to go out and try different ages and brands to discover what you like. Personally, we believe in choosing a Comté based on its flavour profile, rather than age.

LOOK: The natural hard rind is a little crusty at times with yellow-to-brown colouring, which we prefer not to eat. Comté has a yellow, straw-coloured paste when made with summer milk, compared to a lighter ivory paste when made with winter milk. Tyrosine (cheese crystals) can be seen on aged Comtés. Each wheel weighs 45 kg, and will have a green or brown band around it. Choose one with a green label, as this means it has been awarded at least 14/20 by the AOP Syndicate of Comté. The brown label carries a score of 12–14, which means the cheese has a small default. Cheeses that score below 12 are not allowed to be called Comté.

TEXTURE: Smooth and buttery, turning to crumbly when aged.

TASTE & AROMA: Very seasonally dependant. When young, Comté has a sweet and mildly nutty aroma and taste. It can have a ferro taste if eaten too old. There are six flavours that emerge with Comté – lactic, fruity, roasted, vegetal, animal and spicy – so it's best to ask your cheesemonger to try a slice before buying. We enjoy a rich, nutty profile, with a savoury and mineral aftertaste. A good Comté should be tasted from the front to the back of the palate.

EAT WITH: Fresh crusty bread, cured meats and pickles; or for a sweet experience, try honey or chocolate. Dip sticks of Comté into soft-boiled eggs (see page 164).

DRINK WITH: Wine from the Jura, such as Vin Jaune or Champagne; oolong tea; filter coffee.

HOT TIP: Like Manchego, Comté is sensitive to temperature, so warm it up in your hands if you are really trying to consciously taste it.

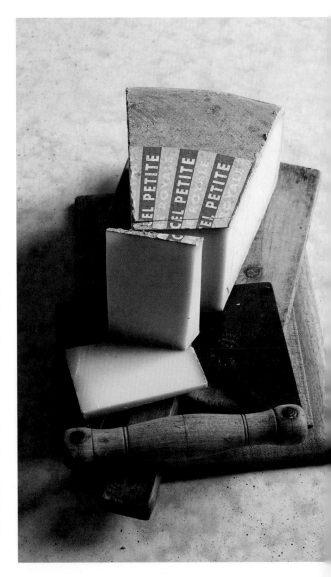

LE GRUYÈRE AOP

Made: Switzerland
Milk: Cow

Don't we all love a cheese that transports you somewhere magical due to its palpable expression of where it is from? Pop a slice of Le Gruyère in your mouth and we'll meet you high in the Swiss Alps, where cows graze on wildflowers and grass, and raw milk is heated in large copper vats.

Gruyère is one of the oldest cheese recipes in the world, dating back nearly 1000 years. This is a cheese born from survival, created as a way to preserve milk and provide sustenance and protein throughout winter, when snow and steep terrain halted the supply of fresh milk and limited herd activity.

The title of Le Gruyère AOP is reserved for those made in Switzerland. Just 170 small village dairies remain, each making 17–20 wheels of cheese a day. Only 10 affineurs are allocated to grading and ageing Gruyère wheels.

Le Gruyère is similar to Comté in its production and taste, which makes sense when you consider their geography, both made on opposite sides of the French Alps. Le Gruyère is made in the west, French-speaking canton of Fribourg. In terms of production differences, Le Gruyère is washed in brine, whereas Comté rind is rubbed with salt by hand.

Due to its consistency in quality, you will find Le Gruyère as a cornerstone product at any good cheese counter. Its taste varies depending on where the cheese is produced and the maturation length.

Gruyère types & grading

Le Gruyère AOP types are distinguished by different maturation periods. Le Gruyère Classic AOP is matured for five to nine months. Its taste is sweet, creamy and nutty, with a softer paste. Rarer types include Le Gruyère Reserve AOP and, rarer still, Le Gruyère d'Alpage AOP, which are most definitely worth experiencing if you see them.

You will also see other cheeses on the market called Gruyère. This is a technical name for the way a cheese is made and often used for mountain cheeses. These include Beaufort, Gruyère de Comté and Asiago, which can be a little confusing. If you are looking for the Swiss variety, look for the 'Le' preceding Gruyère.

LOOK: Each wheel weighs about 36 kg, with a hard beige-to-brown natural rind that we personally do not eat. The interior colour depends on the season, with a buttery yellow paste when made with summer milk, and a lighter ivory paste from winter milk.

TEXTURE: Firm, condensed, smooth and slightly grainy.

TASTE & AROMA: Toasty, nutty, fruity, earthy and complex, with a sweet aftertaste. Younger versions will be sweeter and creamier, whereas aged Gruyère is more complex, with a more pronounced nuttiness.

EAT WITH: This cheese is great in gratins, soups, fondue and quiche, and on toast with ham and mustard. On a cheese board, Gruyère saddles up well with onion jam. It also goes well with dark chocolate or filter coffee, as the sweetness of the cheese can stand up to their bitterness.

DRINK WITH: Aromatic and high-minerality white whites, as well as riesling, Burgundy white and chardonnay.

HOT TIP: Sometimes Gruyère-style cheeses will have small eyes and slits that weep in the paste. This can be a sign of good quality, as the salt is melting in the cheese.

MIMOLETTE

Made: France
Milk: Cow

Like the best-dressed celeb at the Met Gala, Mimolette makes a statement for all the right reasons. It's a head-turner at the cheese counter and on a cheese board. On the outside, Mimolette looks like a mummified bowling ball, while the inside has a striking reddish-orange colour like a chocolate Jaffa.

Mimolette emerged in the 17th century when, following a trade dispute, Louis XIV banned the import of Dutch cheeses. Feeling the sting of the absence of Edam on the cheese platter, Louis and the rest of the French population wanted a French-made version of the popular cheese. Not wanting to blatantly plagiarise the OG cheese, while still very closely copying it, the French made an orange version so it would appear 'different'. There were whispers this 'orangefication' was a not-so-subtle stab at the Dutch House of Orange-Nassau. This colour was originally achieved by stirring carotene from carrot juice into the curds, but was later replaced by annatto.

The other fun fact about Mimolette is that the rind is home to cheese mites, or 'precious little beasts', as the French fondly call them. These microscopic organisms have a symbiotic relationship with the cheese that allows it to breathe and mature. They're invisible to the naked eye, but you'll know they're keeping up their end of the bargain by the cratered rind and powdery residue they leave behind. Don't worry, they don't make it to the paste and are brushed and vacuumed away once a month.

LOOK: With a pock-marked dusty exterior and reddish-orange paste, each ball of cheese weighs 2.4–3.6 kg and is cut to order or portioned.

TEXTURE: Semi-hard to granular, depending on its age.

TASTE & AROMA: When it's young, Mimolette has a soft texture and mild, nutty taste. It's barely worth eating, apart from the novelty of an 'orange cheese'. If you can, try to hunt down an older profile, which is slightly pungent and more sophisticated in flavour. You'll notice fruit, hazelnut, butterscotch and sometimes smoky notes. The interior becomes crunchier and the crust that envelopes the cheese gets harder as the cheese ages.

EAT WITH: We like to shave or grate Mimolette over seasonal steamed veggies, such as asparagus or sweetcorn, slice over tomatoes or add to salads and risottos for a striking effect. It pairs well with candied pecans, cranberries, hazelnuts and pumpkin seeds.

DRINK WITH: A young, dry Fino. Aged Mimolette goes very well with beer, aged Bordeaux, cognac and dessert wines, as they tease out the cheese's caramel notes.

GOUDA

Made: Netherlands
Milk: Cow, goat, sheep

Many people know that Gouda is from the Netherlands, but did you know the correct way to pronounce it is 'how-duh', not 'goo-dah', in Dutch? Sorry to put a stop to your Gouda puns. Gouda is actually a generic term used to describe a large, thick disc of cheese with rounded sides, but the name originally comes from the city of Gouda in southern Holland, where the cheese was distributed. Although the Netherlands is small in size, it is still one of the largest commercial producers of cheese, with Gouda making up around 50 per cent of its production.

Gouda is not name protected, meaning it is used throughout the world as a style of cheese. To make the cheese, curds are washed in hot water and the whey is removed. The curds are then moulded and pressed. The removal of the whey also subtracts the lactose and creates a sweeter cheese that becomes even sweeter as it ages.

It might be hard to get your hands on, but keep your eyes peeled for Boerenkaas, a farmhouse Gouda made from raw milk and aged for 18 months. Failing that, look for Gouda that has been aged. The paste will usually be a more striking orange colour and denser, compared to the pale paste of a young Gouda. As it ages, the cheese develops a gorgeous complexity, with notes of butterscotch, toffee, caramel, toasted nuts and even chocolate, that linger on your palate long after your first bite. You may even be lucky enough to experience biting down on some crunchy tyrosine crystals, which are a true gift for the consumer in aged Gouda. Our favourite is L'Amuse Signature Gouda.

LOOK: Gouda is sold in many stages of maturation. Many Goudas available on the market are mass-produced and identifiable by their yellow wax and supple texture. Most of the sensational-tasting artisan Gouda never makes it out of Holland.

TEXTURE: Gouda varies in texture from supple, to firm and flaky when aged, depending on their affinage.

TASTE & AROMA: These cheeses are generally sold young and will taste buttery, mellow and slightly tangy. There are also Goudas flavoured with spices, such as cumin.

EAT WITH: Bitter chocolate, toasted almonds and cranberries. Try it shaved on rye bread with tomatoes, ham and pickles. Cumin Gouda is particularly agreeable in a cheese toastie.

DRINK WITH: Gin cocktails; whiskey; dessert wine or wine with raisiny notes; malty beers; dry Champagne; stout.

WHAT'S THE DIFFERENCE BETWEEN PROCESSED INDUSTRIAL CHEDDAR & TRADITIONAL CLOTHBOUND CHEDDAR?

LOOK
Traditional clothbound cheddars are made into large cylindrical drums (often 25 kg) that are wrapped in breathable muslin or cloth and sealed with melted lard. Industrial cheddar is produced in large uniform blocks or small wheels. Some are waxed, grated, cubed or sliced. The interior of both can vary from white to golden yellow or dyed orange, depending on where it is made.

CHEESEMAKING
Traditional cheddars rely on intensive hand labour for cheddaring, milling and binding, which takes many hours. Industrial cheddars use highly mechanical and automated processes to control acidity and use a stirred-curd method rather than cheddaring.

AFFINAGE
Traditional clothbounds are matured slowly, with the best aged between 18 and 24 months. The cloth allows the cheese to breathe and slowly release moisture. It creates an open and slightly crumbly texture. They require flipping and brushing throughout ageing. Industrial cheddars are matured in large fridges in plastic, which comes through in the taste with 'baggy' flavours and damp textures.

TASTE
For the effort, clothbounds are rewarded with complexity. Flavours range from buttery and butterscotch to nutty, meaty and earthy. Industrial versions are often predictable and taste as they are labelled, from mild to sharp (acidic). Modern cheesemakers in both camps are creating a new, sweet, candy-like flavour profile by adding cultures like *Lactobacillus helveticus*. Consumers seem to be liking it!

CLOTHBOUND CHEDDARS

Made: Multiple, including England, USA, Australia
Milk: Cow

Our top clothbound cheddars available in Australia are:

- Montgomery's Farmhouse Cheddar, Somerset, England
- Bay of Fires Farmhouse Clothbound Cheddar, Tasmania, Australia
- Quicke's Farm Traditional Farmhouse Clothbound Cheddar, Devon, England
- Cabot Clothbound Cheddar, Vermont, USA
- Long Paddock Granite Clothbound Cheddar, Castlemaine, Victoria
- Pyengana Dairy Traditional Cloth Matured Cheddar, Pyengana, Tasmania
- Westcombe Cheddar, Somerset, England

LOOK: Wrapped in cloth or muslin – simply remove before eating. For clothbound cheddar, it is okay to have cracks near the rind and even blue mould is accepted here. These cheddars come in many different-sized drums.

TEXTURE: Variable, but may be crumbly, firm, flaky, chunky, moist, open or dry.

TASTE & AROMA: Like fingerprints, no two clothbound cheddars are the same. Natural variation occurs for many reasons, such as the time of year the milk was produced, and the particular strains of bacteria in the starter cultures. You will usually notice an array of aromas and flavours, from savoury and brothy (pan-drippings), to caramel, nutty and melted butter, moist grass, clover and, sometimes, citrus notes. Dank and earthy aromas are part of the experience of true clothbound cheddars. A good cheddar leaves a complex and balanced impression that reaches right to the back of your palate and hangs around with a lingering tang. It finds the perfect apex of salty, sweet and acidic. The taste will vary from the centre of the cheddar to the rind, which can bring on flavours of horseradish and earth.

EAT WITH: Cheddar is acidic, so pair acid with acid and go for kimchi, chutney, mustard, pickles and apple. Or play contrasts by adding sweetness, such as raisin toast with caramelised onion, fruit bread or even an Eccles cake, if you can find one. Good cheddar on a ploughman's lunch (hearty bread, relish and pickles) is always welcome.

DRINK WITH: The buttery and acidic nature of cheddar means it was born to be paired with beer, sours and dry cider. Out-of-the-box pairings include a bold, smoky whiskey, a bloody Mary or ginger beer.

CHEDDAR TASTING TIPS: This is a tactile cheese that responds to touch. Try pressing it between your fingers to warm it up. You're looking for elasticity and bounce, or if it's weak, it could collapse. Notice if the cheddar is dry, crumbly or greasy. Always try cheddars from the nose to the rind and chew slowly.

Top Australian firm cheeses

BANKSIA, LONG PADDOCK CHEESE

Made: Castlemaine, Victoria
Milk: Cow

Banksia is a semi-hard cow's milk cheese new to the Australian artisanal cheese scene. A cross between a raclette and gouda-style cheese, it is made with pasteurised certified organic cow's milk. Banksia is the brainchild of Julie and Ivan Larcher, world-renowned cheese masters, who recently relocated from France to set up Long Paddock in Castlemaine on Dja Dja Wurrung country. This cheese is a sign of things to come from the highly respected establishment that emphasises careful monitoring of herd health, milking and small-batch production. The aromatic profile is nutty, fruity, buttery and sweet and, most importantly, an authentic taste of place. The paste is firm and elastic, while also being creamy and melty.

LOOK: Natural, mottled rind, with buttery yellow paste.

TEXTURE: Smooth, semi-firm and fudgy.

TASTE & AROMA: Sweet, fruity, buttery and nutty.

EAT WITH: A wonderful addition to a ploughman's platter.

DRINK WITH: A very light red; creamy stout; IPA.

CURFEW, STONE & CROW CHEESE COMPANY

Made: Yarra Valley, Victoria
Milk: Goat

Jack Holman, head cheesemaker and owner of Stone & Crow Cheese Company, fell into a figurative vat of curds and whey while backpacking in France. He continued his newfound passion for cheesemaking in Canada, before heading back to Australia to work for Yarra Valley Dairy. Stone & Crow existed as Jack's side hustle for five years, but it's now a full-time gig, based in Warrandyte on Wurundjeri Woi Wurrung land. The philosophy behind his business is present in its name: 'stone' represents the rock-solid elements, while 'crow' symbolises an adventurous and mischievous spirit. New to the market is Curfew, a semi-hard goat's milk Tomme made from a single herd of Saanen goats from Mansfield. Born as a result of Covid lockdowns in 2020, Curfew is appropriately named. An approachable and pleasant Tomme, the cheese is aged three to six months.

LOOK: This 2 kg wheel has a natural, light-brown Tomme rind, with an ivory paste.

TEXTURE: Semi-hard with small eyes.

TASTE & AROMA: Earthy, pleasant and sweet flavours, with notes of sweet grass, buttery leeks, parsnip and roasted almonds. The aroma is sweet, goaty and musty.

EAT WITH: Jack says he likes to pair it with apple, pear and walnuts.

DRINK WITH: Chardonnay; sour beer.

GRUYERE, HEIDI FARM

Made: Burnie, Tasmania
Milk: Cow

Heidi Gruyere is Australia's answer to Le Gruyère. Originally produced by passionate and skilled cheesemaker Frank Marchand in the lush green meadows of Northern Tasmania in the 1980s, the recipe and techniques are based on the cheese that Frank used to make in his homeland Switzerland, but are uniquely Australian. Today, this cheese is still made from local Tassie milk, using traditional techniques at the Saputo Dairy in Burnie, on tommeginne land. You would be hard-pressed to tell the difference between this Down Under iteration and the Swiss original when this cheese is melted. Our favourite wheels are made in late spring, when the grasses are rich with herbage that make a more sophisticated and rich cheese.

LOOK: Each wheel weighs 10 kg, with a natural rind and yellow buttery paste.

TEXTURE: Smooth and supple when young; flaky and concentrated when aged.

TASTE & AROMA: Toasty and roasted nuts. Frank believes his Gruyere made in late spring tastes the best, as Tasmania is covered in wildflowers, which translates into the milk.

EAT WITH: Known for its melting properties (like Le Gruyère).

DRINK WITH: Aromatic and high minerality whites; riesling.

MONFORTE, SECTION28 ARTISAN CHEESES

Made: Adelaide Hills, South Australia
Milk: Cow

Cheesemaker Kym Masters was an investment banker at Macquarie for 20 years, before pursuing his passion to make Alpine-style cheeses for the past six years. Monforte is one of his beauties, a delicious raw milk, semi-hard cheese, with a natural brine-washed rind. It is made and matured in shipping containers repurposed as 'cheese caves'. Monforte is multidimensional, dancing with notes of butter, toasted hazelnuts, beef broth and stewed stone fruit. It's a must-try modern Australian icon.

LOOK: Orange-rust hard natural rind with Section28 embossed in it. The interior is buttery to sunny in colour.

TEXTURE: Smooth and semi-firm paste.

TASTE & AROMA: Butter, hazelnuts, meaty and stewed stone fruit.

EAT WITH: Crusty bread, dried fruit or fruit paste.

DRINK WITH: An Adelaide Hills pinot noir, naturally; gamay or Savagnin; session ale.

RAW MILK C2, BRUNY ISLAND CHEESE COMPANY

Made: Bruny Island, Tasmania
Milk: Cow

Founder of Bruny Island Cheese Company, Nick Haddow, spent years overseas and in Australia, studying and refining his cheesemaking skills and knowledge. Nick and his team understand the importance of climate, native pastures, grasses, herbs and using traditional breeds to create a truly Australian cheese in the form of Raw Milk C2. It is a semi-hard cow's milk cheese that draws inspiration from the mountain cheeses of France and Switzerland. C2 is widely regarded as Australia's first raw milk cheese and is imperative for cheese lovers to try. Made on Bruny Island, on nuenonne land, this endemic cheese comes in large formats and is matured for 6–12 months. The rind is wiped every week to encourage the surface bacteria that provide its distinctive and robust integrity. The truth is that when Nick and his team were experimenting with the recipe for this cheese, they didn't have a name. The run sheet (recipe sheet) was denoted as CC, meaning cooked curd. When naming the cheese, it made sense to call it C2.

LOOK: Rugged, cream-coloured natural rind, with a yellow-straw paste.

TEXTURE: Smooth and buttery when young; crumbly when aged.

TASTE & AROMA: Mildly nutty flavour with brothy notes, and a sweet aroma.

EAT WITH: Fresh crusty bread and local honey. A side of caramelised nuts can add a nice sweet crunch.

DRINK WITH: Pale ale or IPA.

OTHER FAVE AUSSIE FIRM CHEESES

Honourable mentions to: Long Paddock's Ironbark, for its umami and brothy flavours; Holy Goat's sensational and seasonal cheese Nectar; all of Elgaar Farm's hard cheeses (seek them out if you are visiting Tassie's farmers' markets); The Peaks Mountaineer Tomme; and Cambray's Traditional Farmhouse Aged Gouda for those in WA.

CHEESY RECIPES

TIPS FOR COOKING WITH CHEESE

For these recipes, our aim was to select cheeses that were reasonably priced and intended for cooking. Most of us can't afford to spoil our palates with the ultra-good stuff on the daily, so we've reserved the artisan speciality cheeses to be the heroes of your cheese board. The only exception to this rule is if the cheesy splurge equals the flavour reward and has a significant impact on the dish. Here are some things to know when it comes to cooking with cheese.

- Aim to use good-quality cheese. If cost is an issue, or a cheese specified in a recipe is not available, look at the qualities and dominant flavour of the cheese used and substitute a similar cheese that is less expensive, but still made well.
- Choose appropriate cheeses for the type of meal you're cooking. For example, if you're making toasties, pizzas or anything where you want a cheese pull (those deliciously stretchy strands), you'll want to grab a cheese from our 'super-melty cheese' list opposite.
- Be aware that some cheeses can change in taste when they're heated. For example, goat's cheese will become less pronounced in flavour, while blue cheese can intensify.
- Under each recipe we've included a shout-out to the trusted brands we love for their consistency and premium quality. You don't have to use these for the recipe, but they are elegant versions, should you care to level up.
- Cheese is a salted ingredient, so try to be a little more present and sensitive to your dish's needs when seasoning, as you may need less than you are habitually used to. Your culinary prowess will go unappreciated if no one can detect the flavours you've created due to all the salt you've tossed in.
- Never buy pre-grated cheese, even for cooking. It's inferior, often oxidised and has additives, such as anti-caking agents and preservatives.
- Room-temperature cheese works best for cooking. However, if a recipe calls for the rind to be removed, do this while the cheese is still cold.
- Always add grated cheese to wet dishes, such as sauces, soups and risottos, at the last minute. Make sure the dish isn't too hot, then cook just long enough for the cheese to melt and combine.

Cheese rinds & what to do with them

Can't bear to throw out those hard ends because you instinctively know there must be some way to coax out the goodness trapped within? Yes, there is. But you can't possibly save them all, bless your heart. So, the ones to keep are Parmigiano Reggiano, Grana Padano and Pecorino.

- **Infuse oil.** Pop those parm rinds and a couple of garlic cloves into a jar of quality olive oil to make a flavourful oil. We recommend infusing the oil for at least 3 days before mopping it up with crusty bread.
- **Add to long-simmering sauces.** Beans, stews or red sauces can develop a lip-smacking umami flavour and richness with the addition of parm rinds. It is (or was) a secret of ours that deludes guests into believing the sauce has been simmering for hours (genius, we know).
- **Add to a broth or stock.** Add Parmigiano or Pecorino rinds to your base stock, broth or simmering rice. Stocks can be used for dishes such as risottos and chicken or vegetable soups. A general guide is that if the cheese tastes good in your dish, it will taste good while infusing. Wash the rinds before popping in the stock and remove before using the stock or someone will end up with a rubbery globule on their spoon.
- **Add to greens.** Add a Parmigiano rind to a pan of simmering or steaming greens, then finish with a dash of balsamic vinegar and freshly grated Parmigiano for an extra Italian hit. We've also found that artichokes absorb the flavour when steaming particularly well.
- **Make parm broth.** See recipe on page 260.
- **Use as dog treats.** Many dogs enjoy chewing on grana or parm rinds. Obviously, don't do this if your dog has a dairy allergy!

THE MELTY CHEESE LIST

SUPER-MELTY CHEESES

As a general rule, higher moisture, higher fat, young-to-middle-aged and semi-firm cheeses are better melters. Think of them as voluptuous seductresses ready to drape themselves on your chaise lounge, by which we mean toast. Cheeses melt in different ways when heated, some become stringy, some oozy, gooey, crisp and some silky. For this reason, we'll often use a combination of cheese types in a recipe to ensure the ultimate texture and flavour, especially in our toasties. These cheeses are up for it.

- Mozzarella, scamorza, provolone and Emmentaler: stringy and stretchy for the ultimate cheese pull.
- Alpine and Alpine-style cheeses, including Gruyère, Comté, Appenzeller, Abondance, Beaufort, Chällerhocker and Asiago: smooth, rich and fat textures with some likely cheese pull.
- Fontina-style cheeses: silky and buttery.
- Burrata: rich, oozy, gooey and melts quickly.
- Raclette-style cheeses, Taleggio, Section28 Monte Rosso and Reblochon styles: funky, oozy and gooey.
- Young Asiago, young Gouda and Havarti: smooth melters.
- Ossau-Iraty: a great smooth melter, but can oil pool a little.
- Non-industrial camembert-style and Vacherin-style cheeses will melt, but can have some oil pooling, so avoid using for cheese sauces. They'll be saucy and gooey.

RESISTANT MELTERS

These cheeses will soften or become crispy rather than melt, which is sometimes exactly what you need.

- Halloumi and paneer both hold their shape and are sizzlers.
- Feta will soften, but not melt.
- Acid-set cheeses, such as fresh goat's cheese, cottage cheese and ricotta, will soften and become creamy when heated.
- Low-fat and fat-free cheeses are resistant to melting, due to their limited fat content.
- Low-moisture aged cheeses, such as Parmigiano Reggiano, aged Gouda and Manchego, are resistant melters and become crispy when heated. They pack a salty umami punch and are best grated and used as 'finishing' cheeses for pastas, risottos and oven-baked meals.

PUNCHY NON-MELTERS

If you're making a toastie (see pages 216–21) or cheese sauce (see pages 192–5) and want to add some X-factor, use one of these punchy non-melters, but make sure it's only 25 per cent of the whole cheese quantity.

- Blues, such as Gorgonzola, Roquefort and Stilton, add plenty of pow.
- Parmigiano Reggiano or Grana Padano are salty, so use sparingly for some nutty and umami punch. Pecorino Romano, Pecorino Sardo and Manchego are great alternatives for a salty kick.
- Strong aged cheddar has a reputation as a good melter, which we strongly disagree with. Be aware that due to its acidity there will be oil pooling and lack of stretch. Grate it first for a better chance of melting.

BRUNCH

For years, we used to join the mass congregations of last night's revellers in long queues for a weekend brunch in the Melbourne madness or Byron bustle. We craved the feeling of being 'amongst it' that only an overpriced omelette at an over-hyped cafe can deliver.

However, every time we'd return home in a somewhat deflated state, $60 poorer, and grumbling deep into the day about the lacklustre breakfast we endured just to feel a part of it all. Peace came a few years later, when we surrendered to the idea that making brunch at home was a much better proposition. Not only was the food infinitely more delicious and cheaper, it could also be enjoyed in pyjamas without a side of attitude from a disinterested waitperson.

The beauty in this epiphany (if you decide to do the same) is becoming so familiar with the recipes in this chapter that you make them with one eye still closed, a coffee in hand and remnants of last night's party still in your hair, before stumbling back to bed.

ONE-POT GREENS & FETA

50 g unsalted cultured butter

2 large leeks, white and pale green parts only, washed well and cut into 1 cm thick rounds

sea salt flakes

½ bunch of silverbeet

½ bunch of cavolo nero

1 tablespoon extra-virgin olive oil

2 teaspoons balsamic vinegar

100 g Greek barrel-aged feta, crumbled

lemon wedges, to serve

This is probably *the* most requested recipe (and thus most cooked) in both our households. It's a truly satisfying and delicious way to use up those tired greens in the crisper drawer that you overbought at the farmers' market, promising yourself 'this week will be different'. It's a greens reset your body will thank you for.

The feta is what levels up this dish, so buy the best quality you can afford (Greek, PDO and barrel-aged, if possible), and go low and slow on the leeks to take this beauty across the finish line.

We often eat this straight from the frying pan, scooped up with freshly buttered sourdough toast, but it also stands up as a refined side dish to roast chicken. Hot sauce certainly doesn't go astray, either. If you know, you know.

Preheat the oven to 200°C conventional.

Melt the butter in an ovenproof frying pan over medium–low heat. Add the leek and a pinch of salt and cook, stirring occasionally, for 15–20 minutes, until softened and lightly caramelised.

Tear the silverbeet and cavolo nero leaves from their stalks and shred the leaves into 5 cm pieces. Add to the pan and cook, stirring frequently, for 5 minutes. Stir in the oil and vinegar, then cover and cook for 10 minutes or until the greens have wilted.

Remove the lid and sprinkle the feta over the top. Transfer to the oven and bake for 15 minutes or until the feta is golden. Serve with lemon wedges for squeezing over.

Serves 4 as a side

STUDD SIBLINGS RECOMMEND

We love Aphrodite Barrel-Aged Feta.

BRUNCH COCKTAILS & CHEESE

We reckon brunch, cocktails and cheese are a direct path to nirvana. The idea of alcohol at brunch was introduced to us when Sam was living in New York City. Hair of the dog paired with a fatty yet delicious and nutritional food source made the heavy hangovers much more bearable.

BLOODY MARY WITH A CELERY-SALT RIM & CLOTHBOUND CHEDDAR

1 litre (4 cups) good-quality tomato juice

100 ml vodka or bourbon

5 cm piece of fresh horseradish, grated, or 1 tablespoon jarred horseradish relish (not cream)

1 teaspoon celery salt

1 teaspoon cornichon brine

2 teaspoons Dijon mustard

Worcestershire sauce, to taste

Tabasco sauce, to taste

sea salt flakes and freshly ground black pepper

CELERY-SALT RIM

1 teaspoon celery salt

1 tablespoon onion powder

½ teaspoon garlic powder

½ teaspoon sea salt flakes

½ teaspoon freshly ground black pepper

TO SERVE

lemon wedges

ice cubes

crinkle-cut pickle slices

100 g clothbound cheddar

Bloody Marys and cheese are not on many people's radar but, lucky for you, we stumbled upon this dynamic and unconventional pairing. The Worcestershire sauce and tomato juice wallop your palate with an insistent 'wake up!' zing and flirt with the cheddar's own acidity. The buttery notes of the cheddar then go to work to calm it all down and balance out the pairing.

Accessories for Bloody Marys are obviously essential. We think the bigger the better, so often poke half a bunch of celery in it. The pickle slices harmonise with the cheddar's earthy notes and add a welcome crunch.

To make the celery-salt rim, combine the ingredients in a bowl. Transfer to a plate and set aside.

Place all the Bloody Mary ingredients in a large jug. Season to taste and stir to combine.

Rub the rims of four glasses with a lemon wedge, then dip the rim of each glass in the celery-salt mixture. Fill each glass with ice, then pour in the Bloody Mary and decorate the rim of each glass with a pickle slice.

Serve the drinks alongside sizeable pieces of cheddar for an earthy, punchy addition to brunch.

Serves 4

STUDD SIBLINGS
RECOMMEND

This drink also goes well with Havarti, burrata or Stilton.

UBRIACO: AN ACCIDENTALLY 'DRUNKEN' CHEESE

This is essentially a class of cheese that is soaked or washed in wine or grape skins. It is very prevalent in the Veneto region in Italy. Rumour has it, this cheese was born out of necessity in World War I by Northern Italian farmers. Apparently, hungry Austro-Hungarian soldiers moving through the Veneto region demanded food and began looting cellars. The farmers were forced to come up with unique hiding spots for their cheese, such as secreting it away in wine barrels. Turns out, not only did it keep the cheese safe from the clutches of ravenous raiders, it also had the surprise bonus of adding flavour and preserving the cheese. Ubriaco cheese is a little hard to get your hands on in Australia, but still possible. Some have rich-purple rinds and dried grape skins stuck to them, while other varieties are soaked in a sparkling bubble bath of Prosecco.

MICHELADA

Michelada, when made well, is one of the most refreshing and bracingly flavourful hangover killers known to the human race. Often served 'bottomless' in the USA, we are campaigning for this trend to come to Australian shores. Alpine cheeses and Manchego surprisingly pair beautifully with the light effervescence of the beer and hit of the chilli-salt rim. We like to be double parked with this number: cheese in one hand, michelada in the other.

Combine the Tajin and 1 teaspoon of sea salt flakes in a shallow dish. Rub the rim of your glass with one of the lime wedges and dip the rim into the Tajin mixture to create a chilli-salt rim.

Combine the lime juice, hot sauce, Worcestershire sauce and a pinch of salt flakes in a tall glass. Fill with ice and top with the beer. Gently stir to combine and add the remaining lime wedge.

Serve the michelada with triangular slices of Alpine cheese or hard Spanish cheese, cured meats and pickles. Enjoy.

Makes 1

1 teaspoon Tajin seasoning

sea salt flakes

2 lime wedges

60 ml (¼ cup) lime juice

2 teaspoons hot sauce of your choice

1 teaspoon Worcestershire sauce

ice cubes

330 ml bottle of light Mexican beer, such as Modelo, Pacífico, Tecate, Victoria or Corona (the colder, the better)

TO SERVE

Alpine cheese or hard Spanish cheese

cured meats

pickles

SPAGHETT

No, we didn't leave the 'i' off spaghetti. This beer cocktail is a refreshing, summery, sparkly salve to dust off the night before. The bitterness of the Aperol works perfectly with the bitey flavours of goat's cheese, Manchego or the tang of a barrel-aged feta.

Add all the ingredients to a pint glass and stir to combine.

Alternatively, if you are in the park having a picnic, take a swig or two out of the beer, then pour the Aperol and lemon juice directly into the beer bottle – no dishes, no worries.

Serve with your choice of cheese and crusty bread.

Makes 1

330 ml bottle of light lager

45 ml Aperol

15 ml lemon juice

ice cubes

TO SERVE

Holy Goat Skyla Log, Jacquin Pyramide de Chabris, Aphrodite Barrel-Aged Feta or quality Manchego

crusty bread

PERFECT CROQUE MONSIEUR

25 g unsalted cultured butter

25 g plain flour

175 ml full-cream milk

sea salt flakes and freshly ground black pepper

generous grating of nutmeg

220 g Gruyère or Comté, finely grated

4 slices of sourdough

1 tablespoon Dijon mustard

180 g sliced honey-roasted ham

This may be the most ballsed-up dish in cafe culture. In theory, it's good. It doesn't seem like something you can truly make a mess of, but often in restaurants the execution is robustly disappointing. You may just have to take matters into your own hands. Thankfully, our version won't leave you with the sour taste of a second-rate sanga.

Preheat the oven to 220°C fan-forced.

Melt the butter in a small saucepan and add the flour. Gently stir for 2–3 minutes, until it smells biscuity and resembles wet sand. Gradually add the milk, one ladleful at a time and whisking constantly to avoid lumps, then bring to a simmer and cook for 2 minutes or until thickened. Remove the pan from the heat and season the béchamel with salt, pepper and the nutmeg. Stir in 50 g of the grated Gruyère or Comté until melted and set aside.

Preheat a grill to high. Place the sourdough on a large baking tray and lightly toast one side under the grill.

Spread the untoasted side of two slices with the mustard, then add the ham and three-quarters of the remaining Gruyère or Comté. Top with the remaining sourdough, toasted-side up.

Spread the top of each sandwich with a large spoonful of the béchamel and sprinkle over the remaining Gruyère or Comté. Bake in the oven for 10–12 minutes, then finish under the grill for 2–3 minutes, until the cheese is golden brown.

Serves 2

STUDD SIBLINGS RECOMMEND

We love La Couronne Fort-Aged Comté.

TURN YOUR MONSIEUR INTO A MADAME

- *If up want to turn this monsieur into a madame, you just need to add eggs. Fry two eggs, sunny-side up, in some butter for 2 minutes or until the whites are cooked through. Top the sandwiches with the fried eggs once they come out from under the grill, season with black pepper and serve immediately.*

DOUBLE CRÈME BRUNCH BAGELS: SWEET & SAVOURY

SWEET

1 x 200 g double cream cheese, removed from the fridge 1 hour before serving

4 sesame seed bagels, split and toasted

105 g (⅓ cup) black cherry or strawberry jam

SAVOURY

4 poppyseed bagels, split and toasted

1 x 200 g double cream cheese, removed from the fridge 1 hour before serving

350 g smoked salmon or gravlax

35 g (¼ cup) baby capers, drained

freshly ground black pepper

PICKLED SHALLOTS

60 ml (¼ cup) white vinegar

60 ml (¼ cup) apple cider vinegar

1 tablespoon caster sugar

1½ teaspoons sea salt flakes

2 large French shallots, finely sliced

STUDD SIBLINGS
RECOMMEND

We love Le Dauphin Petit Double-Crème in this recipe, but if you can't get your hands on it, try substituting Tarago River Triple Cream, Milawa Camembert, Saint Angel Triple Cream or Brillat-Savarin.

Part of our job is manning a stall at cheese tradeshows in NYC every year. It's not quite as romantic as it sounds and involves spending countless hours under convention centre fluorescent lighting for five long days. The thing we look forward to most on those days is lunch and breakfast. 'I'll go get lunch,' one of us pipes up, as if it's a favour, but we both know the sunlight and stretch of the legs is the better deal. Most of the time we get bagels, because, well, it's New York.

The classic smoked salmon, cream cheese and capers is the gold standard. The savoury bagel here is the upgraded fancy version we make for our friends. It's especially good for taking to a morning gathering or afternoon picnic, as it looks as though you've put in an impressive amount of effort, but really, it took two minutes to whip up. You owe it all to good bagels and good cheese.

To make the sweet bagels, thickly spread the cheese on the cut side of the toasted sesame seed bagels and spoon the jam on top. Sandwich the bagel halves together or leave as halves to serve.

To make the savoury bagels, start with the pickled shallots. Place the vinegars, sugar and salt in a small saucepan with 125 ml (½ cup) of water. Bring to the boil over high heat, then pour over the shallot in a heatproof bowl. Set aside to cool completely.

Spread each half of the toasted poppyseed bagels with the cheese, then top with the salmon, pickled shallot and capers. Sprinkle with some black pepper and serve.

Serves 4

SILKY FRENCH 'JACQ' OMELETTE

Jacques Pépin is a French chef and much-adored daytime television personality in the USA. Make sure you check out his highlights on YouTube and become acquainted with him, as he has some really good essential cooking tips. He is pretty hard not to love, especially in omelette form.

Using a fork, beat the eggs with a pinch of salt and pepper and three-quarters of the herbs in a bowl until well combined. It should look homogenised, meaning you can't see the difference between the yolk and the white.

Melt the butter in a 20 cm non-stick frying pan over high heat, until foaming. Add the egg mixture, reduce the heat to medium and stir the egg as fast as you can while shaking the pan with your other hand. Continue to shake and stir simultaneously without stopping for 2–3 minutes, so the egg coagulates uniformly.

Once the egg looks uniform with a slight custardy appearance, scatter the cheese evenly over the top. Remove from the heat and, using a spatula, roll up the omelette.

Plate the omelette, then finish with an extra knob of butter, lots of salt and pepper and the remaining herbs.

Makes 1

4 large eggs

sea salt flakes and freshly ground black pepper

1 tablespoon finely chopped flat-leaf parsley leaves

1 tablespoon finely chopped chives

20 g unsalted butter, plus extra to serve

30 g finely grated hard cheese, such as Comté, Manchego, clothbound cheddar or Parmigiano Reggiano

DIPPY EGGS WITH COMTÉ SOLDIERS

4 eggs, at room temperature
100 g Comté
sea salt flakes and freshly
ground black pepper

Dad whipped up this little treasure one Easter. He thought he was being funny and 'on theme' with the play on eggs and the introduction of cheese. The Comté started to melt a little in the hot egg and made us re-evaluate the need for toast. It was a protein-packed meal if ever we met one.

It must be the action of the dipping that triggers kid-like glee, even as an adult … and, of course, the cheeky replacement of the usual bread soldiers with cheese.

Bring a saucepan of water to a rolling boil. Carefully add the eggs and cook for 5 minutes. Drain and transfer the eggs to egg cups.

Cut the Comté into 'soldiers', then crack open the tops of the eggs and season with salt and pepper. Serve the eggs with the Comté soldiers for dipping.

Serves 4

STUDD SIBLINGS RECOMMEND

We love La Couronne Fort-Aged Comté in this recipe, but you can substitute with Bruny Island C2, aged Gouda, Gruyère or Chällerhocker.

MATURING WITH MITES

Cheese mites are found on natural rind cheeses that are aged, including traditional clothbound cheddar, Stilton, Comté, Tomme de Savoie and Mimolette. Sometimes they are intentionally encouraged (such as Mimolette) to mature the cheese, whereas other times affineurs see them as a plain nuisance. Mites are invisible to the naked eye, but you'll know they're keeping up their end of the bargain by the powdery beige residue they leave behind on the rind and the surface on which the cheese is sitting. Don't worry, they are harmless for consumption, but obviously not appetising, so most are brushed off and vacuumed away.

SLUTTY SCRAMBLED EGG ROLL

Restaurant chain Eggslut is a must-visit if you go to LA. Although the word 'slutty' can be offensive, in this context it essentially refers to someone who invariably 'adds an egg to it' when cooking. This is our rendition of one of the restaurant's famous brekkie sandwiches.

Melt half the butter in a large non-stick frying pan over medium heat. Add the onion and stir for 2–3 minutes, until it starts to turn translucent. Reduce the heat to low and cook, stirring occasionally, for 20 minutes or until the onion is lightly caramelised. Remove the onion from the pan and set aside.

Combine the mayonnaise, sriracha chilli sauce and lemon juice in a bowl and season with salt and pepper.

Preheat the oven grill to high.

Clean your frying pan and return it to low heat. Add the remaining butter and allow it to melt. Crack the eggs into the pan, break up the yolks using a wooden spoon and stir gently for 3–5 minutes, until the egg is almost cooked (think glossy). Remove the pan from the heat, stir through the chives and season with salt and pepper.

Place the brioche buns on a baking tray, cut-side up, and arrange the shaved cheddar on top. Transfer to the hot grill and grill until the cheese is melted.

To assemble the egg rolls, spread a generous amount of sriracha mayo over the melted cheese. Divide the scrambled eggs and caramelised onion among the buns, top with the bacon, if using, and sandwich together. Eat immediately.

Serves 4

80 g unsalted butter

1 large onion, finely sliced

80 g (⅓ cup) mayonnaise

1 tablespoon sriracha chilli sauce

juice of ½ lemon

sea salt flakes and freshly ground black pepper

8 eggs

½ bunch chives, finely chopped

4 brioche buns, halved

100 g cheddar, shaved

8 rashers of cooked bacon (optional)

HOMEMADE MARINATED LABNEH

1 kg pot-set natural yoghurt (Greek-style yoghurt is good)

2 teaspoons sea salt flakes

500 ml (2 cups) extra-virgin olive oil, plus extra for greasing

4 garlic cloves, peeled

2 sprigs of rosemary

1 teaspoon whole black peppercorns

SUGGESTED COATINGS

finely chopped flat-leaf parsley and mint leaves

ground sumac

dukkah

People often ask us what cheese they can make at home. We generally leave it to the expert cheesemakers, but labneh is an exception. An excellent weekend project, it's a recipe that keeps on giving for months to come. Every time you look at the jar in the fridge, you'll proudly blow it a kiss and think 'I made you'.

Labneh is technically not a cheese. It is, however, an ancient form of preserving milk, made by straining yoghurt through muslin or cheesecloth. Labneh can be traced back to the Levant more than 2000 years ago, and it still forms the foundation of many Middle Eastern dishes today.

Labneh varies in thickness and tang, depending on the type of milk and cultures used and whether it is eaten fresh, dried or preserved in oil. You'll need to begin this recipe one day ahead.

Combine the yoghurt and salt in a bowl, then transfer to a sieve lined with muslin or cheesecloth set over a bowl. Twist the muslin to enclose the yoghurt, then refrigerate overnight, allowing the whey to drain from the yoghurt into the bowl.

The next day, dip your fingers in olive oil and roll the strained yoghurt into balls about the size of a cherry tomato. Roll the labneh in your desired coating: chopped herbs, sumac or dukkah.

In a small saucepan, blanch the garlic cloves in boiling water for 1–2 minutes, until softened. Drain and refresh under cold running water.

Pour the olive oil into a large clean jar, along with the rosemary, peppercorns and garlic. Add the labneh balls, then seal with a lid and store in the fridge for up to 1 month.

Makes 1 kg

STUDD SIBLINGS RECOMMEND

Try using the infused oil for cooking or as a salad dressing.

SERVING UP YOUR HOMEMADE LABNEH

- *Spread on toast with tomatoes, olive oil and mint.*
- *Serve alongside breakfast burritos.*
- *Sprinkle with za'atar, drizzle with olive oil and serve as an accompaniment to a Middle Eastern spread – think pita, grilled meat, cucumber and olives.*
- *Place on top of tomato-baked eggs or roasted veggies.*
- *Use as a healthy substitute for sour cream on baked potatoes or nachos.*

EASY-PEASY FETA SOURDOUGH TOAST

Sammy didn't name this dish for nothin! It can be whipped up in 10–15 minutes and enjoyed at any time of the day. When it's broad bean season, we double shell them and use them instead of the peas.

In a bowl, mash the feta with the yoghurt to form a paste. Set aside.

Heat a chargrill pan over high heat until smoking. Add the bread and grill, turning after each side has been gently charred. Remove the bread from the pan and rub the cut sides of the garlic clove over each side. Set aside.

Cook the peas in a saucepan of salted boiling water for 1–2 minutes, until just tender. Drain and run under cold water to stop the cooking process.

Melt the butter in a non-stick frying pan over medium–high heat until slightly browned. Add the peas to the pan with the chilli and mint and, using a fork, lightly mash. Remove from the heat and mix through the olive oil and lemon juice, then season with salt and pepper.

Spread a generous amount of the feta mixture onto the toast and top with the peas. Sprinkle a few mint leaves over the top, season with salt and pepper and serve.

Serves 4

100 g Greek barrel-aged feta

80 g (⅓ cup) Greek-style or pot-set natural yoghurt

4 slices of sourdough

1 garlic clove, halved

300 g (2 cups) frozen or fresh peas

25 g unsalted butter

1 small red chilli, finely chopped (deseeded if you prefer less heat)

½ bunch of mint, leaves picked and torn, plus extra to serve

1½ tablespoons extra-virgin olive oil

juice of 1 lemon (they taste better stolen from a neighbour's tree or homegrown)

sea salt flakes and freshly ground black pepper

STUDD SIBLINGS RECOMMEND

We love Aphrodite Barrel-Aged Feta.

GALOTYRI WITH BLISTERED CHERRY TOMATOES & MIXED HERBS

500 g mixed cherry truss tomatoes

60 ml (¼ cup) extra-virgin olive oil

½ teaspoon sugar

2 garlic cloves, finely sliced

4 sprigs of oregano

2 sprigs of thyme

¼ bunch of basil, leaves picked, plus extra to serve

sea salt flakes and freshly ground black pepper

180 g Galotyri

sliced seeded baguette, to serve

Galotyri can be a little hard to track down but can easily be replaced with goat's curd or labneh. We make at least a double portion of the tomatoes, especially when they're cheap in late summer, so we can eat this a few days in a row. The charriness of the tomatoes adds a deep, sweet complexity that dances with the creaminess and acidity of the mixed milk Galotyri.

Preheat the oven to 200°C fan-forced.

Place the tomatoes in a baking dish (make sure the tomatoes fit snugly). Combine the olive oil, sugar, garlic and herbs in a small bowl, then drizzle the mixture over the tomatoes. Season to taste.

Transfer to the oven and roast for 20–25 minutes, until the tomatoes bubble and blister. Remove from the oven and allow to cool slightly.

Spread the Galotyri over the base of a large shallow serving dish. Top with the hot tomatoes and a few extra basil leaves, if you like, and spoon over a generous amount of the tomato juices in the dish. Serve with slices of seeded baguette to dip in immediately.

Serves 4 as a side

STUDD SIBLINGS
RECOMMEND

We love Aphrodite Galotyri, but you can sub in goat's curd or labneh – for a labneh recipe, see page 168.

HALLOUMI, EGG & BACON MUFFIN WITH EGGPLANT PICKLE

250 g packet of Cypriot sheep and goat halloumi, drained and patted dry

2 tablespoons extra-virgin olive oil

8 rashers of streaky bacon

4 eggs

4 English muffins, halved and toasted

softened butter, for spreading

80 g (⅓ cup) Indian eggplant pickle (sweet pickle/chutney)

1 avocado, sliced

sea salt flakes and freshly ground black pepper

Halloumi enjoys a relatively long shelf life, so we always have a few blocks stashed at the back of the fridge, ready to whip out for the many meals you can make with it. This muffin may only be the size of your palm, but it sure leaves you full and satisfied with its fried, salty and hearty goodness. For the vegos out there, you can simply skip the bacon.

Preheat the oven to 140°C conventional.

Cut the halloumi in half horizontally, then cut each half into two pieces.

Heat 1 tablespoon of the oil in a non-stick frying pan over medium–high heat. Add the halloumi and cook for 2–3 minutes each side or until golden brown. Transfer the halloumi to a small baking tray and place in the oven to keep warm.

Add the bacon to the pan and cook for 2–3 minutes each side until crispy. Transfer to the tray in the oven.

Add the remaining oil to the pan and fry the eggs for about 3–4 minutes or until the edges are crisp and the whites are set.

Spread the toasted muffins with butter and the eggplant pickle, then layer with the avocado, halloumi, bacon and fried eggs. Season with salt and pepper, sandwich together and eat immediately.

Serves 4

STUDD SIBLINGS
RECOMMEND

*We love Aphrodite
Mixed Milk Halloumi.
It's hand folded.*

MEXICAN-STYLE CORN & FETA FRITTERS

Good moods only after eating this one. It's a meal that teleports you to where you'd rather be. Sometimes we serve it with a side of smoked salmon or smoked prawns (if we have them, thanks to Freckle, the local fisho in Byron). Please eat in a patch of sun, if available.

Place the sweetcorn kernels, 125 g of the feta, the flour and panko in a large bowl. Season with salt and pepper and mix well to combine. Add the egg, chives and jalapeños and stir until a batter forms.

Heat 1 tablespoon of the olive oil in a large non-stick frying pan over medium heat. Working in batches, scoop ½ cup portions of batter into the pan and gently flatten with the back of a spoon. Cook for 3–4 minutes each side, until golden brown. Continue with the remaining oil and batter.

Stack the fritters on top of each other and scatter the remaining feta and the coriander over the top. Sprinkle the paprika over the avocado and season with salt and pepper. Serve the avo alongside the fritters, with the lime quarters and hot sauce.

Serves 4

4 sweetcorn cobs (about 1 kg), husks and silks removed, kernels stripped

250 g Greek barrel-aged feta, crumbled

75 g (½ cup) self-raising flour

15 g (¼ cup) panko breadcrumbs

sea salt flakes and freshly ground black pepper

4 eggs, lightly beaten

small bunch of chives, cut into 3 cm pieces

60 g pickled jalapeños, chopped

60 ml (¼ cup) extra-virgin olive oil

½ bunch of coriander, leaves picked and chopped

1 teaspoon smoked paprika

2 avocados, quartered

1 lime, quartered

green chilli hot sauce of your choice, to serve

PRO FRITTER TIPS

- *Once you dollop the fritter mixture into the pan, use the back of a spoon or a spatula to help you flatten and shape the fritter into a circle.*
- *Fritters take time, so don't rush. They need 3–4 minutes each side to cook through and turn golden. If your pan is too hot, the fritters will not cook properly on the inside.*
- *Store leftover fritters in the fridge to enjoy for breakfast, brunch or lunch the next day.*
- *Don't use tongs to turn your fritters; use a spatula and gently flip to prevent them from falling apart.*

STUDD SIBLINGS
RECOMMEND

We love Aphrodite Barrel-Aged Feta.

MATES & DATES

The dishes in this chapter are all about eliciting emphatic 'ooohs' and 'ahhhs' from your friends. They are showstopping entrance-makers that kickstart a party with a cheesy wallop. That doesn't mean they're difficult, though. As any seasoned entertainer will tell you, the key to an accomplished host who looks like they have their shit together is preparation, not last-minute panic stations.

These recipes are also great for 'bring-a-plate' events. They're the equivalent of arriving bare-chested on horseback given the impressed eyebrow raises they'll extract as you slap down your goods with confidence.

BAKED CHEESE IN ITS BOX

It's the wooden box in which you serve the cheese that makes it fancy. Essentially, instant cheese fondue. These recipes (pictured on the previous spread) are molten and melty in all the right ways. People may think you're showing off. Let them!

GOOEY BAKED CAMEMBERT

2 garlic cloves, peeled
250 g Normandy Camembert, in its box
2 tablespoons cider
4–5 sprigs of thyme, leaves picked
freshly ground black pepper
crusty bread, to serve

We recommend using the best camembert available to you for this recipe. We love ones from Normandy for their barnyard funk. Industrial versions of camembert will taste bland and don't melt as well, and they'll often ooze a pool of oil, which isn't the sultry look we're going for here, especially on those hot date nights.

Preheat the oven to 200°C conventional.

In a small saucepan, blanch the garlic cloves in boiling water for 1–2 minutes, until softened. Drain and slice the garlic.

Remove the wax paper from the cheese and return it to the box, with the lid on the bottom. Pierce the cheese in six places with a small, sharp knife and gently push the garlic into the cheese.

Spoon over the cider, making sure it seeps into the cheese, and scatter the thyme over the top. Season with freshly ground pepper, to taste.

Wrap the base of the box tightly in foil or tie with string to keep the box together. Place the cheese on a baking tray and bake for 10–15 minutes, until hot and bubbling and the cheese centre is liquid.

Serve immediately, dipping the crusty bread into the molten cheese.

Serves 4 as a starter

STUDD SIBLINGS
RECOMMEND

We love Le Conquérant Camembert.

BAKED LE DUC VACHERIN

This recipe is based on the famous whole baked Mont d'Or from France that is strictly seasonal. Le Duc Vacherin is the closest thing you can get to it in Australia, made from the rich milk from the same region and girdled in a ring of spruce bark harvested by hand in the summer months. Baking the cheese activates the spruce bark, adding forest/pine notes to the cheese. Smother it on potatoes or serve with cornichons and cured meats for dipping as a centrepiece at a winter dinner party.

Preheat the oven to 200°C conventional.

In a small saucepan, blanch the garlic clove in boiling water for 1–2 minutes, until softened. Drain and cut the clove into 4–6 thin slices.

Remove the plastic cheese packaging and return the cheese, uncovered, to the wooden box.

Pierce the top of the cheese four to six times with a small, sharp knife. Gently push the garlic and rosemary leaves into the holes, then pour over the wine, making sure it seeps into the cheese, and season with freshly ground pepper, to taste.

Wrap the base and top of the Vacherin tightly with foil and bake for 15 minutes. Remove the foil on top and bake for a further 5–10 minutes, until hot and bubbling.

Serve with crusty bread or boiled potatoes to scoop up the cheese, alongside cornichons, salami and/or cured ham.

Serves 4 as a starter

1 garlic clove, peeled

200 g Le Duc Vacherin, in its box

1 sprig of rosemary, leaves picked

1–2 tablespoons white or red wine

freshly ground black pepper

TO SERVE

crusty bread or boiled potatoes

cornichons

salami and/or cured ham

STUDD SIBLINGS RECOMMEND

Long Paddock Driftwood also works well in this recipe if you can't find Le Duc Vacherin.

CHARRED SWEETCORN WITH CHIPOTLE MAYO & TWO CHEESES

1–2 chipotles in adobo sauce, chopped

125 g (½ cup) whole-egg mayonnaise

4 sweetcorn cobs

60 g Parmigiano Reggiano, finely grated

40 g quality Manchego, finely grated

lime wedges, to serve

This recipe is made for barbecue season and takes just moments to prepare. Leaving the husks on the corn adds a visual effect – sometimes we tie them with string to up the fanciness. The flavours fly on the perfect apex of spicy, salty and acid. This recipe is adapted from our dear family friend, Bob Hart, the barbecue man, but we've added an additional cheese, because we're cheese people. The Manchego adds sweet, nutty and grassy notes, while the Parmigiano Reggiano delivers its signature umami punch.

Polite table etiquette is not required here. Don't overthink it, just get stuck in and enjoy the interactive experience of deliciousness.

Preheat a barbecue with a lid to high.

Place the chipotle and mayonnaise in a bowl and stir well, then set aside.

Peel back the sweetcorn husks, leaving them attached to the base of the cobs. Tie the husks together with kitchen string, and remove and discard the silks.

Place the sweetcorn cobs on the grill and lower the lid, ensuring that the husks are sticking outside the lid to stop them burning. Barbecue the corn for 6–8 minutes, turning regularly, until charred. Remove the corn from the barbecue and immediately brush with the chipotle mayonnaise.

Sprinkle the corn with the cheese and serve hot with lime wedges for squeezing over and extra mayo on the side.

Serves 4

STUDD SIBLINGS
RECOMMEND

We love Cravero Parmigiano Reggiano and El Esparto Manchego.

MAC 'N' CHEESE, THREE WAYS

Some like their mac 'n' cheese crunchy on top, some like it spicy, some like it smooth, creamy and traditional. We have made it three ways to cover most bases for you.

CREAMY COMFORT MAC 'N' CHEESE

It has to be elbow or macaroni pasta to bring those big, warm hug feels to mac 'n' cheese. Perhaps it's nostalgia or those crafty Italians and their pasta science that engineers the best shapes for the right sauce. In any case, step away from the risoni, it's not gonna cut it. Oddly, though, we don't get too caught up on the type of cheese used here – most cheeses work. But, similar to the Borough Market toastie on page 220, the secret ingredient is the leek – don't skip it.

Cook the pasta in a large saucepan of salted boiling water over high heat for 3 minutes less than the packet instructions. Drain, reserving 2 tablespoons of the cooking water. Set aside.

In the same saucepan, melt the butter over medium–low heat, add the leek and a pinch of salt and cook for about 8 minutes, until softened but not browned. Add the flour and cook, stirring, for 2 minutes. Gradually add the milk, one ladleful at a time and stirring constantly to prevent lumps, until incorporated. Add the mustard and half the thyme, then reduce the heat and simmer, stirring often, for 3–4 minutes, until thickened. Remove the pan from the heat, add three-quarters of the cheese and stir until melted. Season well with salt and freshly ground black pepper, then stir through the lemon zest.

Preheat the oven grill to high.

Add the macaroni to a 2.5 litre baking dish, along with the reserved cooking water. Pour over the cheese sauce and mix through, then sprinkle the remaining cheese on top. Place the mac 'n' cheese under the hot grill and cook for 10–15 minutes, until golden brown and bubbling. Scatter with the remaining thyme leaves and serve with a side of green salad.

Serves 4–6

400 g dried macaroni

75 g unsalted butter

1 leek, white part only, washed well and finely sliced

sea salt flakes and freshly ground black pepper

50 g (⅓ cup) plain flour

750 ml (3 cups) full-cream milk

2 teaspoons Dijon mustard

4 sprigs of thyme, leaves picked

200 g sharp cheddar, grated

100 g firm mozzarella or melty cheese of your choice (see our list on page 149)

finely grated zest of ½ lemon

STUDD SIBLINGS RECOMMEND

We couldn't have all three mac 'n' cheese recipes with a golden panko breadcrumb top, but, truth be told, we often add it to this version too, for extra mouthfeel.

CRISPY KEFALOTYRI SAGANAKI MAC 'N' CHEESE

300 g dried macaroni

50 g unsalted butter

1 small onion, finely chopped

35 g (¼ cup) plain flour

2 teaspoons Dijon mustard

1 teaspoon smoked paprika

¼ teaspoon cayenne pepper

750 ml (3 cups) full-cream milk

170 g Kefalotyri saganaki, grated

150 g cheddar, grated

sea salt flakes and freshly ground black pepper

60 g (1 cup) panko breadcrumbs

1 tablespoon extra-virgin olive oil

Here's a little insider secret: Kefalotyri adds a golden, crunchy top to dishes like this. Kefalotyri can be grated or is often fried whole in traditional saganaki dishes. 'Kefla' translates to hat or head, a fitting name, as the mould and size of the cheese is similar to that of a brimless hat. It is brine washed and aged for a minimum of 3–4 months, over which time a hard, natural and irregular rind develops, resulting in a salty and savoury cheese. Some are aged up to a year, for a saltier, more robust cheese that's perfect for grating.

Kefalotyri is the oldest hard cheese in Greece, with origins dating back to the Byzantium era. Traditional Kefalotyri is made from a combination of goat's and sheep's milk, with the ratio of each varying seasonally. This affects the colour and taste of the cheese, from ivory white to buttercup yellow. Due to the natural landscape in Greece, many farms still allow animals to freely forage on the steep, rugged mountain slopes.

Preheat the oven to 200°C conventional.

Cook the pasta in a large saucepan of salted boiling water over high heat for 3 minutes less than the packet instructions. Drain, reserving 2 tablespoons of the cooking water. Set aside.

In the same saucepan, melt the butter over medium heat. Add the onion and cook, stirring, for about 7 minutes, until softened. Add the flour and stir for 1 minute, then reduce the heat to low and add the mustard, paprika and cayenne pepper. Gradually add the milk, one ladleful at a time and stirring constantly to prevent any lumps, until incorporated. Increase the heat to medium, bring to a simmer and cook, stirring occasionally, for 5–7 minutes, until the sauce is thickened. Remove from the heat.

Add 150 g of the Kefalotyri saganaki and all of the cheddar to the sauce and stir to melt. Stir through the macaroni and the pasta water, and season with salt and pepper. Transfer the mixture to a 2.5 litre baking dish.

Combine the breadcrumbs, olive oil and remining Kefalotyri saganaki in a bowl and scatter over the top of the mac 'n' cheese. Bake for 20–25 minutes, until golden. Serve immediately.

Serves 4

STUDD SIBLINGS RECOMMEND

We love Aphrodite Kefalotyri, but if you can't find any you can sub in halloumi.

HALL-PASS MAC 'N' CHEESE

We have chosen to name this mac 'n' cheese in hall-pass spirit, unshackled from negative connotations. This is possibly one of the most indulgent dishes you could make, but in all the right ways. Trust us, like any good hall-pass encounter, you'll be having flashbacks for weeks after eating it. We can't help ourselves when it comes to mac 'n' cheese, we have to whack it with sriracha. Serve with a crunchy salad involving iceberg lettuce and a lemon juice dressing to cut through the ooze.

Preheat the oven to 220°C conventional.

Cook the pasta in a large saucepan of salted boiling water over high heat for 3 minutes less than the packet instructions. Drain, reserving 2 tablespoons of the cooking water. Set aside.

Place the bacon in a cold, large, deep non-stick frying pan over medium–high heat and cook for 3–4 minutes, until golden. Using a slotted spoon, remove the bacon from the pan leaving the fat behind. Add the butter to the pan and allow it to melt, then reduce the heat to medium–low, stir through the flour and cook, stirring, for 1 minute. Gradually add the milk, one ladleful at a time and stirring constantly to prevent any lumps forming, until incorporated. Add the Le Dauphin Double-Crème and half the Comté and stir until completely melted and the sauce is smooth. Add the sriracha (if using) and stir through.

Add the macaroni, reserved pasta water and bacon to the pan and stir well to completely coat in the cheese sauce. Transfer to a 25 cm round baking dish and sprinkle with the breadcrumbs and remaining Comté. Bake for 8 minutes or until golden brown and bubbling. Serve immediately, sprinkled with chopped parsley.

Serves 4

250 g dried spiral macaroni

180 g rindless smoky bacon rashers, finely sliced (unsmoked is also fine)

50 g unsalted butter

1 tablespoon plain flour

125 ml (½ cup) full-cream milk

120 g Le Dauphin Double-Crème, rind removed (or use Fromager d'Affinois or 125 ml/½ cup cooking cream)

80 g Comté, grated

1–2 teaspoons sriracha chilli sauce, to taste (optional)

20 g (¼ cup) sourdough breadcrumbs

chopped flat-leaf parsley leaves, to serve

STUDD SIBLINGS
RECOMMEND

We love La Couronne Fort-Aged Comté, but if you can't find Comté, any Alpine cheese will work well here.

FLAVOURED BUTTER, THREE WAYS

125 g unsalted cultured butter

HERBED BUTTER
1 tablespoon chopped oregano leaves
1 tablespoon chopped chives
1 tablespoon chopped flat-leaf parsley leaves

HARISSA BUTTER
1 teaspoon harissa

ANCHOVY & CAPER BUTTER
2 teaspoons baby capers, rinsed and drained
4 anchovy fillets
finely grated zest of 1 lemon

Flavoured butter is also known as compound butter, but we really don't like the way that rolls off the tongue. Whatever you call it, flavoured butter is only as good as the base butter you use. Our fave is cultured 'beurre de baratte' French butter (from Normandy, specifically), where the cows graze on dandelions and daises in summer. It is slow-churned, so the fat and protein matrix doesn't get destroyed, the culture develops slowly and the butter doesn't lose flavour.

We spread a knob of flavoured butter on crispy baguette, add lashings to finish a piece of pan-fried fish or steak, stuff into fish parcels steamed in the oven, tuck under the skin of a roasting chicken, or slice into a pot of steaming mussel or pipi soup.

Choose the type of butter you would like to make and take the butter out of the fridge for 1 hour to soften.

Beat the butter with a wooden spoon until it is soft and creamy, then beat in your chosen flavouring.

Lay a square of plastic wrap on a work surface and add the butter. Form the butter into a log, then roll up the plastic to encase the butter and twist the ends to seal. The butter will keep in the fridge for up to 3 days or in the freezer for up to 2 months.

Serves 6

STUDD SIBLINGS RECOMMEND

We love Ortiz anchovies and Le Conquérant Beurre de Baratte, but any French or quality cultured butter can be used.

MARIE ANTOINETTE'S PLEASURE DAIRY

Although we may not agree with her indulgent behaviours, we are, at the very least, captivated by the most famous Queen of France, Marie Antoinette. We have a story to add to this woman's cauldron of exuberant lifestyle choices. History tells us the queen used to dress up as a milkmaid with her friends and pretend to churn butter at a fake dairy, known as a 'pleasure dairy'. These dairies were built in France as meeting points for elite women for pleasure, healing and empowerment. Marie built hers right next door to the castle's working dairy, and it was almost an exact replica. However, she had it decorated with luxurious materials, including white marble benches.

ROGUE RIVER BLUE CHEESE DRESSING WITH PEAR WALDORF SALAD

115 g (½ cup) caster sugar

100 g (1 cup) walnuts, toasted

1 witlof, trimmed, leaves separated

100 g celeriac, peeled and sliced into matchsticks

2 celery stalks, trimmed and finely sliced

1 green pear, cored and cut into matchsticks

¼ cup dill fronds

ROGUE RIVER BLUE CHEESE DRESSING

110 g wedge of Rogue River Blue Cheese Special Reserve, crumbled

80 g (⅓ cup) crème fraîche

1 French shallot, finely chopped

1 spring onion, finely sliced

60 ml (¼ cup) full-cream milk

1 tablespoon champagne vinegar or white wine vinegar

sea salt flakes and freshly ground black pepper

This recipe has been passed down over two decades and tweaked numerous times by a collection of cheese legends. David Gremmels from Rogue Creamery, Peggy Smith and Sue Conley from Cowgirl Creamery, Cathy Strange from Whole Foods and our dad, to name a few, have all bequeathed this salad with their own personality and, as such, it's in a constant state of evolution. When we have been present at gatherings of such people, this dressing is always made … and you can hear the delighted gaggles in the kitchen by those preparing it.

This metamorphosising will undoubtedly continue in the coming decade but, for now, it is getting rave reviews at the table in its current guise. The pear adds crunch to the saltiness, creaminess and funk of the blue.

To make the Rogue River Blue Cheese dressing, place the cheese, crème fraîche, shallot, spring onion, milk and vinegar in a bowl. Season with salt and pepper and mix together with a fork.

Transfer two-thirds of the dressing to the bowl of a food processer and blend until smooth. Return to the bowl and mix to combine. Set aside.

Place the sugar and 2 tablespoons of water in a small saucepan over high heat, bring to the boil and cook, without stirring, for 4–5 minutes, until you have a golden caramel. Quickly add the walnuts and toss to completely coat them in the caramel. Spread the sticky walnuts on a baking tray lined with baking paper and set aside to set.

Arrange the witlof, celeriac, celery and pear on a serving platter and drizzle over the dressing. Break over the candied walnuts and sprinkle with the dill.

Leftover dressing will keep in an airtight container in the fridge for 2–3 days. It is great with other green-leaf salads.

STUDD SIBLINGS RECOMMEND

If you can't get your hands on Rogue River, you can also use Roquefort, Cashel Blue, Fourme d'Ambert or Berry's Creek Riverine Blue.

Serves 4–6

PERFECT CHEESE SAUCE, THREE WAYS

Like a warm, silky blanket, cheese sauce drapes itself comfortingly over everything, from tortilla chips and nachos, to raw and blanched veggies, baked potatoes, mac 'n' cheese and lasagne. It's a must-know to keep tucked in your recipe arsenal, ready to go to work livening up dishes with its savoury, salty and creamy flavour.

CLASSIC WHITE SAUCE

30 g unsalted butter

30 g plain flour

500 ml (2 cups) full-cream milk

¼–½ teaspoon garlic powder (optional)

¼–½ teaspoon smoked paprika (optional)

¼ teaspoon finely grated nutmeg

½ teaspoon sea salt flakes

½ teaspoon ground white pepper

250–350 g 'melty' cheeses, grated (we use a mix of Alpine cheeses, such as Gruyère and Comté; see page 149 for our super-melty cheese list)

Everyone needs a go-to cheese sauce and this is it.

Melt the butter in a saucepan over medium–low heat. Stir in the flour and cook for 1–2 minutes, to make a thick roux (you don't want any colour here, you want to keep it 'blonde').

Slowly add the milk a ladleful at a time, stirring constantly with a rubber spatula or whisk to stop lumps forming. Continue to stir until you have a smooth, lump-free sauce, making sure you get your spatula or whisk into the edge of the pan. Reduce the heat to low and simmer for 10 minutes or until the sauce has thickened and coats the back of a spoon. Stir through the garlic powder and paprika (if using).

Remove from the heat and stir through the nutmeg, salt and white pepper. Gradually add the cheese, stirring, until it is completely incorporated and the sauce is smooth. Store leftovers in an airtight container in the fridge for up to 1 week.

Makes about 600 ml

CHEESE SAUCE UPGRADES

To take your traditional cheese sauce to new places, there are multiple ways to upgrade. Remember, a high-quality cheese should be your star ingredient and the upgrades used only to enhance, not hide, the cheese. Try adding the following.
- *Spices: paprika, garlic powder, freshly grated nutmeg, onion powder, mustard powder, ground fenugreek, ground turmeric. Add 1/4–1/2 teaspoon of each.*
- *Aromatics: 1 garlic clove, ¼ onion, thyme or rosemary sprig, bay leaf. Add these before the cheese, while the sauce simmers. Discard before use.*
- *Heat: jalapeños, hot sauce or finely chopped long green chilli.*

AMERICAN CHEESE SAUCE

This is a *very* American version of cheese sauce, with its sweetness and the addition of cornflour to prevent curdling. It's velvety, thick, smooth and a little sweeter due to the evaporated milk. It certainly doesn't need to be made with expensive cheeses, just cheese scraps you have lying around will do. Its consistency makes it perfect for mac 'n' cheese or lasagne.

100 g Alpine cheese, grated (we use Gruyère, Emmentaler or Comté)

50 g cheddar, grated

50 g Fontina or Raclette, grated

1 tablespoon cornflour

375 ml (1½ cups) full-fat evaporated milk

Place the cheeses and cornflour in a bowl and toss well to evenly coat.

Transfer the cheese mixture to a saucepan, along with the evaporated milk, and cook over low heat, whisking constantly, for 5–7 minutes, until the cheese melts. Cook for a further 2 minutes, until the sauce thickens and comes together. (If you would like a thinner sauce, add the evaporated milk once removed from the heat.) Store leftovers in an airtight container in the fridge for up to 1 week.

Makes 500 ml (2 cups)

PRO TIPS FOR VELVETY CHEESE SAUCE

- *First, you need a good melting cheese as your base. Feel free to use two cheeses, but make sure the dominant cheese is a 'melter' to ensure your sauce is smooth and gooey. Aim for 75 per cent of the cheese quantity to come from our super-melty cheese list (see page 149). Your second cheese should be no more than 25 per cent of the total quantity. It can be a punchy non-melter (see page 149), chosen for its stronger flavour.*
- *Don't buy pre-grated cheese; always grate it from the block.*
- *A roux is basically equal parts flour and butter, which thickens your cheese sauce. It's important to cook it into a paste, as this cooks out the flour so it doesn't taste starchy. Some of our friends still don't like using flour as the base, as they claim they don't like the starchy taste, so we added our American cheese sauce made with cornflour. Try both versions, so you can pick a side.*
- *Make sure your milk is cold when you add it to the pan, as this helps prevent lumps from forming.*
- *Stir like it's going out of fashion; nobody likes lumps. This applies to the flour and the milk. Feel around the edge of the saucepan with a rubber spatula for trapped flour.*
- *Have confidence and use your intuition to take the pan off the heat if the sauce is 'moving too fast'. Continue to stir while it's off the heat, so the ingredients can catch up and combine. Sometimes you'll need to add more milk if the sauce is too thick, or more cheese if it's too thin. But make sure to only add more cheese while the sauce is hot.*
- *The sauce should be thinner than your desired consistency for the finished dish, as it will thicken when cooked again, such as in mac 'n' cheese.*

DID YOU SAY … FOUR-CHEESE SAUCE?

Is it possible to have too many cheeses in the one sauce? Let us think … no. The secret to this sauce's addictiveness is twofold. Firstly, it uses chicken stock, which adds a familiar 'I can't figure out why this sauce is so good' ring to it. And secondly, it's gifted with umami by the blue cheese.

Heat a large saucepan over low heat and melt the butter. Stir in the flour and cook for 1–2 minutes to make a thick roux (you don't want any colour here, you want to keep it 'blonde').

Gradually add the stock, one ladleful at a time, stirring constantly to prevent lumps. Repeat with the milk, stirring the whole time, until you have a smooth, lump-free sauce. Add the mustard and season with salt and pepper. Cook for 3–5 minutes, stirring frequently to prevent the sauce from sticking to the base of the pan, until thickened.

Remove the pan from the heat, add the mozzarella, Fontina and blue cheese and stir until melted. Add the Parmigiano Reggiano and stir until well combined, then finish with the nutmeg. Check the seasoning and add more if needed.

If you are making this sauce in advance, place a cut-out circle of baking paper (cartouche) on top of the hot sauce to prevent a skin from forming. The sauce will thicken as it cools. When you reheat this sauce, make sure you stir constantly with a spatula to avoid burning. Store leftovers in an airtight container in the fridge for up to 1 week.

Makes about 1 litre

70 g unsalted butter

75 g (½ cup) plain flour

500 ml (2 cups) chicken stock (or use the Parm Rind Broth on page 260)

500 ml (2 cups) full-cream milk

1 teaspoon Keen's mustard powder

sea salt flakes and freshly ground black pepper

100 g low-moisture mozzarella, grated

100 g Fontina, grated

50 g creamy blue cheese, such as Fourme d'Ambert, Cashel Blue or Roquefort, crumbled

50 g Parmigiano Reggiano, grated

¼ teaspoon freshly grated nutmeg

STUDD SIBLINGS
RECOMMEND

We love Vannella Mozzarella, Mauri Fontina and Le Roi Roquefort by Carles.

QUICK BREAD & BUTTER PICKLES FOR YOUR CHEESE BOARD

3 Lebanese cucumbers (about 400 g), trimmed and finely sliced into rounds

1 small onion, finely sliced

1 tablespoon sea salt flakes

250 ml (1 cup) white vinegar

80 g (⅓ cup) caster sugar

¼ teaspoon chilli flakes

¼ teaspoon ground turmeric

½ teaspoon roughly crushed black peppercorns

1 teaspoon fennel seeds

2 tablespoons chopped dill fronds

This is a satisfying creation to have in your fridge with little effort. We add a small bowl of these pickles to our cheese boards. They're especially good with cheddar and stinky washed rinds as the acidity bounces off the meatiness of the cheese. They're also great in a cheddar or Comté toastie.

Place the cucumber, onion and salt in a bowl and mix well. Transfer the mixture to a colander in the sink and allow to drain for 2 hours.

Place the vinegar, sugar, chilli flakes, turmeric, peppercorns and fennel seeds in a small saucepan over medium heat and stir until the sugar dissolves. Bring to the boil, then reduce the heat to a simmer and cook for 5 minutes. Remove from the heat.

Squeeze the excess liquid from the cucumber and onion and place in a clean 1 litre glass jar. Pour over the vinegar mixture to cover and stir to combine. Set aside to cool completely.

Place the pickles in a bowl, sprinkle over the dill and add to your cheese board. Leftover pickles will keep in the fridge for up to 1 week.

Makes 1 x 1 litre jar

SUMMER HALLOUMI & WATERMELON SALAD

1 x 220 g packet of Cypriot sheep and goat halloumi, drained and patted dry, thickly sliced

1 tablespoon extra-virgin olive oil, plus extra for brushing

1 kg wedge of watermelon, rind removed, cut into wedges or chunks

45 g (¼ cup) pitted kalamata olives, chopped

1 tablespoon pomegranate molasses

¼ cup mint leaves

¼ cup basil leaves

When we visit our producers in Cyprus, this is how they eat their halloumi. It's a Cypriot take on the Greek version of feta and watermelon salad.

We eat at the same restaurant every time we visit – a rustic, open-air local that backs onto the black-pebbled beach with crystal water. Plonking down here for a meal is a welcome reward after visiting the sheep and goats in the dry inland mountains. We sit on plastic chairs and do our best to exchange funny stories with the waitstaff, despite the language barrier. This dish sits next to fried fish, chips, lamb and seemingly bottomless glasses of Zivania, a traditional, and lethal, Cypriot brandy!

For this recipe, we've added olives (slightly off tradition), but we find they add an extra salty, briny kick that bounces off the sweet, crunchy watermelon. This is a great one to make in summer when it's too hot to cook and watermelon is at its juiciest and sweetest.

Heat a chargrill pan over medium–high heat or barbecue flat plate to medium–high. Brush the halloumi slices with olive oil and grill for 1–2 minutes each side, until golden brown.

Arrange the watermelon on a large serving platter and top with the halloumi and olives. Drizzle over the olive oil and pomegranate molasses, sprinkle with the herbs and serve.

Serves 4

STUDD SIBLINGS
RECOMMEND

We love Aphrodite Mixed Milk or Goat Milk Halloumi.

EASY RICOTTA GNOCCHI WITH TOMATO SUGO & FRESH BASIL

These gnocchi are *sooooo* light and fluffy, and damn easy to make! TBH, we have stuffed up homemade gnocchi a few times, but we have mastered these like true champions, so consider them foolproof!

Because there are so few ingredients in this recipe, it's worth spending the money on the more expensive Italian cherry tomatoes, plus some high-grade Parmigiano Reggiano.

Don't freak out about the gnocchi dough – it's meant to be a moist batter, so you only need a small amount of flour to bind it. Use too much and the gnocchi will taste floury.

Bring a large saucepan of salted water to the boil over medium–high heat. Get a bowl of iced water ready and place it next to the stove.

In a large bowl, combine the ricotta, egg, flour and salt and gently mix until a sticky, moist dough has formed. Working in batches, gently drop heaped teaspoons of the dough into the boiling water. The gnocchi will initially sink, but then rise to the top when they are ready – this will only take 5 minutes. As soon as they rise, scoop out the gnocchi using a slotted spoon and add to the iced water.

Drain and wipe out the saucepan, then return it to medium–high heat. Add the olive oil, garlic, tomatoes and most of the basil and bring to the boil, then reduce the heat to medium–low and simmer for 3–5 minutes, until slightly thickened.

Using the slotted spoon, carefully transfer the gnocchi to the sauce and simmer for a further 3–5 minutes, until heated through.

Divide the gnocchi and sugo among serving bowls, top with the Parmigiano Reggiano, remaining basil leaves and chilli of your choice, then serve.

Serves 4

iced water

500 g fresh ricotta

2 eggs, lightly beaten

100 g (⅔ cup) plain flour

1 teaspoon sea salt flakes

60 ml (¼ cup) extra-virgin olive oil

2 garlic cloves, peeled and smashed with the back of a knife

3 x 400 g cans Italian cherry tomatoes

small bunch of basil, leaves picked

50 g Parmigiano Reggiano, finely grated

Japanese chilli oil or chilli flakes, to serve (optional)

STUDD SIBLINGS
RECOMMEND

We love Cravero Parmigiano Reggiano.

RAINBOW TROUT, SWEET-PICKLED CUCUMBER & FRESH DILL BRUSCHETTA WITH GALOTYRI

1 x quantity Quick Bread & Butter Pickles (see page 196)

4 slices of sourdough, toasted

140 g (⅔ cup) Galotyri

1 x 350 g whole smoked rainbow trout, skin and bones removed, flesh flaked

⅓ cup dill fronds

Crunchy, acidic, salty, creamy – this dish is a great way to whet the appetite before mains arrive.

Place the bread and butter pickles on some paper towel to remove any excess liquid.

Spread the toast with the Galotyri, then top with the pickles and trout and sprinkle over the dill fronds. Serve immediately.

Serves 4 as a starter

STUDD SIBLINGS
RECOMMEND

We love Aphrodite Galotyri, but if you can't find it, sour cream, goat's curd or crème fraîche will all work well.

SPICY SALAMI & SCAMORZA CASARECCE

100 g spicy salami

60 ml (¼ cup) extra-virgin olive oil

1 onion, finely chopped

small bunch of flat-leaf parsley, stems and leaves separated and finely chopped

5 garlic cloves, finely sliced

2 tablespoons tomato paste

2 x 400 g cans cherry tomatoes

400 g dried casarecce

50 g unsalted butter, chopped

sea salt flakes and freshly ground black pepper

150 g white or smoked scamorza, grated

This pasta hits ALL the right comfort spots in your body. The combo of tomatoes and tomato paste adds a beautiful richness and tanginess, the scamorza provides cheese pull and the spicy salami brings a little kick. Most of the ingredients you will often find hiding in your pantry, so it's a good one to whip up your when you've been postponing a grocery shopping trip a little too long. The scamorza can be substituted for any melty cheese (see our super-melty cheese list on page 149), and the salami for chorizo.

Place the salami in a food processor and whiz until coarsely chopped. Transfer to a bowl and set aside.

Heat the olive oil in a large frying pan over medium–low heat. Add the onion and cook, stirring occasionally, for 7–8 minutes, until softened. Add the parsley stems, garlic, chopped salami and tomato paste, then cook, stirring frequently, for 3–4 minutes, until aromatic. Add the cherry tomatoes, then reduce the heat to low and simmer for about 15 minutes, until the mixture is slightly reduced.

Meanwhile, cook the casarecce in a large saucepan of salted boiling water according to the packet instructions. Drain, reserving 125 ml (½ cup) of the pasta cooking water.

Add the pasta cooking water to the tomato sauce and stir over low heat for 2–3 minutes, until slightly thickened. Add the pasta and butter, and stir to coat the pasta in the sauce and melt the butter. Season to taste with salt and pepper, then divide among serving bowls. Scatter the scamorza and parsley leaves over the top and serve.

Serves 4

ROASTED BABY BEETROOT, MOZZARELLA & MIXED SEED SALAD

Best eaten on a balmy summer evening, this salad is all about the sweetness of the beets, the creaminess of the mozzarella, and crunch from the seeds. We encourage you to drag a big hunk of sourdough or warmed flatbread through it to mop up the purple cream.

Preheat the oven to 220°C conventional.

Place the beetroot in a small roasting tin, drizzle with the olive oil and season with salt. Transfer to the oven and roast for 50–60 minutes, until cooked through (test by piercing a beetroot with a knife through the centre to make sure it is tender). Remove the beetroot from the oven and set aside to cool to room temperature, then slip the skins off with your fingers (wear kitchen gloves if you don't want to end up with red hands).

Meanwhile, place the hazelnuts, pumpkin seeds and coriander seeds on a small baking tray and place in the oven for 1–2 minutes, until lightly roasted. Set aside to cool.

To make the honey–mustard dressing, place all the ingredients in a jar, screw on the lid and shake until well combined. Set aside.

Cut the beetroot in half and arrange on a serving plate with the watercress and toasted nuts and seeds. Tear the buffalo mozzarella over the top and drizzle over the honey–mustard dressing just before serving.

Serves 4 as a side

500 g mixed baby beetroot, trimmed and scrubbed

1 tablespoon extra-virgin olive oil

sea salt flakes

35 g (¼ cup) hazelnuts, roughly chopped

1 tablespoon pumpkin seeds

1 teaspoon coriander seeds

40 g (1⅓ cups) watercress

2 x balls of buffalo mozzarella

HONEY–MUSTARD DRESSING

½ teaspoon Dijon mustard

1 teaspoon honey

juice of 1 lemon

2 tablespoons extra-virgin olive oil

sea salt flakes and freshly ground black pepper

STUDD SIBLINGS
RECOMMEND

We love Vannella Mozzarella.

ONE-PAN CHEESY NEW POTATOES WITH BACON & GALOTYRI

1 kg chat potatoes

50 g unsalted cultured butter, chopped

1 garlic bulb, top trimmed to expose the cloves

sea salt flakes and freshly ground black pepper

180 g streaky bacon rashers

200 g Gruyère or other Alpine cheese, grated

4 sprigs of thyme, leaves picked and chopped

100 g Galotyri or crème fraîche

½ bunch of flat-leaf parsley, leaves picked and chopped

Galotyri is our favourite alternative to sour cream due to its savoury tang and complexity, but if you can't find it, sour cream or crème fraîche will also satisfy. This is a good F-off dish if you ever get assigned a side for pot luck.

Preheat the oven to 220°C fan-forced.

Place the potatoes in a large saucepan of cold salted water and bring to the boil over medium–high heat. Reduce the heat to a simmer and cook the potatoes for 12 minutes or until just tender. Drain and pat dry with a clean tea towel.

Place the potatoes in a baking dish with the butter and garlic. Season with salt and pepper, then transfer to the oven and cook, turning occasionally, for 30 minutes or until the potatoes start to colour. Reduce the temperature to 180°C, then carefully weave the streaky bacon through the potatoes and cook for another 15 minutes or until the potatoes are golden and the bacon is crispy. Sprinkle the Gruyère over the top and cook for a final 8–10 minutes, until the cheese is melted and golden.

Remove the dish from the oven, dollop with the Galotyri or crème fraîche and scatter the herbs over. Serve immediately. If you like, you can fish out the roasted garlic and squeeze the cloves over the potatoes.

Serves 4–6 as a side

STUDD SIBLINGS
RECOMMEND

We love Aphrodite Galotyri and Isigny Sainte-Mère Crème Fraîche.

STICKY VINEGAR CHORIZO WITH FETA

2 cured chorizo, cut diagonally into 5 mm thick slices
2 tablespoons brown sugar
60 ml (¼ cup) sherry vinegar
100 g Greek barrel-aged feta
crusty sourdough, to serve

This makes a sexy side or could be moved to brunch or antipasto hour, if you wanted. Buttered sourdough as a shovel and for mopping is mandatory.

Place the chorizo in a cold frying pan over medium–high heat and cook, stirring frequently, for 3–5 minutes, until starting to colour. Add the sugar and vinegar and cook, stirring, for a further 3–5 minutes, until the vinegar is reduced and sticky.

Transfer the chorizo to a serving bowl, crumble over the feta and serve with the sourdough.

Serves 2–4 as a side or snack

STUDD SIBLINGS RECOMMEND

We love Aphrodite Barrel-Aged Feta.

SEXUAL IRISH QUEEN KILLED BY A HUNK OF CHEESE

Whether or not Queen Maeve existed or is mere Irish folklore is still debated. Described as a beautiful, strong-willed warrior who knew what she wanted and deserved (including five husbands), she got into some fearsome battles over the years, but perhaps her gnarliest attack was deliberately killing her pregnant sister. The child, Furbaide, grew up resenting his aunty (obvi) for killing his mum. He planned revenge by becoming a pro at the sling shot. According to legend, Queen Maeve was also a woman of routine and enjoyed a bath at the same time every day, which made the job of a would-be assassin much easier. One day, Furbaide took a hard piece of cheese and, with expert aim, slung it at her head. Queen Maeve died. One has to ask, though, wasn't there a rock nearby? Still, it goes to show what you can do with a well-chosen piece of cheese.

LAMB, FETA & ZA'ATAR KOFTA KEBABS WITH SUMAC YOGHURT

Kofta kebabs are one of our favourite Middle Eastern delicacies and take us back to our backpacking days and the smells and tastes of Istanbul. The feta and yoghurt make the end result exceptionally refreshing and zesty. This dish will sneak into your dreams, and you will find yourself craving it at the strangest of times. It also smells as good as it tastes, so get ready to make your neighbours jealous.

Remove the sausage mince from the casings into a bowl and discard the casings. Add the olives, za'atar and feta and mix well to combine. Shape the mixture into eight oval shapes and refrigerate for 30 minutes.

Meanwhile, place the onion, lemon juice and half the sumac in a bowl and season with salt. Toss well to coat and set aside.

Heat a chargrill pan over medium heat or preheat a barbecue flat plate to medium. Brush the koftas with olive oil and grill for 10–12 minutes, turning frequently, until browned all over and cooked through.

Add the parsley leaves and tomato to the onion mixture and drizzle with a little olive oil.

Dollop the yoghurt or Galotyri onto the warmed pitas and sprinkle with the remaining sumac. Place two koftas on each pita and top with the onion and parsley salad, then wrap it all up and serve.

Serves 4

8 good-quality thick lamb sausages (about 1 kg)

30 g (¼ cup) pitted black olives, chopped

2 teaspoons za'atar

100 g Greek barrel-aged feta, crumbled

1 small red onion, finely sliced

juice of 1 lemon

1 teaspoon ground sumac

sea salt flakes

extra-virgin olive oil, for brushing and drizzling

1 cup flat-leaf parsley leaves

1 large vine-ripened tomato, cut into wedges

185 g (¾ cup) Greek-style yoghurt or Galotyri

4 Greek pitas, warmed

STUDD SIBLINGS
RECOMMEND

We love Aphrodite Barrel-Aged Feta and Galotyri.

MIDNIGHT SNACKIES

A lot of thought and a few sibling arguments went into deciding just which recipes belonged in this chapter. It was a modern-day Goldilocks tale of trying to find dishes that ticked all the boxes for witching-hour cook-ups. We were looking to straddle the just-right balance between opulence and ease. Sam passionately campaigned Ellie to move recipes that would take too long late at night, required too much effort or were definitely not going to be made by someone four-beers-deep into another section.

Midnight snackies is for those of us awake and ravenous between the stroke of midnight and dawn. Perhaps these recipes are the post-script to a boozy night filled with moments of low inhibitions; a simple win at a time of limited brain function; a balm to post-break-up sleeplessness; study-break sustenance; or the cure for an unexpected hangry tsunami that makes landfall mid-binge of your latest series. No matter the reason, the call to ooey-gooey cheesy goodness is the only answer for those keeping the hours of a lusty vampire. Trust us when we say we have never regretted making one of these recipes late at night or early in the morning. And nor will you.

BEST CHEESE TOASTIES

Nobody likes a toastie with hunks of cheese that are half melted. What we all want is a toastie that is golden brown and crunchy on the outside and soft and gooey on the inside. Here are our tips for making perfect melt-in-your-mouth toasties and jaffles.

Bread: It depends on the kind of toastie you're making. For sandwich-press and pan-fried toasties, we often reach for a dense, quality sourdough. We're even fans of day-old bread, as it's more crunchy! For jaffles, you have to go for the basic white sandwich bread or Japanese sandwich bread, such as shokupan (milk bread).

Cheese: Choose at least one cheese with perfect meltability for maximum 'cheese pull' and ooey-gooey goodness, and then a stronger cheese for flavour (see our lists on page 149). Cheese-pull cheeses include low-moisture mozzarella, Comté, Gruyère, Emmentaler, Appenzeller, Abondance, Beaufort, Fontina, Raclette and scamorza. Consider using more than one cheese in your toastie.

Preparation: Grate or finely slice your cheese as it will melt quicker and the bread is less likely to burn before the cheese melts. Use your own judgement, but around 60 g or one large handful of grated cheese should do the job.

Fat: We like to spread the bread with shitloads of softened butter to ensure a crisp exterior. Cold butter will likely rip your bread when you spread it. Great alternatives include ghee or grapeseed oil, or you can get creative by using flavoured butters such as the ones on page 188.

Filling: Don't overstuff your toastie – less is more.

Scoring: Score your toastie with a knife before cutting, so the melted cheese doesn't go everywhere when you slice it.

Grill methods: Mood dependent (see below).

Jaffle maker

- *The forgiving jaffle suits cheeses that ooze, as the firmly sealed edges contain it and moisture is not lost.*
- *Make sure your jaffle maker is nice and hot before adding your jaffle.*
- *Melt your butter and brush it onto your unashamedly white bread. Don't be shy about it, this is the time and place where white bread slathered in butter is okay.*
- *Think of your jaffle like a soft burrito; avoid getting overexcited and overstuffing. Nobody likes broken jaffle clips or benchtop carnage.*

Pan

- *Choose your pan (preferably a cast-iron griddle so you can achieve grill marks) and place over medium heat.*
- *Butter both sides of your bread, then place in the pan and toast for 2 minutes on one side.*
- *Flip the bread over, add your chosen fillings to one slice, then place another slice on top (toasted-side down). Reduce the heat to medium–low and toast the sandwich for 2 minutes each side.*
- *Consider using a weight, such as a plate with a couple of cans on top, to press it all down.*
- *Optional steaming step: Add 1 tablespoon of water to the pan (not the sandwich) once toasted. Cover the pan with a lid for 1–2 minutes. This steams the sandwich, which makes it extra gooey.*

Sandwich press

- *Don't slam the lid, press it down gently.*
- *Flip the toastie halfway through cooking and then rotate it 180 degrees for even melting.*
- *Cook it low and slow. Finding the proper temperature is essential and a true art form. You want to toast the bread, while allowing the rich oils from the cheese to come through without burning.*

TRIPLE X STUDD SIBLING TOASTIE

This toastie always turns heads when it comes out on a plate. We originally saw the cheese crown party trick performed by Jamie Oliver and, after we tried it, we just couldn't go back to a normal toastie. Don't worry too much about how your crown looks; the flip action can take a little while to master, but you will get better the more you make it. We do not use the steaming method mentioned opposite for this pan-fried toastie, due to the Parmigiano crown.

Butter both sides of the bread and then only one side with the mustard.

Heat a large non-stick frying pan over medium–low heat. Place two slices of bread, butter-side down, in the pan. Divide the cheddar between the bread slices, then top with the sliced pickles and a pinch of white pepper. Sandwich with the remaining bread slices, butter-side up.

Fry the sandwiches, with a weight on top (a plate weighted down with two cans will do), for 3–5 minutes each side or until golden, rotating the sandwiches in the pan as you cook them to ensure they are evenly toasted. Using a spatula, carefully remove the toasties from the pan and set aside.

Add half the Parmigiano Reggiano to the centre of the pan and cook until melted. Place one of the sandwiches on top of the melted cheese and cook for 1–2 minutes, until the Parmigiano Reggiano is golden.

Use the spatula to firmly scoop under the cheese and toastie. Hold it in air for around 30 seconds, so the cheese has a chance to firm up in long spikes, creating a cheese crown (see image on the next page). Repeat with the remaining sandwich. Eat immediately.

Makes 2

40 g unsalted butter, softened

4 slices of dense sourdough or rye bread

2 teaspoons Dijon mustard

120 g cheddar, grated

2 Polish dill pickles, finely sliced lengthways

pinch of ground white pepper

40 g Parmigiano Reggiano, grated

STUDD SIBLINGS
RECOMMEND

We love clothbound cheddar in this toastie, but any cheddar can be used.

PICTURED

Triple X Studd Sibling Toastie (page 217); Monterey Jack, Mozzarella & Kimchi Jaffle (page 221); Borough Market Caramelised Leek & Cheddar Melt (page 220)

BOROUGH MARKET CARAMELISED LEEK & CHEDDAR MELT

50 g unsalted butter, softened

1 tablespoon extra-virgin olive oil

1 small leek, white and pale green part only, washed well, finely sliced

4 slices of dense sourdough

60 g Comté, coarsely grated

60 g clothbound cheddar, coarsely grated

1 spring onion, finely sliced

freshly ground black pepper

This toastie pays homage to our childhoods, when we would visit Borough Market in London en route to Neal's Yard Dairy. We could smell the toastie filled with Montgomery cheddar way before we could see the little stand that sold it. As we're mates with Jamie Montgomery, we can confirm the secret here is the inclusion of leek and spring onion. There is a high risk of this dish not tasting exactly like it does in London, but we think this version comes close enough to stoke the fires of nostalgia.

Montgomery cheddar can be a little hard to find in Australia, so snap it up if you see it. If you can't source it, a good-quality, clothbound cheddar will work. But, a caveat: if you use only cheddar, it will likely be oily, hence the addition of Comté. They still make a version of this toastie at the market today; smell your way there.

Heat 10 g of the butter along with the olive oil in a large non-stick frying pan over medium–low heat. Add the leek and cook, stirring occasionally, for 7–10 minutes, until softened and starting to caramelise. Transfer the leek to a bowl and wipe the pan clean.

Butter both sides of the bread with the remaining butter. Combine the cheeses and spring onion in a bowl. Place half the cheese mixture on two slices of bread, top with the cooked leek and then the remaining cheese mixture. Season with pepper and sandwich together with the remaining slices of bread.

Return the pan to medium heat or preheat a sandwich press. Cook the sandwiches, rotating them and pressing down with a spatula to ensure they toast evenly, for 4–5 minutes each side, until golden brown and the cheese has melted.

Makes 2

STUDD SIBLINGS
RECOMMEND

We love La Couronne Fort-Aged Comté and Montgomery, Cabot, Westcombe or Pyengana clothbound cheddars.

MONTEREY JACK, MOZZARELLA & KIMCHI JAFFLE

If you haven't owned a jaffle maker since the '80s, it might be the best $15 you spend at Kmart this year. Did you know the jaffle iron was invented by a Sydney resident in 1949?! We didn't realise it was an Australian thing, either, until a few American pals DM'd us after an Instagram post about jaffles, asking: 'sorry, what is a jaffle?'.

Glad you asked ... a jaffle is defined by its two carby bread triangles that are firmly sealed. Its edges are crunchy and the centre is golden and puffed up. Be as inventive as you like, you can't go wrong with the cheese. Compared to toasties, we feel jaffles are more forgiving when it comes to what you stuff them with, because the sides act as decent barriers. You lose less moisture, so you can afford to add a super melty, melty cheese. White bread is a must, forget fancy. A jaffle is classless and we love it.

Kimchi goes mad well with cheese. If you don't have Monterey Jack, it swoons equally with Comté and cheddar, too.

Preheat a jaffle maker.

Butter both sides of the bread slices, then divide the cheeses and kimchi between two slices of bread and top with the remaining bread.

Cook in the jaffle maker until the cheese has melted and the corners are slightly charred – about 3–5 minutes, depending on your machine. Serve immediately.

Makes 2

40 g unsalted butter, softened

4 slices of white bread or Japanese shokupan (milk bread)

60 g Monterey Jack, grated

60 g low-moisture mozzarella, grated

80 g (⅓ cup) kimchi

OTHER WINNING TOASTIE & JAFFLE FILLINGS

- *Fontina, green Sicilian olives and chèvre.*
- *Manchego, Gruyère, caramelised onion relish and pickles.*
- *Mozzarella, Raclette, sage and prosciutto.*
- *Taleggio with sautéed mushrooms, thyme and truffled Pecorino (add truffle oil if using regular Pecorino).*
- *Normandy Camembert with smoked tomato chutney.*
- *Mascarpone, Nutella and banana.*
- *Ham, caramelised onion, Comté and Dijon mustard.*
- *Asiago, roasted red capsicum, rocket and olive tapenade.*

THE OH-SO-SIMPLE CACIO E PEPE

400 g dried spaghetti

60 ml (¼ cup) extra-virgin olive oil

2 teaspoons freshly ground black pepper, plus extra to serve

350 g Pecorino Romano, finely grated

100 g Parmigiano Reggiano, finely grated

It's a wild and beautiful alchemy that unites just a handful of quality ingredients to make this dish a thing of reverence! Some recipes call for either Pecorino or Parmigiano Reggiano, but we think it's the combination of both that makes hearts skip (side note: this dish is only as good as the best cheese you can find). The Pecorino adds a sharp punch and the Parmigiano Reggiano balances that fist-in-the-face with its nutty and umami flavours. The starchy pasta water in the sauce makes it stick beautifully to the spaghetti, adding the right amount of 'sauciness' to proceedings. Now, prepare to lie down in that carby, cheesy bed you've just made.

Cook the pasta in a large saucepan of salted boiling water for 1 minute less than the packet instructions. Reserve 500 ml (2 cups) of the pasta cooking water, then drain the pasta.

Heat the olive oil in a large non-stick frying pan over medium heat. Stir in the pepper and cook for 15 seconds or until fragrant, then add half the reserved cooking water and bring to the boil. Reduce the heat to low, add the pasta to the pan and cook, stirring, for 1–2 minutes, until the pasta is coated in the cooking water.

Sprinkle three-quarters of the Pecorino Romano and Parmigiano Reggiano over the pasta. Stir constantly for 2–3 minutes, until the cheese is melted and the sauce coats the pasta. Stir in the remaining cooking water, a spoonful at a time, to create a creamy sauce.

Divide the pasta among bowls. Sprinkle the remaining cheese over the top and scatter with extra ground black pepper to serve.

Serves 4

STUDD SIBLINGS
RECOMMEND

Other types of Pecorino will work fine if you can't get your hands on Pecorino Romano.

EIGHTIES CHEESE STRAWS

2 sheets of frozen puff pastry, just thawed

1 egg, lightly beaten

1 teaspoon smoked paprika

100 g (1 cup) Parmigiano Reggiano, finely grated

60 g halloumi, finely grated

sea salt flakes

CHILLI BUTTER

50 g unsalted butter, melted

1 teaspoon chilli oil

½ bunch of chives, finely sliced

A twizzle of puffed pastry with cheese – a totally primo party starter circa 1985! These take two seconds to make. We mix and match our cheese topping for this recipe – it's great for using up those off-cuts that are skulking at the back of the fridge.

Preheat the oven 200°C conventional. Line a large baking tray with baking paper.

Brush the pastry sheets with some of the beaten egg and sprinkle over the paprika. Combine the cheeses and sprinkle over the top, then use a rolling pin to roll over the cheese and press it into the pastry.

Fold the pastry sheets in half and roll again with the rolling pin to firmly enclose the cheese layer. Cut the pastry sheets into 2 cm wide strips, then twist each strip and place on the prepared tray. Brush with the remaining beaten egg, then sprinkle with salt and bake for 15–20 minutes, until golden brown.

Meanwhile, to make the chilli butter, combine the butter, chilli oil and chives in a bowl. Remove the cheese straws from the oven, brush with the chilli butter and serve.

Makes 24

STUDD SIBLINGS
RECOMMEND

We love Cravero Parmigiano Reggiano and Aphrodite Halloumi.

IMPRESSIVE WHOLE-LOAF GARLIC BREAD

The thing that makes this garlic bread so impressive is that you're serving a whole loaf of good-quality sourdough, instead of a pre-packaged, store-bought soggy baguette. The Hasselback cutting technique is intentional as it stops the butter from seeping out and encourages the garlic to further infuse the bread without burning. We have been known to sneakily add some mozzarella in between some of the slits for a surprise cheesy hit.

Preheat the oven to 200°C fan-forced.

Trim the top off the garlic bulb to just expose the cloves. Drizzle the bulb with olive oil and wrap in foil, then transfer to the oven and bake for 30–40 minutes, until the bulb feels soft. Squeeze the cloves into a bowl with the butter, parsley, sage and Parmigiano Reggiano. Season with salt and pepper and mix well to combine.

Using a serrated knife, slice the sourdough into 1 cm thick slices, without cutting all the way through. Spread the butter mixture in between the cuts, then wrap the bread in foil, place on a baking tray and bake for 15–20 minutes, until the butter has melted. Remove the foil and continue to bake for a further 5 minutes, until the bread is browned and crisp.

Serve warm with your choice of saucisson, pickled veg or kimchi.

Serves 4–6

1 large garlic bulb

extra-virgin olive oil, for drizzling

200 g cultured butter, at room temperature

½ cup chopped flat-leaf parsley leaves

¼ cup chopped sage leaves

80 g Parmigiano Reggiano, grated

sea salt flakes and freshly ground black pepper

1 sourdough loaf (about 640 g)

TO SERVE
saucisson
pickled vegetables
kimchi

STUDD SIBLINGS
RECOMMEND

*Our fave butter is
Le Conquérant Beurre
de Baratte.*

CHEESE DIP, THREE WAYS

Nosh on these dips with crusty bread, pita chips or Jatz crackers.

PICTURED

Green Dip with Manchego & Roasted Almonds (page 230);
Fromage Fort (Cheesy French Dip, page 231); Gooey Mexican
Cheese & Jalapeño Dip (page 230)

GREEN DIP WITH MANCHEGO & ROASTED ALMONDS

200 g Manchego, rind removed, cut into large pieces

50 g (⅓ cup) roasted almonds

1 bunch of basil, leaves picked

¼ bunch of flat-leaf parsley, leaves picked

1 garlic clove, crushed

finely grated zest of 1 lemon

100 ml extra-virgin olive oil

sea salt flakes, to taste

vegetable sticks or corn chips, to serve

This dip relies on quality Manchego, otherwise it risks tasting bitter or gamey. We use El Esparto Manchego, but any hard Spanish cheese can be used, as long as it isn't too aged and bitey.

Add the Manchego to the bowl of a food processor and pulse for 15–20 seconds, until the cheese is finely crumbled. Add the almonds, basil, parsley, garlic, lemon zest and olive oil and blend until combined and the almonds are coarsely chopped. Season with salt to taste.

Transfer the dip to a serving bowl and serve with fresh vegetable sticks or corn chips.

Serves 4

GOOEY MEXICAN CHEESE & JALAPEÑO DIP

25 g unsalted butter

2 tablespoons plain flour

250 ml (1 cup) full-cream milk

60 g (¼ cup) sour cream

2 tablespoons chopped pickled jalapeños

50 g (½ cup) grated cheddar

50 g fresh firm ricotta

75 g (½ cup) low-moisture mozzarella, grated

sea salt flakes and freshly ground black pepper

corn chips, to serve

Serve this one when you're settling in to watch a good movie or a big game. It's a show-stopper dip in itself.

Place the butter in a saucepan over medium–low heat and stir until melted. Add the flour and cook, stirring constantly, for 2 minutes or until the flour has cooked out and the mixture resembles wet sand. Add the milk in two batches, whisking constantly to ensure no lumps form. Whisk in the sour cream, then increase the heat to medium and bring to a simmer. Cook for 5 minutes, whisking constantly, until slightly thickened. Remove from the heat and stir in the jalapeños, cheddar, ricotta and 25 g of the mozzarella. Season to taste with salt and pepper.

Preheat the oven grill to high.

Transfer the mixture to a small ovenproof dish and sprinkle with the remaining mozzarella. Place the dish on a baking tray and grill for 3–4 minutes, until golden and bubbling. Set aside for 10 minutes to cool (the dip will be very hot), before serving warm with corn chips for dipping.

Serves 4–6

FROMAGE FORT (CHEESY FRENCH DIP)

Fromage fort (which translates literally to 'strong cheese') is a traditional French recipe. Historically, it was made from a mixture of random cheese odds and ends mashed together in a ceramic pot with whey, milk or broth and left to ferment. Once the desired stank profile had developed and the cheesy mush had expanded to double the size, a fortified wine, such as brandy or eau-de-vie, was added to stop or slow the fermentation. As you can imagine, this dish was often an acquired taste. Thankfully, we have a modern recipe that is not quite as offensive on the nose.

There are no strict rules regarding fromage fort, but it is best to stick to the cheeses and tastes you like. As a general rule, adding something creamy, such as brie, double cream or chèvre, gives the spread a smooth texture. If you are chasing something punchy, try adding blue cheese or a washed rind to give it more oomph. Alpines will bring a nice umami flavour.

For this one, we find it goes best dipped with your version of Jatz crackers to add crunch.

Heat the olive oil in a small non-stick frying pan over medium–low heat, add the garlic and thyme and cook for 1–2 minutes, until the garlic is softened and perfumed. Remove from the heat.

Transfer the garlic mixture to the bowl of a food processor, along with the cheeses, and process until finely crumbled. Slowly add the wine or eau-de-vie and blend until the mixture is smooth and spreadable. Transfer to a bowl, season with salt and pepper and refrigerate, covered, overnight.

Serve the fromage fort on slices of toasted French baguette or crackers and pair with dried fruits of your choice and some nice low-tannin wine.

Serves 4–6

1 tablespoon extra-virgin olive oil

2 garlic cloves, crushed

2 teaspoons thyme leaves

250 g mixed cheese (at least two types), rinds removed, coarsely chopped (soft cheese examples: feta, brie, camembert, chèvre; hard cheese examples: Asiago, Gruyère, Parmigiano Reggiano, Manchego, Pecorino Romano)

60 ml (¼ cup) dessert wine or eau-de-vie

sea salt flakes and freshly ground black pepper

TO SERVE

toasted slices of French baguette or crackers

dried fruit, such as figs, apricots and dates

PARM CHIPPIES

These gems are perfect for a nibbles and beer situation. They're also the business on top of soup or as a garnish for a salad. We always make extra and store them in an airtight container.

Preheat the oven to 160°C conventional. Line a baking tray with baking paper.

Scatter the Parmigiano Reggiano in a thin, even layer on the prepared tray. Sprinkle over the oregano, cayenne pepper, paprika and black pepper. Bake for 12–15 minutes, until deep golden.

Remove from the oven and allow to cool completely. Break into shards to serve or store in an airtight container for up to 1 week.

Serves 4

100 g Parmigiano Reggiano, finely grated

1 teaspoon dried Greek oregano

¼ teaspoon cayenne pepper

¼ teaspoon paprika

¼ teaspoon freshly ground black pepper

DOES CHEESE GIVE YOU 'CHEESEMARES'?

Nope. We give you full permission to head to the fridge this evening! Cheese actually contains high levels of an amino acid called 'tryptophan', which has been shown to PROMOTE sleep and reduce stress. From tryptophan, our brains manufacture the chemical serotonin.

In 2005, a study gave 200 participants 20 g of cheese before bed for a week and told them to record their dreams. No nightmares were recorded, but there was evidence that different cheeses resulted in different types of dreams.

Stilton – vivid dreams

Red Leicester – childhood memories/nostalgia

Cheddar – dreams about celebrities (LOL)

Please note, this study did not have a control group and was relatively small in sample size and sponsored by the British Cheese Board. So, take these results with a cracker!

STUDD SIBLINGS RECOMMEND

We love Cravero Parmigiano Reggiano.

JAPANESE-STYLE CRISPY SPICED HALLOUMI SANDWICH

75 g (½ cup) plain flour

1–2 teaspoons cayenne pepper, to taste

2 teaspoons garlic powder

sea salt flakes and freshly ground black pepper

2 eggs, lightly beaten

60 g (1 cup) panko breadcrumbs

2 x 250 g packets of Cypriot sheep and goat halloumi, drained and patted dry

vegetable oil, for cooking

8 slices of white bread or Japanese shokupan (milk bread)

1 cup shredded iceberg lettuce

SPICY MAYO

125 g (½ cup) Kewpie mayonnaise

¼ cup chopped sweet dill pickles

2 tablespoons sriracha chilli sauce

sea salt flakes and freshly ground black pepper

One long Covid lockdown, we would entertain ourselves with *Iron Chef*–style cook-offs using the same cheese as a base ingredient. We would drag Mum in from next door to be the judge. Sammy won this particular Japanese halloumi challenge fair and square with a 10/10 score (El made halloumi katsu burgers that were 7.5/10).

To us, it's kind of like a Filet-O-Fish burger from Maccas, but in the best possible way.

To make the spicy mayo, combine all the ingredients in a small bowl and season with salt and pepper. Set aside.

Combine the flour, cayenne pepper and garlic powder in a bowl. Season with salt and pepper. Place the lightly beaten eggs in another bowl and the panko breadcrumbs on a large plate.

If you're using Aphrodite Halloumi, cut the cheese in half horizontally. If you're using blocks of halloumi, cut the cheese into thick slices. Coat the halloumi in the spiced flour, then dunk in the egg and finally coat in the panko breadcrumbs.

Heat enough oil to cover the base of a large non-stick frying pan. Cook the halloumi for 2–3 minutes each side or until golden brown, then transfer to a wire rack to drain.

Spread the bread with the spicy mayo, top half the bread slices with the shredded lettuce and halloumi, then sandwich together with the remaining bread. Using a serrated knife, trim the crusts off the sandwiches and cut in half to serve.

Makes 4

STUDD SIBLINGS
RECOMMEND

We love Aphrodite Mixed Milk Halloumi.

TRIPLE CHEESY QUESADILLAS

30 g unsalted butter

1 French shallot, finely chopped

50 g frozen spinach

sea salt flakes and freshly ground black pepper

juice of ½ lemon

4 x 16 cm flour tortillas

300 g mixed cheese 'leftovers', grated

½ bunch of dill, leaves picked, plus extra to serve

TO SERVE

Tabasco sauce

lemon wedges

This is another recipe you can rustle up with limited ingredients and scrappy pieces of cheese in your fridge. You almost don't need a recipe – this is more of an invitation for you to improvise in the kitchen.

Our secret here is we always use two melty cheeses (see our list on page 149) and one salty.

Melt the butter in a non-stick frying pan over medium heat and cook the shallot for 2–3 minutes, until starting to soften. Add the spinach and cook for 5 minutes or until thawed, then transfer the mixture to a sieve and drain any excess water from the spinach. Place the mixture in a bowl, season with salt and pepper, add the lemon juice and mix to combine.

Spread the spinach mixture over half of each tortilla. Top with the cheese leftovers and dill, then fold the empty half of each tortilla over the filling, to form a half-moon shape.

Place a chargrill pan over medium–low heat and lightly grease with butter or oil. Cook the tortillas, one at a time, for 3 minutes each side or until golden brown and the cheese has melted. Scatter over some extra dill and season with salt and pepper. Serve with Tabasco sauce and lemon wedges.

Serves 4

STUDD SIBLINGS
RECOMMEND

For this recipe, we use equal amounts of Gruyère, Aphrodite Barrel-Aged Feta and low-moisture mozzarella.

SAMMY'S HALLOUMI BURGERS WITH SPECIAL SAUCE

60 ml (¼ cup) extra-virgin olive oil

2 x 250 g packets of Cypriot sheep and goat halloumi, drained and patted dry, halved horizontally

4 brioche buns, cut in half

80 g unsalted butter, at room temperature

¼ iceberg or butter lettuce, trimmed and leaves separated

2 small vine-ripened tomatoes, sliced

1 small white onion, finely sliced into rings

SPECIAL SAUCE

2 dill pickles, drained, finely chopped

2 tablespoons tomato sauce

60 g (¼ cup) whole-egg mayonnaise

2 teaspoons Dijon mustard

½ teaspoon garlic powder

¾ teaspoon onion powder

sea salt flakes and freshly ground black pepper

This is Sammy's signature dish; he takes great pride in having nailed Maccy D's 'special sauce'. Who said meat-free Mondays need to take salad form? This is anything but boring.

To make the special sauce, place all the ingredients in a small bowl, season with salt and pepper and stir to combine. Set aside.

Preheat the oven grill to high.

Heat the oil in a non-stick frying pan or chargrill pan over medium–high heat. Cook the halloumi, in batches if necessary, for 2 minutes, turning once, until golden. Transfer to paper towel to drain, then set aside and keep warm.

Place the buns, cut-side up, under the grill for 30–60 seconds, until golden and toasted. Spread each cut side with the butter, then generously spread the special sauce on top. Layer the base of each bun with the lettuce, tomato, halloumi and onion. Finish with the bun tops and serve immediately.

Makes 4

STUDD SIBLINGS
RECOMMEND

We love Aphrodite Mixed Milk Halloumi.

WHY DOES HALLOUMI SQUEAK?

Because of its molecular structure! Halloumi has strong intact protein structures and lots of calcium. This combo makes the protein strands rub against the enamel on your teeth, causing it to squeak. Our personal observation is that cow's milk halloumi squeaks more than sheep and goat halloumi.

WEEKNIGHT MANCHEGO & HAM CARBONARA

100 g quality Manchego, finely grated, plus extra to serve

1 egg, plus 4 egg yolks

1 teaspoon freshly ground black pepper

100 g leg ham or bacon, chopped

400 g dried spaghetti

This recipe is a dark horse for its simplicity. The piquant, peppery flavours of the Manchego add a welcome dimension to this classic, and the simplicity will have you fretting that you will be found out. Quality Manchego is the key – but any quality hard cheese can be subbed in, such as truffle Pecorino or Parmigiano Reggiano. The ham provides salt and fat, while the Manchego and egg yolks mixed with pasta water create the velvety sauce. A hearty, easy meal, no matter what time of day.

Whisk the Manchego, egg, egg yolks and pepper together in a large bowl and set aside.

Place the ham or bacon in a cold, large non-stick frying pan over medium–low heat. Cook for 5–6 minutes, until crisp. Remove the pan from the heat.

Meanwhile, bring a large saucepan of salted water to the boil, add the spaghetti and cook according to the packet instructions. Drain, reserving 60 ml (¼ cup) of the pasta cooking water.

Add the pasta to the bowl with the cheese and egg, tossing to evenly coat. Add the ham and any rendered fat from the pan to the bowl and toss again. Add the reserved pasta cooking water 1 tablespoon at a time until the sauce reaches a creamy consistency. Serve with extra Manchego sprinkled over the top.

Serves 4

STUDD SIBLINGS RECOMMEND

We love El Esparto Manchego.

HALLOUMI SCHNITZELS WITH POTATO SALAD & SAUERKRAUT

One of the many things we have learnt about halloumi from the Cypriots is to 'think chicken' when it comes to recipes. You won't miss the meat here, because this faux chicken schnitty tastes just like it!

Place the potatoes in a saucepan of cold, salted water and bring to the boil over high heat. Reduce the heat to a simmer and cook the potatoes for 15 minutes or until tender. Drain and set aside to cool slightly, then slice into 1 cm thick discs.

In a large bowl, whisk together the olive oil, mustard, vinegar, spring onion and dill. Season with salt and pepper, add the potato and carefully toss to coat in the dressing. Set aside.

If you're using Aphrodite Halloumi, cut the cheese in half horizontally so you have four flat pieces. If you're using blocks of halloumi, cut the cheese into thick slices.

Place the flour in a shallow bowl and season with salt and pepper, then place the egg in a second bowl and the panko breadcrumbs and caraway seeds in a third shallow bowl. Coat the halloumi schnitzels in the flour, followed by the egg and the breadcrumbs, then re-dunk in the egg and finish with a second crumb of panko. Place the halloumi schnitzels on a plate and refrigerate for 15 minutes.

Heat enough vegetable or sunflower oil to generously cover the base of a large, deep frying pan. Place over medium heat until the oil reaches about 180°C (the oil is ready when you add a halloumi schnitzel and it bubbles immediately). Working in batches if necessary, add the halloumi schnitzels and shallow fry, turning occasionally, for 1–2 minutes each side, until golden brown. Remove the schnitzels using a slotted spoon and place on a wire rack over a baking tray (don't drain on paper towel or they risk turning soggy).

Serve the halloumi schnitzels hot and crisp, alongside the potato salad and sauerkraut, with a little extra dill sprinkled over the potato salad.

Serves 4

500 g small kipfler potatoes, peeled

2 tablespoons extra-virgin olive oil

2 teaspoons wholegrain mustard

60 ml (¼ cup) apple cider vinegar

1 spring onion, finely sliced

¼ cup dill fronds, finely chopped, plus extra to serve

sea salt flakes and freshly ground black pepper

2 x 250 g packets of Cypriot sheep and goat halloumi, drained and patted dry

35 g (¼ cup) plain flour

2 eggs, lightly beaten

120 g (2 cups) panko breadcrumbs

1 teaspoon caraway seeds

vegetable or sunflower oil, for shallow frying

sauerkraut, to serve

STUDD SIBLINGS RECOMMEND

We love Aphrodite Mixed Milk Halloumi.

SLOW SUNDAYS

Whether your Sunday follows on from a somewhat sleazy and late-night cheesy Saturday or arrives with a sense of renewed calm, this day is reserved for taking it easy on yourself. And for us, that means borderline inertia, where all we do is cook at a perfectly leisurely pace and then enjoy the spoils of our efforts with loved ones and friends.

These recipes are perfect for laid-back gatherings and days where time feels elastic. Stretch it out and serve with bottomless glasses of whatever you fancy.

CREAMY FRENCH FONDUE

800 g grated Alpine cheese (use a mix of at least two cheeses; see suggestions opposite), at room temperature

1 teaspoon cornflour

1 garlic clove, halved

375 ml (1½ cups) dry riesling or gewurztraminer

1 tablespoon dry junmai (pure rice) sake

juice of ½ lemon, or to taste

ground white pepper, to taste

pinch of freshly grated nutmeg, plus extra to serve

TO SERVE

crusty sourdough or baguette, cut into cubes (ideally use day-old bread as it will stay on your fondue fork better)

cured meats, such as bresaola and pepperoni

pickled vegetables

The word 'fondue' can conjure up hilarious and cringe-inducing images of 1970s recipe books. But an updated version can bring a mouth-watering 'ooh la la' factor to any contemporary gathering.

Fondue is basically the combination of cheese, wine and bread. It's a traditional dish from Switzerland and France. Both countries use a hard cow's milk cheese, but they differ in how they change its viscosity: the Swiss use a thickening agent such as flour; the French use ... more cheese.

Early mentions of fondue date back as far as Homer's *The Iliad*, around 800 BCE. The climate and geography of the snow-covered Alps played a significant role in the creation of modern fondue – dated to the 1800s – as cheesemakers and farmers were cut off in the wintertime with no access to fresh food. Fondue was therefore an ingenious way to make use of old cheese, wine and stale bread.

The French word 'fondre' translates as 'to melt', and it has become traditional to cook the cheese in a ceramic pot over a fire or flame. With guests dipping and swirling bread on long, slender forks into a communal pot of bubbling cheese, we truly can't think of a more delicious or fun way to spend a wintry evening!

Here, we've added junmai, a pure rice sake, instead of the traditional kirsch, as it adds an umami kick and is far more drinkable.

Place the grated cheese in a large bowl with the cornflour. Toss to combine and set aside.

Rub the cut sides of the garlic down the side of a large fondue pot or cast-iron saucepan. Place the pot or pan over medium–high heat and add the wine. Bring to a simmer, then reduce the heat to medium and gradually add the cheese, a handful at a time and stirring until melted, until the fondue is smooth and thick. Add the sake and lemon juice and gently stir, then season with white pepper and the nutmeg.

If you have one, place the pot over a fondue burner to keep warm; otherwise, just dip in from your saucepan, which can be intermittently heated if needed. Sprinkle over a little extra nutmeg and serve with cubes of bread, cured meats and pickled veg.

Serves 4

PRO TIPS FOR PERFECT FONDUE

- *Mature, firm Alpine cheeses work best at room temperature. We repeat: room temperature. Use a classic melter as your base and add at least one other cheese. We use 300 g of Emmentaler, 200 g of Fontina and 300 g of Comté.*
- *Avoid copper or stainless-steel pans as the cheese will burn and stick. Use a caquelon (traditional fondue pot) or a deep cast-iron saucepan.*
- *Do NOT rush. Add the cheese slowly, making sure each handful has fully melted before adding more. Let the fondue simmer, not boil.*
- *Stir the pot slowly and continually in a figure-eight motion, as you would for gently scrambled eggs, so the cheese doesn't stick to the base of the pot.*
- *If your fondue starts to curdle or become a gluggy mess, try adding a few drops of lemon juice, then stir vigorously.*
- *Stir as you dip, so the fondue remains creamy to the end.*

CAESAR SALAD WITH TRUFFLED PECORINO

4 eggs, at room temperature

4 bacon rashers

4 baby cos lettuce, halved lengthways

20 g truffled Pecorino, freshly shaved (or use Parmigiano Reggiano or Manchego)

¼ cup each of chopped chives, dill fronds and flat-leaf parsley leaves

ANCHOVY CRUMB

1 tablespoon extra-virgin olive oil

3 anchovy fillets

70 g fresh or dried breadcrumbs (or use day-old bread blitzed in a food processor)

sea salt flakes and freshly ground black pepper

½ teaspoon chilli flakes

½ garlic clove, crushed

CAESAR DRESSING

80 g (⅓ cup) crème fraîche

½ garlic clove, crushed

2 tablespoons finely grated Parmigiano Reggiano

1 teaspoon Worcestershire sauce

juice of ½ lemon

sea salt flakes and freshly ground black pepper

This is a crunchy, punchy salad with a lingering truffle satisfaction from the Pecorino. Add chicken, if you'd like some extra protein.

To make the anchovy crumb, heat the olive oil in a large non-stick frying pan over medium heat. Add the anchovy fillets and stir until they start to dissolve. Add the breadcrumbs, season with salt and pepper and cook, stirring frequently, for 4–5 minutes, until the breadcrumbs are golden. Add the chilli flakes and garlic and stir for another 2–3 minutes, until the breadcrumbs are brown and crisp. Transfer to a bowl and set aside to cool.

To make the dressing, whisk all the ingredients together in a bowl until smooth. Season with salt and pepper. Add a splash of water if you want a runnier consistency.

Cook the eggs in a saucepan of boiling water for 5 minutes for soft-boiled. Run under cold water to stop the cooking process, then gently peel and set aside.

Cook the bacon in the same pan as the breadcrumbs, over medium heat, for 3–4 minutes each side, until brown and crisp. Transfer to a plate lined with paper towel to drain.

Arrange the lettuce in a serving bowl. Cut the eggs in half and add to the lettuce, along with the bacon and anchovy crumb. Drizzle over the dressing, scatter with the Pecorino and herbs and serve.

Serves 4

STUDD SIBLINGS RECOMMEND

We love Ortiz anchovies and Cravero Parmigiano Reggiano.

HEARTWARMING FRENCH ONION SOUP WITH COMTÉ CROUTONS

This recipe is from our dear friend and mentor, Cathy Strange. While we were travelling with her in Italy, visiting Parmigiano Reggiano productions, we had cravings for French onion soup on a particularly cold day. She was convinced she had 'the best recipe in the world' back in Austin.

A woman always true to her word, when she returned home, she sent a copy cut out from an old newspaper. We removed the sugar, though, as we prefer a more savoury soup. It's the kind of soup that hugs you from the inside. The key to this recipe is going low and slow on the onions.

Melt 75 g of the butter in a large heavy-based saucepan over medium heat until it starts to sizzle. Add the onion, then reduce the heat to medium–low and cook, covered and stirring occasionally, for 20 minutes or until the onion has completely collapsed.

Stir through the thyme, season with salt flakes and the pepper and continue to cook, uncovered and stirring frequently, for 10–12 minutes, until caramelised (watch carefully to ensure the onion doesn't burn). Increase the heat to medium and add half the stock, then bring to a simmer and cook for 15 minutes. Add the remaining stock and the port, sherry or Madeira, then cover with the lid and cook for a further 30–40 minutes, until the soup tastes rich.

Meanwhile, preheat the oven to 180°C fan-forced.

Rub the garlic over both sides of the bread slices and spread with the remaining butter. Place the bread slices on a baking tray, transfer to the oven and bake for 3–4 minutes, until lightly toasted.

To serve, place ovenproof soup bowls on a baking tray and ladle in the hot soup. Top the bread slices with the grated cheese, then place on top of the soup. Transfer to the oven and bake for 4–5 minutes, until the cheese is melted and golden. Serve hot.

Serves 4

100 g unsalted cultured butter

4 large brown onions, sliced

3 sprigs of thyme

sea salt flakes

½ teaspoon freshly ground black pepper

1.5 litres good-quality beef stock

2 tablespoons ruby port, sherry or Madeira

½ garlic clove

4 slices of baguette or sourdough

100 g Comté, grated

STUDD SIBLINGS RECOMMEND

We love La Couronne Fort-Aged Comté. If you can't find Comté, sub in any Alpine cheese.

PIZZA, THREE WAYS

One of our dad's side hustles when we were growing up was part-owning one of the first wood-fired pizza shops down the Mornington Peninsula – The Smokehouse – with two of his closest mates. While we were playing 'kick the bucket' on weekends at the back of the restaurant, our dad was obsessed with perfecting the dough with the chefs, including the slow-fermented dough opposite. He was convinced that wood-fired pizza would be 'the next big thing' in Melbourne's food scene, which in the '90s did not feature any wood-fired oven cooking, including pizza. A little like our cheese knowledge, the understanding of what made a good pizza infiltrated our hungry little stomachs as we smashed a mozzarella and Parmigiano-stuffed calzone or an oozing Taleggio pizza between kicks.

If you have the time and inclination, the effort to make the slow-ferment pizza dough is very well paid back with interest.

PRO TIPS FOR PIZZA PERFECTION

- *Dough takes time to rise, so make sure you plan ahead. There is definitely a time and place for store-bought pizza bases.*
- *Baking is a science, so weigh the ingredients for the dough on a scale and don't guess.*
- *If you are using a pizza stone, make sure it's heated in the oven for at least 1 hour before cooking.*
- *Don't use cold dough; bring it to room temperature.*
- *Stretch, don't roll, the dough.*
- *If you are using fresh herbs, such as basil, place them under your cheese so they don't burn.*
- *Pat dry cheeses in brine, such as buffalo mozzarella and feta, on paper towel, to prevent your base from going soggy. A thin layer of passata will also help to avoid sogginess.*
- *Don't overload your pizza – less is more.*
- *Make sure your oven is properly preheated (this will ensure a crisp base).*
- *A white base pizza basically means drizzling your base with extra-virgin olive oil, rather than passata. Leave the crust edge naked.*

QUICK PIZZA DOUGH

500 g (3⅓ cups) tipo 00 flour, plus extra for dusting

10 g (1½ teaspoons) dried yeast

½ teaspoon caster sugar

1½ teaspoons sea salt flakes

350 ml lukewarm water

60 ml (¼ cup) extra-virgin olive oil, plus extra for drizzling

Place the flour, yeast, sugar and salt in a stand mixer fitted with the dough hook attachment and mix on low speed to combine.

Combine the warm water and olive oil in a jug, then, with the motor running, gradually add to the flour mixture, mixing to form a very soft dough. Increase the speed to medium and knead for 5 minutes or until the dough is smooth and elastic.

Transfer the dough to a lightly oiled bowl, cover with a tea towel and leave to prove in a warm place for 1–2 hours, or until doubled in size.

Punch down the dough and knead on a lightly floured work surface with your hands for 1 minute, then divide into four equal portions, ready to roll out and bake.

Makes 4

SLOW-FERMENT PIZZA DOUGH

10 g (1½ teaspoons) dried yeast

½ teaspoon caster sugar

450 ml lukewarm water

750 g (5 cups) tipo 00 flour

1 tablespoon sea salt flakes

2 tablespoons extra-virgin olive oil, plus extra for drizzling

Combine the yeast, sugar and water in a bowl, then cover and set aside for 10–15 minutes, until frothy.

Combine the flour and salt in a stand mixer fitted with the dough hook attachment, add the yeast mixture and olive oil and knead on medium speed for 10 minutes or until smooth and elastic.

Transfer the dough to a lightly oiled bowl, cover with a tea towel and leave to prove in a warm place for 2 hours, or until doubled in size.

Divide the dough into four balls and place on a tray. Cover and refrigerate for 24 hours (the dough can also be frozen for up to 6 months).

Allow the dough to come to room temperature for 1 hour before baking.

Makes 4

TALEGGIO & POTATO PIZZA

60 ml (¼ cup) extra-virgin olive oil, plus extra for brushing

3 large brown onions, finely sliced

1 teaspoon caster sugar

sea salt flakes and freshly ground black pepper

360 g desiree potatoes (about 2), finely sliced

plain flour, for dusting

1 x quantity pizza dough of your choice (see page 253)

1 tablespoon thyme leaves

400 g Taleggio, finely sliced

We're throupling hard with this trio: tangy and meaty Taleggio melting like a dream over the potatoes and flirting heavily (and going all too well) with the sweet caramelised onions. We add eyebrow-raising amounts of freshly cracked pepper to finish, but that is our personal taste. Crack as you wish.

Preheat the oven to 220°C fan-forced. Grease four large baking trays and line with baking paper.

Heat the olive oil in a non-stick frying pan over medium heat. Add the onion and sugar and cook, stirring occasionally, for 1–2 minutes. Reduce the heat to low and cook, stirring frequently, for 20–30 minutes, until the onion is caramelised. Season with salt and pepper and set aside.

Cook the potato in a large saucepan of salted boiling water for 3–5 minutes, until par-cooked. Drain and pat dry with a clean tea towel or paper towel. Set aside.

On a lightly floured work surface and working with one piece of dough at a time, stretch the dough into a rough 30 cm x 25 cm rectangle. Transfer the dough to one of the prepared trays and brush with olive oil. Repeat with the remaining dough to make four pizza bases.

Transfer two pizza bases to the oven and cook for 10–12 minutes, until lightly golden. Repeat with the remaining pizza bases.

Divide the caramelised onion among the bases, spreading it evenly and leaving a 1 cm border. Top each pizza with the potato, thyme leaves and Taleggio.

Cook two pizzas at a time for 12–15 minutes, until the edges are golden and crispy, and the cheese is melted. Scatter with freshly ground black pepper and serve while hot.

Makes 4

STUDD SIBLINGS
RECOMMEND

Our fave is Mauri Taleggio, but Normandy Camembert and Pont-l'Évêque also work very well.

ROQUEFORT, CARAMELISED ZUCCHINI, ROCKET & PEAR PIZZA

60 ml (¼ cup) extra-virgin olive oil, plus extra for brushing

3 garlic cloves, sliced

3 large zucchini, finely sliced into rounds

sea salt flakes and freshly ground black pepper

plain flour, for dusting

1 x quantity pizza dough of your choice (see page 253)

200 g Roquefort, crumbled

2 green pears, cored and finely sliced

rocket, to serve

lemon wedges, to serve

Opposites attract here, with the assertive salty punch of Roquefort dancing with the sweetness of the caramelised zucchini, the tartness of the pear and the bitterness and crunch of the rocket.

Preheat the oven to 220°C fan-forced. Grease four large baking trays and line with baking paper.

Heat the olive oil in a non-stick frying pan over medium heat. Add the garlic and zucchini and cook, stirring, for 1–2 minutes. Reduce the heat to low and cook, stirring frequently, for 20–30 minutes, until the zucchini is caramelised. Season with salt and pepper, then remove from the heat and set aside.

On a lightly floured work surface and working with one piece of dough at a time, stretch the dough into a rough circle. Transfer the dough to one of the prepared trays and brush with olive oil. Repeat with the remaining dough to make four pizza bases.

Transfer two pizza bases to the oven and cook for 10–12 minutes, until lightly golden. Repeat with the remaining pizza bases.

Divide the caramelised zucchini among the pizza bases, spreading it evenly and leaving a 1 cm border. Top with the Roquefort.

Cook two pizzas at a time for 12–15 minutes, until the edges are golden and crispy, and the cheese is melted. Top with the pear and rocket, and serve with the lemon wedges and freshly ground black pepper.

Makes 4

STUDD SIBLINGS
RECOMMEND

We love Le Roi Roquefort by Carles.

BROCCOLINI, PORK SAUSAGE, CHILLI & SCAMORZA PIZZA

Broccolini is more tender than broccoli and the stalks add a nice visual interest here. Pork sausage satisfies the meat heads, then the smokiness of the scamorza brings it all together, along with the cheese pull that you will probably want to 'gram as it stretches from your mouth to the crisp pizza base.

Preheat the oven to 220°C fan-forced. Grease four large baking trays and line with baking paper.

Place the garlic, rosemary and olive oil in a small saucepan over low heat and cook for 5–7 minutes, until the garlic has started to soften. Remove from the heat and use a fork to lightly crush the garlic into the oil. Set aside.

Blanch the broccolini in a saucepan of salted boiling water for about 1–2 minutes, until just tender. Drain and refresh under cold water, then set aside.

On a lightly floured work surface and working with one piece of dough at a time, stretch the dough into a rough circle. Transfer the dough to one of the prepared trays and brush with olive oil. Repeat with the remaining dough to make four pizza bases.

Transfer two pizza bases to the oven and cook for 10–12 minutes, until lightly golden. Repeat with the remaining pizza bases.

Brush the infused oil over the pizza bases and top with the Pecorino. Remove the sausage mince from the casings and scatter over the pizza bases, then top with the broccolini, chilli flakes (if using) and scamorza.

Cook two pizzas at a time for 13–15 minutes, until the edges are golden and crispy, and the cheese is melted. Scatter with extra Pecorino and drizzle with any remaining infused oil and a little honey, if you like.

Makes 4

4 garlic cloves, halved

4 sprigs of rosemary, leaves picked

125 ml (½ cup) extra-virgin olive oil, plus extra for brushing

2 bunches of broccolini, trimmed, sliced on the diagonal

plain flour, for dusting

1 x quantity pizza dough of your choice (see page 253)

100 g Pecorino, finely grated, plus extra to serve

6 thick good-quality pork and fennel sausages

1 teaspoon chilli flakes (optional)

400 g smoked scamorza, grated (or substitute low-moisture mozzarella)

honey, for drizzling (optional)

WHOLE BAKED CAULIFLOWER WITH COMTÉ & PARMIGIANO SAUCE

1 large head of cauliflower (about 1 kg)

80 g unsalted butter, softened

4 sprigs of thyme, leaves picked

pinch of cayenne pepper

finely grated zest of 1 lemon

sea salt flakes and freshly ground black pepper

20 g (⅓ cup) panko breadcrumbs

COMTÉ & PARMIGIANO SAUCE

40 g unsalted butter

2 garlic cloves, crushed

2 tablespoons plain flour

500 ml (2 cups) full-cream milk

150 g Comté, grated

90 g Parmigiano Reggiano, grated

1 tablespoon crème fraîche

¼ teaspoon smoked paprika

pinch of ground white pepper

STUDD SIBLINGS RECOMMEND

We love La Couronne Fort-Aged Comté and Cravero Parmigiano Reggiano. If you can't find Comté, sub in any Alpine cheese.

There is something about seeing a whole baked cauliflower in its full, resplendent glory, rather than florets, that makes you automatically think, 'I did *gooood*!'.

Preheat the oven to 200°C fan-forced.

Place the cauliflower in a saucepan large enough to cover it with a lid. Add enough boiling water to come 4 cm up the side of the cauliflower, cover with the lid and place over high heat. Bring to the boil and cook for 10–12 minutes, until tender. Carefully remove the cauliflower using two large metal spoons and allow to cool for 10–15 minutes.

Combine the butter, two-thirds of the thyme, the cayenne pepper and lemon zest in a bowl and season with salt and pepper. Place the cauliflower in a snug-fitting ovenproof frying pan or small baking tray and rub with the butter mixture. Transfer to the oven and bake for 20 minutes.

Meanwhile, to make the sauce, melt the butter with the garlic in a saucepan over medium heat. Add the flour and whisk to form a roux, then cook, stirring, for 2–3 minutes, until it starts to smell biscuity.

Add the milk gradually, whisking constantly to stop lumps forming, until you have a thick white sauce. Bring to the boil, then reduce the heat to low and gradually add the Comté and two-thirds of the Parmigiano Reggiano. Mix until the cheese has melted and the sauce is smooth. Remove from the heat and stir through the crème fraîche, paprika and white pepper.

Pour the sauce over the roasted cauliflower and sprinkle over the remaining Parmigiano Reggiano, thyme leaves and the panko breadcrumbs. Roast the cauliflower for another 10–12 minutes, until the breadcrumbs are golden and the sauce is bubbling.

Carve up the cauliflower and serve with pilaf rice and your choice of steamed greens, or as part of a bigger spread.

Serves 4–6

MAKE YOUR OWN PANEER

2 litres full-cream milk

1½–2 tablespoons freshly squeezed lemon or lime juice

We don't usually make cheese at home, but paneer is an exception as it's so simple and remarkably different to the supermarket version.

Heat the milk to just below boiling point – it's ready when you see bubbles form around the edge of the pan – and turn off the heat. Add the citrus juice, 1 teaspoon at a time, gently stirring until the milk separates into tiny particles of curds and watery whey. Leave to cool for 30 minutes.

Drain through a fine-mesh sieve lined with muslin. Bring together the corners of the muslin to enclose the curds and squeeze out the whey. Press into a flat shape, then top with a plate and two cans. Refrigerate for 3–4 hours, until the curds knit together. The longer you leave it, the harder it will get, improving the texture. Alternatively, soak the cheese in cold water for 2 hours for the same result.

This paneer is best eaten fresh, but can be stored in the dampened muslin cloth inside an airtight container in the fridge for up to 2 days. Serve with honey, or add to your favourite Indian dish.

Makes about 300 g

PARM RIND BROTH

60 ml (¼ cup) extra-virgin olive oil

1 large brown onion, unpeeled, quartered

1 leek, white part only, washed and chopped

1 garlic bulb, cut in half horizontally

250 ml (1 cup) dry white wine

3–5 large Parmigiano Reggiano rinds (about 500 g)

½ bunch of thyme, stems and leaves

2 bay leaves (preferably fresh)

½ bunch of flat-leaf parsley, stems and leaves

8 black peppercorns

2 teaspoons sea salt flakes

Whenever we finish a block of Parmigiano Reggiano we throw the rind in a bag and store it in the freezer. This broth is adaptable, so add whatever tired-looking veggies you have in your fridge.

Heat the olive oil in a large saucepan over medium–high heat. Add the onion, leek and garlic and cook, stirring occasionally, for 8–10 minutes, until caramelised. Add the wine, bring to a simmer and cook, scraping the base of the pan to loosen any stuck-on bits, for 4–5 minutes, until the liquid is reduced by half.

Add the rinds, thyme, bay leaves, parsley, peppercorns and 2 litres of water and bring to the boil. Reduce the heat to a simmer and cook, stirring occasionally to prevent the rinds from sticking, for 2–3 hours, until reduced by half. Add the salt and strain into a large heatproof bowl. Cool, then store in an airtight container in the fridge for up to 4 days. Use for soups, pasta sauces, risottos, cheese sauces and as a stock to cook beans.

Makes about 1 litre

ITALIAN EGG-DROP SOUP (STRACCIATELLA)

Cam's Kiosk in Abbotsford Convent is a cauldron huddle for me and my Melbourne friends. Nestled in an outer wing, it backs onto a courtyard of large leafy oak trees. Its Danish minimalist wooden interiors, open kitchen, seductive wine list and simple, heart-warming Italian-inspired menu lure us in time and time again, but it is especially good for a mid-week meal to break up a Melbourne winter. It also helps that head chef Julie Blum is our dear pal who always greets us with a warm hug.

My favourite item on the menu is her signature stracciatella … I may have had to beg Julie for this recipe, so it is an honour to share a slightly easier version of it below. Julie makes hers with a brown stock cooked for more than three hours from roasted chicken carcasses, parm rinds and plenty of aromatics, so free to do the same if you have time.

Stracciatella is made quite differently by every individual – it's one of those easy/hard things. In asking permission to share this recipe, Julie stood by a few non-negotiable methods, the most passionate one being to pour the egg into the boiling broth, then drop the temp and leave it undisturbed. This creates thicker rags of egg that you can really pick up with a spoon. More traditional methods may use a fine curd, but Julie (and I) like a thicker-textured broth. – *Ellie*

1.8 litres very good-quality chicken stock
parm rinds (optional)
8 eggs
100 g Parmigiano Reggiano, finely grated, plus extra to serve
sea salt flakes and ground white pepper
bunch of cavolo nero, leaves stripped and finely shredded
chopped flat-leaf parsley leaves, to serve
crostini, to serve
extra-virgin olive oil, for drizzling

Place the stock (and parm rinds if you have them) in a large heavy-based saucepan over high heat. Whisk the eggs in a large bowl until well combined. Stir through half the Parmigiano Reggiano and season with salt and white pepper.

Add the remaining Parmigiano Reggiano to the stock, season with salt and white pepper and bring to the boil. Add the cavolo nero and cook for 3 minutes or until tender. Reduce the heat to low, pour in the egg mixture and cook for 4 minutes without stirring. Using a large spoon, gently and slowly agitate the soup to create 'rags' of egg, until the egg is just set.

Divide the soup among bowls and serve topped with chopped parsley, a few crostini, extra Parmigiano Reggiano and a drizzle of olive oil.

Serves 4

STUDD SIBLINGS
RECOMMEND

We love Cravero Parmigiano Reggiano.

AUSSIE SPANAKOPITA

1 bunch of English spinach, stalks removed, leaves finely chopped

1 bunch of kale, leaves stripped and finely chopped

sea salt flakes and freshly ground black pepper

320 g Australian marinated curd, crumbled, plus 80 ml (⅓ cup) strained oil from the jar

3 spring onions, finely sliced

3 garlic cloves, crushed

finely grated zest of 1 lemon

3 large eggs, lightly beaten

1 roasted red capsicum, roughly chopped

½ teaspoon hot paprika

¼ bunch of dill, finely chopped

16 sheets of filo pastry

125 ml (½ cup) extra-virgin olive oil, for brushing

black sesame seeds, for sprinkling

tomato relish, to serve

This Greek-inspired spanakopita-style dish is super fun to make and features a unique Aussie all-star curd-in-oil cheese. It also has an unconventional addition of roasted red capsicum, which we refuse to apologise for.

Combine the spinach and kale in a large colander and toss through ½ teaspoon of salt. Stand for 20 minutes or until the spinach and kale leaves are just softened. Rinse under cold running water and drain.

Preheat the oven to 200°C conventional. Grease a 22 cm round baking dish.

Heat 2 tablespoons of the curd oil in a large frying pan over medium heat. Add the spinach and kale and cook, stirring occasionally, for 6–8 minutes, until wilted. Remove from the heat and set aside until cool enough to handle, then place the mixture in a clean tea towel and squeeze out the excess water. Transfer to a large bowl.

Wipe out the frying pan and heat the remaining 2 tablespoons of curd oil over medium heat. Add the spring onion and garlic and cook for 2–3 minutes, until softened. Remove from the heat and allow to cool slightly, then transfer to the spinach and kale mixture. Add the marinated curd, zest, egg, capsicum, paprika and dill, season to taste with salt and pepper and stir to combine. Divide the mixture into four equal portions.

Brush three sheets of filo pastry with olive oil and stack them on top of each other. Top with another sheet of filo, then spoon one portion of the spinach and kale mixture along a long edge of the pastry, 2 cm in from the edge. Fold the pastry over the mixture and roll up into a 2 cm thick log, then place the log around the edge of the prepared dish. Brush the log with oil, then repeat with the remaining pastry, oil and filling, coiling the logs in towards the middle. Brush the top of the spanakopita with more oil, sprinkle with a few black sesame seeds, then transfer to the oven and bake for 35–45 minutes, until the top is golden and crispy.

Cool the spanakopita on a wire rack for 15 minutes before serving. Serve with tomato relish.

STUDD SIBLINGS RECOMMEND

We love Yarra Valley Persian Fetta or Meredith Dairy Marinated Goat Cheese.

Serves 4

ALIGOT

1 kg floury potatoes, such as King Edward, Dutch cream, desiree, all roughly the same size

50 g unsalted butter

250 g (1 cup) crème fraîche

1 garlic clove, crushed

120 ml full-cream milk

300 g Comté, grated

150 g low-moisture mozzarella, grated

sea salt flakes and ground white pepper

Aliwhattttt?! This is the gnarliest, gooiest, ooziest cheese and potato mash you will ever make. A speciality of Auvergne in Central France, it was the last meal we ate overseas pre-Covid, at a French cheese show in Paris. Aligot is usually made with Tomme, but we've swapped it for our all-time fave, La Couronne Fort-Aged Comté – though any Alpine cheese will do the trick. Most recipes call for a potato ricer to mash the potatoes, which we find most people don't have in their kitchen arsenal. If you do have one, go for it, but we use a sieve with equally pleasing results.

Aligot translates as 'something to eat' in Latin, and it used to be served with soup and potatoes when meat was scarce.

Scrub the potatoes, if necessary, then submerge them in a saucepan of lightly salted cold water. Bring to the boil and simmer for 15–20 minutes, until the potatoes are tender and easily pierced with a knife. Drain, then use a tea towel to rub off their skins cos they will be hawwwtt! Do this quickly before they cool, though, as they're easier to peel.

Push the potatoes through a fine-mesh sieve into a saucepan, creating a smooth purée. Place the saucepan over low heat and stir through the butter, crème fraîche and garlic. Slowly add the milk, whisking, until you have a viscous purée (you may not need all the milk). Whisk in the Comté and mozzarella a handful at a time, then beat the mixture vigorously until the cheese is melted and the texture is smooth (be patient as it can take time for the cheese to really melt). The aligot is ready when it starts to come away from the side of the pan and has a slightly glassy sheen. Add a little extra milk if it seems too firm.

Season with salt and white pepper and scoop up immediately with a spoon, or mop up with a hunk of bread, like the French.

Serves 4

STUDD SIBLINGS RECOMMEND

We love Isigny Sainte-Mère Crème Fraîche.

PRO TIPS FOR ALIGOT

- *Always use floury, starchy potatoes.*
- *Cook the potatoes whole and unpeeled to retain their starchiness, which is key for perfect aligot.*
- *Don't use a food processor to purée the potatoes, as it will makes the aligot gluey, rather than creamy.*
- *If it's not thick enough for your liking, add more mozzarella.*
- *If you make a big pot and have leftovers, we suggest using the cold aligot for topping shepherd's pie, lasagne or tuna mornay.*

CRÈME FRAÎCHE ORECCHIETTE WITH ASPARAGUS, PEAS, MINT & TOASTED WALNUTS

Orecchiette, aka 'little ears', is one of our favourite types of pasta, as the deep pockets help to capture the flavour of the sauce with every bite. This easy recipe is superbly balanced, with the freshness of the asparagus, peas and mint, the creaminess and zing of the crème fraîche and the earthiness and crunch of the toasted walnuts. This dish, of course, shines brightest when it's asparagus season.

Cook the pasta in a large saucepan of salted boiling water, according to the packet instructions. In the last minute of cooking add the asparagus and peas. Drain, reserving 250 ml (1 cup) of the pasta cooking water.

In the same saucepan, heat the olive oil over medium heat, add the spring onion and cook, stirring, for 3–4 minutes, until softened. Add the crème fraîche and 125 ml (½ cup) of the pasta cooking water and stir until smooth.

Remove from the heat and add the pasta and vegetables to the pan, stirring to coat in the sauce. Add the lemon zest and juice and Pecorino, and season with salt and pepper, adding extra pasta water if you like a looser sauce. Transfer to serving bowls and top with the walnuts and mint. Serve immediately.

Serves 4

400 g dried orecchiette

bunch of asparagus, woody ends trimmed, cut into 4 cm lengths

155 g (1 cup) frozen peas

2 tablespoons extra-virgin olive oil

4 spring onions, finely chopped

250 g (1 cup) crème fraîche

finely grated zest and juice of 1 lemon

100 g Pecorino, finely grated

sea salt flakes and freshly ground black pepper

50 g (½ cup) toasted walnuts, chopped

½ small bunch of mint, leaves picked and chopped

ROSEMARY & RED WINE LAMB SHANKS WITH THE ULTIMATE CHEESE MASH

4 lamb shanks

35 g (¼ cup) plain flour

sea salt flakes and freshly ground black pepper

2 tablespoons extra-virgin olive oil

4 garlic cloves, peeled and smashed with the back of a knife

1 brown onion, cut into wedges

250 ml (1 cup) red wine

500 ml (2 cups) chicken stock

2 tablespoons brown sugar

4 sprigs of rosemary

roughly chopped flat-leaf parsley leaves, to serve

finely grated lemon zest, to serve

ULTIMATE CHEESE MASH

1 kg desiree potatoes, peeled and chopped into 4 cm pieces

60 ml (¼ cup) pouring cream

60 ml (¼ cup) full-cream milk

100 g unsalted butter, chopped

60 g cheddar, grated

35 g Parmigiano Reggiano, finely grated

60 g Fontina, grated

sea salt flakes and freshly ground black pepper

STUDD SIBLINGS RECOMMEND

We love Mauri Fontina.

Glenny, my partner's stepdad, makes this lamb wonder every time we visit them in Meroo Meadow, NSW. The ley lines of the property run along the same latitude as Glastonbury in the UK, which triggers an immediate state of relaxation. A creek cuts through the centre of my partner's mum Deb's garden and Murphy, the resident Shetland pony, trots towards us expectantly for his feed of local apples. In anticipation of our arrival, the menu is shared over the phone days before and, without fail, 'Glenny's lamb' is front and centre. Also without fail, the fire will be lit and accompanied by a glass of Glenny's cab sav and Deb's family flower decorative napkins. – *Ellie*

Preheat the oven to 150°C conventional.

Dust the lamb in the flour and season with salt and pepper. Heat the olive oil in a flameproof casserole dish over medium heat, add the lamb and sear, turning frequently, for 10 minutes, until browned all over. Add the remaining ingredients, apart from the parsley and zest, to the pan, season with salt and pepper and bring to the boil. Cover with the lid, transfer to the oven and cook for 3½–4 hours, until the meat is falling off the bone.

Meanwhile, to make the ultimate cheese mash, place the potato in a large saucepan of cold salted water. Bring to the boil over high heat, then reduce the heat to medium–low and simmer for 15 minutes or until the potato is tender and easily pierced with a knife. Drain, then return the potato to the pan and cover with a lid. Place over low heat and allow the potato to steam and dry out for 1–2 minutes.

Heat the cream and milk in a small saucepan over low heat until warmed through. Using a potato masher, mash the potato in the saucepan until smooth, then add the butter and half the cream mixture and mix with a spatula until combined. Add the remaining cream mixture and all the cheese, and stir until the cheese is completely melted into the mashed potato. Season with salt and pepper, then set aside and keep warm.

Remove the shanks from the dish and set aside, covered. Strain the cooking juices into a small saucepan and discard the solids. Cook the juices over high heat for 10 minutes or until the liquid is reduced by half.

Divide the mash among plates and top each with a lamb shank. Spoon over the cooking juices, sprinkle with parsley and lemon zest and serve.

Serves 4

CHICKEN, LEEK & STILTON PIE

2 tablespoons extra-virgin olive oil

1 kg skinless chicken thigh fillets, cut into 3 cm pieces

60 g unsalted butter

1 leek (about 200 g), white and pale green part only, washed well and finely sliced

8 sprigs of thyme, leaves picked

2 tablespoons plain flour

500 ml (2 cups) chicken stock

125 ml (½ cup) pouring cream

2 tablespoons Dijon mustard

sea salt flakes and freshly ground black pepper

100 g Stilton, crumbled

1 sheet of frozen puff pastry, just thawed

1 egg yolk, lightly beaten

½ teaspoon sesame seeds

This recipe makes us feel as though we are in a pub somewhere in England. Serve this pie with a dark ale and grey skies to really get your Brit on.

Heat the olive oil in a large, deep non-stick frying pan over medium–high heat. Working in batches, add the chicken and sear, turning frequently, for 6–8 minutes, until golden brown. Using a slotted spoon, remove the chicken from the pan and set aside.

Add the butter to the same pan and melt over medium–low heat. Add the leek and thyme and cook, stirring occasionally, for 4–5 minutes, until softened. Add the flour and cook, stirring, for 1 minute. Slowly pour in the stock and cream and continue to cook, stirring, for about 2 minutes, until the mixture comes to the boil and thickens. Return the chicken to the pan, stir through the mustard and season with salt and pepper. Set aside to cool, then stir through the Stilton.

Preheat the oven to 200°C fan-forced.

Spoon the cooled filling into a 23 cm round baking dish or ovenproof frying pan and top with the pastry sheet, tucking in the edges. Brush the pastry with the egg yolk, sprinkle with the sesame seeds and cut two small slits in the centre of the pie for steam to escape. Transfer to the oven and bake for 25–30 minutes, until puffed and golden brown.

Serves 6–8

STUDD SIBLINGS RECOMMEND

We love using Colston Basset or Cropwell Bishop Stilton for this pie.

CHEESE ROLLING

Every year in the English city of Gloucester, people participate in the extreme sport of cheese rolling. These cheese-loving non-athletes race each other as they chase a wheel of double Gloucester down a tediously steep hill. If you win first place, the wheel is yours. Otherwise, you earn the distinct pleasure of somersaulting downhill in pursuit of cheese, while endeavouring to keep your bones intact. The first written evidence of this nonsensical yet entertaining cheese tumbling event can be found in a message to the Gloucester Town Crier in 1825. However, historians suggest that the tradition has close links to old pagan customs. We recommend you do yourself a favour and watch this event on YouTube. It's a wild romp.

SWEETIE TREATIES

We grew up as sugar-free kids and, 98 per cent of the time, we would be offered fruit for dessert. Sometimes it was ice cream, with the rule being as much as you could stuff into a tiny cone. The limitations on sweetie treaties have relaxed as we've grown older, and our mum Bonnie now holds the title of baking queen in our family unit. Without fail, Bon rolls out a decadent, flawless dessert every time there is a family gathering. Due to our rationing in early life, however, it means that when guests come over, we also overcompensate.

Having said all this, when it comes to 'cheese being in a dessert' we have kept this chapter quite limited in the number of recipes. Even after reading all our cult cheese magazines, which are often filled with weird dessert flavours, such as Roquefort ice cream or cheese s'mores, personally, we find this combination too easily tips into NQR, and we ask ourselves, 'is that really necessary?'. So for this sweetie treatie finale, we have condensed it to desserts people actually want to eat.

SAGANAKI WITH HONEY, OREGANO & FIG JAM

2 tablespoons plain flour

½ teaspoon sesame seeds

¼ teaspoon nigella seeds

2 x 170 g pieces of Kefalotyri saganaki

60 ml (¼ cup) extra-virgin olive oil

4 sprigs of oregano

90 g (¼ cup) orange blossom honey

1 lemon, halved

sticky fig jam, to serve

This classic and winning combo of salty and sweet is a no-fuss dessert that could technically also fit in our Midnight Snackies chapter. The fig jam can be replaced with grilled fresh figs, when in season.

Combine the flour, sesame seeds and nigella seeds in a shallow bowl. Rinse the Kefalotyri under cold water, then pat dry with paper towel and lightly coat it in the flour mixture, shaking off the excess.

Heat the olive oil in a non-stick frying pan over medium heat. Add the Kefalotyri saganaki and cook for 1–2 minutes each side, until golden, adding the oregano in the final minute of cooking. Remove the cheese and oregano and wipe the pan clean with paper towel.

Place the pan over low heat and return the Kefalotyri and oregano to the pan, along with the orange blossom honey, and cook, swirling, for 1 minute or until the honey starts to bubble. Squeeze one of the lemon halves over the top.

Serve the Kefalotyri, either in the pan or plated, with the other lemon half for squeezing over and the fig jam on the side.

Serves 2–4

STUDD SIBLINGS
RECOMMEND

We love Aphrodite Kefalotyri, but Kefalograviera, kasseri or Cypriot halloumi also work really well in this recipe.

BRILLAT-SAVARIN BASQUE CHEESECAKE

200 g Brillat-Savarin, chopped, at room temperature

600 g cream cheese, chopped, at room temperature

2 teaspoons vanilla bean paste

400 ml pure cream

300 g caster sugar

2 tablespoons cornflour, sifted

6 egg yolks

2 whole eggs

We suggest making this cheesecake for a special occasion, rather than as an everyday cake (mainly due to the expense of using a whole Brillat-Savarin). We guarantee that the rich lactic tang and complexity does elevate the dish and make it sing on a whole new delectable level, so is worth it.

Preheat the oven to 240°C conventional. Grease and line the base and side of a 22 cm springform cake tin with baking paper, with a 5 cm overhang above the top of the tin.

Place the Brillat-Savarin, cream cheese and vanilla in the bowl of a stand mixer fitted with the paddle attachment and beat on medium speed for 3–4 minutes, until smooth, stopping to scrape down the side of the bowl with a spatula. Gradually beat in the cream until combined.

Add the sugar and beat for 2 minutes, then add the cornflour and egg yolks and beat for 1–2 minutes, until combined. Scrape down the side of the bowl again, then add the whole eggs, one at a time and beating well between each addition, and beat for a further 5 minutes until combined.

Pour the mixture into the prepared tin, transfer to the oven and bake on the middle shelf for 35–40 minutes, until the top of the cheesecake is deeply caramelised and almost burnt, but still slightly wobbly in the centre. Turn off the heat and leave the cheesecake to cool in the oven for 2 hours, then transfer to the fridge and chill overnight.

Carefully remove the cheesecake from the tin. Transfer to a serving plate and allow to come to room temperature before serving.

Serves 10–12

STUDD SIBLINGS
RECOMMEND

We love Will Studd Brillat-Savarin or Le Dauphin Petit Double-Crème.

BONNIE'S MASCARPONE, RASPBERRY & ROSEWATER TART

2 sheets of titanium strength gelatine

2 tablespoons full-cream milk

500 g (2 cups) mascarpone

60 g (½ cup) pure icing sugar, sifted, plus extra for dusting

1 teaspoon vanilla bean paste

2 teaspoons rosewater

250 g raspberries

2 tablespoons slivered pistachios

SHORTCRUST PASTRY

390 g plain flour, plus extra for dusting

200 g cold unsalted butter, chopped

90 g (¾ cup) pure icing sugar, sifted

3 egg yolks

1 tablespoon iced water

STUDD SIBLINGS RECOMMEND

We love Mauri Mascarpone in this recipe.

Mascarpone is an Italian dairy sweetheart made from full-fat cultured cream. Dating back to the 16th century, mascarpone is native to Lombardy in Northern Italy, where the milk, once skimmed, is often used to make Parmigiano Reggiano.

This tart encapsules the energy and spirit of our gorgeous mum, Bonnie. Described by most people who meet her as 'a real diamond', her essence is mesmerising and comforting, with true kindness and playfulness. Although largely denied sugar as kids, in our later years, sweetie treaties have found their way into our family gatherings. Bon will bake the goods the day before, claiming that it is better to do it then, so she can be calm when hosting. Whether she makes a mascarpone tart, banoffee pie or hummingbird cake, a slice is always enjoyed with a cup of Japanese tea and, sometimes, a side game of backgammon. They all taste especially delightful having been made with Bonnie's magic and love.

When we are time poor, we don't bother with the pastry and simply serve the flavoured mascarpone with the berries and pistachios.

To make the pastry, place the flour, butter and icing sugar in the bowl of a food processor and whiz until it resembles fine breadcrumbs. Add the egg yolks and iced water, and whiz until the mixture forms a dough. Place the pastry on a lightly floured surface and gently knead into a ball. Flatten into a disc, wrap in plastic wrap and chill in the fridge for 1 hour.

Preheat the oven to 180°C conventional. Lightly grease a 22 cm tart tin with a removable base.

Roll out the pastry between two sheets of baking paper until it is 5 mm thick, then carefully transfer to the tin, pressing it into the base and side, and trimming any excess. Refrigerate for 30 minutes.

Prick the pastry base all over with a fork, then line with a sheet of baking paper and fill with baking weights or uncooked rice. Bake for 20–25 minutes, until the pastry is lightly golden, then remove the weights and baking paper and bake for a further 10 minutes or until golden. Allow the pastry to cool completely in the tin.

Soak the gelatine in a bowl of cold water for 5–7 minutes. Remove the gelatine and gently squeeze out the excess water.

Heat the milk in a small saucepan over low heat or in a microwave on high until warm. Remove from the heat, add the gelatine and stir until completely dissolved. Set aside to cool.

Place the milk mixture, mascarpone, icing sugar, vanilla and rosewater in a bowl and mix well. Spoon into the tart shell and smooth with a palette knife. Refrigerate, uncovered, for 2 hours or until set. To serve, top with the raspberries and pistachios and dust with extra icing sugar, if you like.

Serves 8

CARROT & APPLE CAKE WITH RICOTTA CREAM

300 g (2 cups) self-raising flour

1 tablespoon mixed spice, plus extra for sprinkling

2 teaspoons ground ginger

1 teaspoon bicarbonate of soda

140 g unsalted butter, softened

250 g caster sugar

2 eggs

1 teaspoon vanilla extract

sea salt flakes

170 ml (⅔ cup) buttermilk

220 g carrots, peeled and grated

2 large granny smith apples (about 365 g), cored, peeled and grated

RICOTTA CREAM

70 g pure icing sugar

340 g cream cheese

160 g fresh ricotta

2 tablespoons full-cream milk

It's all about the lusciously thick icing on this cake. It has a lovely nutritious vibe to it, with the ricotta, apple and carrot, which also help to keep everything super moist.

Preheat the oven to 180°C conventional. Grease a 20 cm round cake tin and line the base and side with baking paper.

Sift the flour, mixed spice, ground ginger and bicarbonate of soda into a large bowl.

Beat the butter and sugar in a stand mixer fitted with the paddle attachment for about 7 minutes, until thick and pale, stopping occasionally to scrape down the side of the bowl with a spatula. Add the eggs, one at a time, beating well between each addition, then add the vanilla and mix until well combined. Fold through the flour mixture and add a pinch of salt flakes, the buttermilk, carrot and grated apple, stirring until just combined.

Spoon the batter into the prepared tin and bake for 65–70 minutes, until a skewer inserted into the centre of the cake comes out clean. Remove from the oven and allow the cake to cool in the tin for 5 minutes, before turning out onto a wire rack to cool completely.

To make the ricotta cream, place all the ingredients in the bowl of a stand mixer fitted with the paddle attachment and beat for 3–5 minutes, until smooth.

Top the cake with the ricotta cream, sprinkle with a little mixed spice and cut into slices to serve.

Any leftover cake will keep in an airtight container in the fridge for 2–3 days.

Serves 8–12

RICOTTA, NUTMEG & DARK RUM TIRAMISU

750 ml (3 cups) strong black filter coffee

125 ml (½ cup) dark rum

400 g savoiardi biscuits

100 g dark chocolate (70% cocoa solids), chopped into shards

cocoa, to serve

chocolate-coated coffee beans, roughly chopped, to serve (optional)

NUTMEG RICOTTA CREAM

750 g fresh ricotta

375 ml (1½ cups) thickened cream

160 g (1⅓ cups) pure icing sugar, sifted

60 ml (¼ cup) strong black filter coffee

2 tablespoons dark rum

¾ teaspoon freshly grated nutmeg, plus extra for dusting

We wanted to do a cheeky twist on classic tiramisu flavours. You have creaminess and tang from the ricotta, the sweetness of the rum, a traditional coffee kick and a dash of nutmeg for some spice. Don't tell your guests what this dessert is made with until after they've eaten it, especially if they're a little health conscious. As with most Italian sweets, any attempts to curb indulgence is thoroughly preposterous.

You will need to start this recipe four hours ahead.

To make the nutmeg ricotta cream, place all the ingredients in the bowl of a stand mixer fitted with the paddle attachment and beat for 3 minutes or until well combined and smooth. Set aside.

Combine the coffee and rum in a shallow bowl. Working with one biscuit at a time, dip the savoiardi quickly into the coffee mixture and place in the base of a deep 23 cm (3 litre capacity) serving dish. Repeat this process to create a single layer across the base of the dish.

Spread one-third of the nutmeg ricotta cream over the base layer of savoiardi biscuits and sprinkle with half the dark chocolate. Repeat the layering of savoiardi biscuits (this time submerging them in the coffee mixture for slightly longer), nutmeg ricotta cream and chocolate to create three layers, finishing with a final layer of ricotta cream. Refrigerate for 4 hours or until set.

To serve, dust the tiramisu with nutmeg and cocoa and scatter with chocolate-coated coffee beans, if desired.

Serves 10–12

PASTEL DE TRES LECHES (THREE MILKS CAKE)

Sponge cake soaked in three types of milk is an OG classic that rose to fame in the 1930s in Mexico and never really left. This is one of our favourite guilty pleasures. Sweet and syrupy, with a light flavour and texture that will make you reminisce about that one hot Mexican summer. We really enjoy this cake served cooled.

Preheat the oven to 180°C conventional. Grease and line a 30 cm x 20 cm slice tin with baking paper.

Place the eggs and vanilla in the bowl of a stand mixer fitted with the whisk attachment and beat on high speed until pale and thick. Slowly add the sugar, a tablespoon at a time, whisking well after each addition. Whisk on high speed for a further 4 minutes or until the mixture is thick and glossy.

Reduce the mixer speed to low and gradually add the melted butter in a steady stream until incorporated. Sift together the flours, then add to the egg mixture and mix until combined. Pour the batter into the prepared tin and gently tap it on a work surface to remove any excess air bubbles.

Transfer the tin to the oven and bake for 30–35 minutes, until the cake is firm to the touch and a skewer inserted into the centre comes out clean.

Pour the condensed milk, evaporated milk and milk into a large jug and whisk until well combined. Use a skewer to prick deep holes all over the cake, then evenly pour the milk mixture over the warm cake, allowing it to soak into the holes. Allow the cake to cool to room temperature, then refrigerate, uncovered, for at least 3 hours.

Cut the cake into pieces and serve. Any leftover cake will keep in an airtight container in the fridge for up to 2 days.

Optional topping: Whisk 375 ml (1½ cups) of pure cream to soft peaks with 2 tablespoons of sifted icing sugar and 1 teaspoon of vanilla extract and add to the top of the cake when serving.

Serves 8–10

5 eggs, at room temperature

1 teaspoon vanilla extract

230 g (1 cup) caster sugar

125 g unsalted butter, melted

150 g (1 cup) plain flour

75 g (½ cup) self-raising flour

395 g can sweetened condensed milk

150 ml evaporated milk

250 ml (1 cup) full-cream milk

STUDD SIBLINGS
RECOMMEND

This cake also goes well with seasonal fruits – our favourites are mango slices and fresh berries.

CAMEMBERT WITH CARAMELISED APPLE & ROASTED HAZELNUTS

50 g unsalted butter

2 red apples, peeled, cored and quartered

1½ tablespoons caster sugar

80 g (⅓ cup) crème fraîche

1 x 250 g Normandy Camembert, halved horizontally

2 tablespoons roasted hazelnuts, chopped

Another baked cheese, but this time, sweet. If there is a wood-fired oven in your vicinity, use it, as this recipe works very well in one. However, a regular oven is perfectly adequate.

Preheat the oven to 220°C conventional.

Melt the butter in a large saucepan over medium heat, add the apple and sugar and cook, stirring occasionally, for 10 minutes or until the sugar starts to caramelise. Remove the apple mixture from the pan and set aside to cool.

Divide the crème fraîche between two small round ovenproof ramekins that will comfortably fit the cheese. Top each with half of the Normandy Camembert and the cooked apple, then transfer to the oven and bake for 8–10 minutes, until oozy (don't let the cheese melt too much).

Sprinkle with the hazelnuts and serve with spoons.

Serves 4 as a shared dessert

STUDD SIBLINGS
RECOMMEND

We love Isigny Sainte-Mère Crème Fraîche and Le Conquérant Camembert.

CURD NERD TERMS

ACID CURD/ACID-SET
See Lactic-Set.

ACIDIFICATION
The step in cheesemaking where lactose turns into lactic acid and sours the milk.

AFFINAGE
In French, affinage means 'to refine' and is the process of ageing or ripening cheese to its optimum condition for consumption.

AFFINEUR
A person whose job is to mature cheese and bring it up to peak flavour, ripeness and texture. This can be done by inoculating, piercing, rubbing, turning, washing and tasting to establish how a cheese is maturing.

ALPAGE
A French term for Alpine pastures and fields where animals graze, usually in the summer months.

ALPINE
A cheese that is from the Alps. It can also be used to describe a style of cheese that is hard and smooth textured, with nutty and caramel flavours, similar to those made in the Alps.

AMMONIA/AMMONIATED
Condition and description of a cheese that is nearing its maximum shelf life and tipping into over-ripe. Ammonia smells and tastes pungent with some describing it as similar to cat litter or cleaning products such as Windex. Cheeses can be unwrapped and allowed to breathe before serving to reduce ammonia (a small amount of ammonia is okay).

ANNATTO
A natural orange colouring from annatto seeds from the achiote tree, native to Central and South America. It does not add any flavour to the cheese. It is used in Mimolette and some cheddars.

ARTISAN/ARTISINAL
Cheeses that are made with traditional cheesemaking techniques and only in small batches by hand. Usually, the milk has been collected from a small herd.

BACTERIA
Bacteria are microscopic living organisms that essentially decompose their ecosystems. The most important bacteria in cheese are lactic acid bacteria (LAB), which break down lactose (sugar) and turn it into lactic acid. LAB are essential in producing healthy and safe cheese by making the milk more acidic. Bacteria in cheese have an intricate relationship with other microbes, especially yeasts and moulds, and contribute to flavour by breaking down fats and proteins. Bacteria can naturally occur in raw milk, in the environment or can be intentionally added to the cheese in the form of cultures.

BRINE
Salty water solution used to wash or store cheese. Washing or 'brining' cheeses mitigates bacterial growth, which influences flavour. Brine helps semi-hard and hard cheeses develop a skin or rind by extracting moisture. Storing cheeses in brine helps preserve them and stop mould growth.

BUTTERFAT
The fat component in milk.

CAROTENE/β-CAROTENE
Yellow colour pigment found in vegetation such as grass and clover that is digested by animals and deposited in their milk, contributing to a cheese's yellow paste. Particularly expressed in cow's milk cheeses. Other animals, such as goats, digest carotene into colourless vitamin A, thus these cheeses have a white paste.

CASEIN
The main protein in milk. Casein solidifies in cheesemaking when the coagulant (rennet) is added.

CHEDDARING
'Cheddaring' is a technique that occurs specifically in traditional cheddar making. The process involves the cutting, stacking and turning of large curd blocks to drain moisture, then milling them.

CHEESEMONGER
A person who sells cheese, usually in a cheese shop.

CHÈVRE
Translates to 'goat' in French. Often used to describe goat's cheese with a creamy, tangy flavour.

CLOTHBOUND
Cheeses that are wrapped in muslin or calico cloth to protect the cheese, prevent rind growth and allow the cheese to breath as it matures. This is usually seen on traditional cheeses such as cheddar.

COAGULATION
Term used in cheesemaking for when liquid milk turns into a solid (curd). It occurs when rennet is added. Curds have a texture like soft tofu when they are ready to be cut.

COOKED CURD CHEESE
A specific classification of cheese that Food Standards Australia New Zealand use to define cheeses with cooked curds and a low moisture content.

COOKED CURDS
When curds are heated to high temperatures to expel moisture in cheesemaking. Often used in Alpine and Alpine-style cheeses.

CREAMLINE
The layer between the rind and the paste, particularly seen in bloomy and washed rind cheeses. It's usually soft and translucent and occurs when the cheese is ripening due to the breakdown of fats and proteins.

CULTURES

There are two main types of cultures used in cheesemaking.

Starter cultures: Primarily a collection of bacteria called lactic acid bacteria, which break down lactose and turn it into lactic acid to begin the fermentation process. They are essential in producing healthy and safe cheese by making the milk more acidic. As the name suggests, these are often added at the start of cheesemaking. *See also* Bacteria.

Adjunct cultures: Intentionally added cultures for flavour and texture in cheese. These include bacteria, yeasts and moulds.

Today, most cultures are made in laboratories as commercially freeze-dried powders; however, there are also naturally occurring cultures in raw milk and the cheesemaking environment.

CURD

The soft solids formed when milk has been coagulated and cut.

DOUBLE CREAM/DOUBLE CRÈME

A cheese that has extra cream added to make it creamier and buttery. It is defined by the amount of Fat in Dry Matter (FDM), which is usually 60–75 per cent. *See also* Fat in Dry Matter.

ENZYMES

Enzymes are complex groups of proteins. In relation to cheese, enzymes are used to coagulate milk (*see* Rennet). They are also present in milk and break down substances to impact the flavour and texture.

EWE

A female sheep. A term commonly used by both cheesemakers and farmers alike. Often noted on cheese labels, which indicate it has been made from sheep's milk.

EYES

Round holes of varying sizes in the paste of a cheese, created from gas formation by particular bacteria.

FARMSTEAD/FARMHOUSE

Interchangeable terms for cheeses made on the farm where the animals are raised and milked. Usually small-batch cheesemaking and made by hand.

FAT IN DRY MATTER (FDM)

A measurement used to determine the percentage of fat in a cheese. Calculated by the amount of solids left in the cheese *after* the moisture/water has been removed.

GEO (GEOTRICHUM CANDIDUM)

A yeast that behaves like a mould. Can be identified by squiggly brain/coral ridges on top of bloomy cheeses and washed rinds.

GEOGRAPHICAL INDICATORS/ NAME PROTECTED CHEESES

The European Union has a strictly controlled system that aims to regulate and preserve traditional food and manufacturing in certain geographical regions.

The intention for this open system for producers is to ensure fair competition and help customers recognise products stamped PDO or PGI as a guarantee of authentic cheese with specific geographical origins, rather than fakes masquerading under the name. This is why you will see industrial cheeses called parmesan, as they are not allowed to call it Parmigiano Reggiano. There are two levels of classification.

Protected Designation of Origin (PDO)

PDO is the highest form of certification. For a cheese to qualify as a PDO, it must meet certain criteria, including the way it is made within a defined region with specific manufacturing and processing techniques. For example, a cheese may have to be made with raw milk from specific breeds of cow, which have grazed on a certain feed at a particular time of year, made within a designated region and aged for a particular amount of time.

Protected Geographical Indication (PGI)

There are fewer requirements to achieve this status compared to PDO. This indicates that at least one of the steps of cheese production takes place within a defined region.

The PDO and PGI regulations for each cheese are vastly different, with some stricter than others. We encourage you to note it with curiosity, remembering it's an effort to preserve and hold onto tradition.

The name and protection of cheeses is an historical and ongoing debate outside the European Union by those who argue they should be able to call a cheese what they want. Some are honoured through bilateral agreements; others are ignored outside the EU.

Some countries still use their original appellation systems in the title as an acronym or a stamp, but know they are PDO and PGI equivalent. We acknowledge this can be highly confusing.

- **France:** Appellation d'Origine Protégée (AOP)/Indication Géographique Protégée (IGP)
- **Italy:** Denominazione d'Origine Protetta (DOP)/Indicazione Geografica Protetta (IGP)
- **Spain:** Denominación de Origen Protegida (DOP)/Indicación Geográfica Protegida (IGP)
- **Switzerland:** Not part of the EU, so doesn't use PDOs/PGIs; instead, has its own naming system: Appellation d'Origine Protégée (AOP) and Indication Géographique Protégée (IGP).
- **United Kingdom:** Still has access to PDO protection and status, even though it is no longer part of the EU.

HARD CHEESE

A cheese that has been aged, usually salted, and pressed, with a low moisture content.

HOOPING

A part of the cheesemaking process where curds are put into forms or 'hoops' to drain whey and create a cheese's shape.

INDUSTRIAL

Large-scale production often focused on quantity rather than quality. Milk is usually heat treated and standardised, with commercial starters used. It is machine operational to decrease labour costs and increase profit.

INOCULATION

The additions of cultures and moulds to milk.

LACTIC
Taste descriptor for cheeses with high acidity, which are milky and sour in flavour.

LACTIC ACID
A type of acid that starter cultures expel after they eat lactose. It increases the acidity in cheesemaking, aiding coagulation.

LACTIC-SET/LACTIC CHEESES/ LACTIC FERMENTATION
Cheeses that have been made where acid is used to coagulate the milk with little to no rennet. These cheeses usually take a long time to coagulate, and their curd is soft. They are also known as acid-set cheeses.

LACTOSE
The natural sugar component in milk. It is converted to lactic acid in cheesemaking.

LADLING
Transferring the cut curd directly into moulds via a ladle or hand pan.

MICROBES
Microscopic living organisms, including yeasts, moulds and bacteria. Microbes are fundamental to cheesemaking.

MILLING
A mechanical or hand process in cheesemaking to make the curds smaller and shape them into shards. Typical but not endemic to most traditional British cheeses.

MONASTIC CHEESES
Cheeses that were originally created by monks in a monastery. Usually washed rind cheeses, which the monks used to call 'white meat'.

MOULD
Microscopic fungi that are essentially large, fluffy puffballs with filaments that search for nutrients (anything made of carbon) to decompose. Spores of mould can be cultivated from cheese caves or grown in labs. The purpose of moulds is to break down fats and proteins, which in turn impacts the flavour of the cheese. Moulds grow on the rind and surface of cheeses (or inside in the case of blue cheeses). Examples include: *Penicillium candidum*, *Penicillium camemberti*, *Penicillium glaucum* and *Penicillium roqueforti*. They are white, blue or grey in colour.

MOUTHFEEL
How a cheese feels in your mouth and the experience of it in your mouth and throat.

NATURAL RIND
A rind that develops naturally from moulds and bacteria in a cheese, without washing. Usually found in semi-hard cheeses such as Tomme de Savoie or hard cheeses such as Parmigiano Reggiano.

PASTE
The interior part of the cheese that is not the rind.

PASTEURISATION
The process of heating milk to a high temperature, with the intention to kill harmful pathogens. The temperature and time the milk is heated varies depending on the country. Pasteurisation kills almost everything in milk – including 'good' bacteria, enzymes and flavour.

PDO/PGI
See Geographical Indicators.

pH
In relation to cheese, pH is a measure of acidity. The acidity of a cheese will affect the flavour and texture.

PIQUANT
A taste in cheese that is usually spicy, bright and tangy, such as black pepper. It is often used to describe goat's cheese, sheep's milk cheeses and cheddar. It is not the same as bitter.

RANCID
Soapy, bitter or off-tasting cheese.

RAW MILK/UNPASTEURISED MILK
Milk that has not been heat treated or pasteurised so has all its natural bacteriological and enzyme qualities.

RAW MILK CHEESE
Cheese that has been made with raw milk that has not been pasteurised or thermised before the addition of rennet. In Australian standards, raw milk cheeses are defined as cheeses that have not undergone a heat treatment step during production, including pasteurisation, thermisation or high-temperature curd cooking. Food Standards Australia New Zealand classifies cheeses such as Parmigiano Reggiano as cooked curd cheeses, rather than raw milk cheeses. Only raw milk cheese that is covered by a recognised foreign government certificate can be imported.

RENNET
Enzymes added intentionally by the cheesemaker to coagulate milk and affect the texture, aroma and flavour of a cheese. Today, there are three types.

Traditional animal rennet: The most powerful and widely considered to contribute the best flavour. It is derived from the stomach of young ruminants and often used in aged hard cheeses. Only a minuscule amount of rennet is needed to coagulate milk – a mere 0.0003 g of rennet for 1 kg of cheese. Rennet has been used since cheese was first invented.

Vegetable rennet: Derived from several plants, including figs, stinging nettles and even pineapple, but the most common is from thistle flowers. This type of rennet often has a distinct taste and can leave a slightly bitter flavour. In Spain and Portugal, thistle rennet was often used for sheep's milk cheeses.

Microbial rennet: Created in a lab by adapting yeast or mould cultures. It is the cheapest and most convenient form of rennet, but can sometimes leave bitterness in aged cheeses.

RIND
The exterior crust or surface of a cheese.

RUMINANT
Hoofed grazing mammals that acquire nutrients from pastures by fermenting it in a specialised stomach(s). 'Ruminant' comes from the Latin 'ruminare', which means 'to chew over again'. When it comes to cheese, think cow, goat, buffalo and sheep.

SALTING
The process of salting helps to draw off moisture and slow the growth of bacteria and acidity development in cheese. Salting is typically done in one of three ways: sprinkling salt directly onto the curd in the vat; placing cheese in a brine bath; or rubbing salt into the rind. Salting also plays a crucial role in preserving cheese.

SILAGE

A type of fermented feed (grass, plants and legumes) often fed to farming animals. Advantages are that it allows feed to be stored longer and is nutritionally dense, while disadvantages are that it can affect the quality of the cheese (i.e. inflated or 'blown' cheeses, as well as causing off flavours). Most PDOs stipulate that silage cannot be used.

STARTER CULTURES

See Cultures.

SURFACE-RIPENED

Cheeses that are ripened from the outside in by yeasts or moulds. Bloomy and washed rind cheeses fall into this category.

TERRITORIALS

A group of British cheeses that have a long history of production and are named after the area in which they are made: Cheddar, Red Leicester and Cheshire, for example.

TERROIR

A taste of place. In French it translates to 'earth' or 'soil', so in relation to cheese this means how the unique environment of where a cheese is made affects its taste.

THERMISATION

Milk that is heated to a slightly lower temperature than pasteurised milk and for a longer period of time. Retains some good microflora, compared to pasteurisation.

TRANSHUMANCE

Seasonal movement of animals and humans to new pastures. Transhumance usually occurs from the valley to high mountains/ Alpine pastures in summer. A dying tradition that is becoming rarer in the modern world.

TRIPLE CREAM

Cheese that is enriched by cream and as a result has a rich, velvety mouthfeel. Usually 75 per cent of Fat in Dry Matter (FDM). See also Fat in Dry Matter.

TYROCINE

Crunchy crystals in aged cheeses, such as Parmigiano Reggiano or Gouda. They are clusters of amino acids. You can hear them crunch when you bite.

UMAMI

A Japanese word translating to the taste of savoury or 'delicious'. In cheese this is usually tasted as meaty and brothy notes.

VAT

A vessel or container where cheese is made. Made of metal, wood or plastic.

WHEY

The liquid left over after the curds have been cut. Whey is rich in water, lactose and proteins. It is often seen as a by-product of cheesemaking. Sometimes it is fed to animals or made into whey cheeses, such as ricotta, or whey butter.

YEAST

Belonging to the fungi (mushroom) family, yeasts play a supportive role in cheesemaking. They are smaller than moulds but larger than bacteria and affect flavour by breaking down fats and proteins in cheese. They can be intentionally added but are also found naturally in the environment and find a home in cheese. Yeast types include *Debaryomyces hansenii*, a common yeast, and *Geotrichum candidum*, which is more complex and has a buttery smell. See also Geo.

ENDNOTES

1. Kehler, M., Donnelly, C. (Ed.), *The Oxford Companion to Cheese*, Oxford, Oxford University Press, 2016.
2. Salque, M., Bogucki, P., Pyzel, J. et al, 'Earliest Evidence for Cheese Making in the Sixth Millennium BC in Northern Europe', *Nature*, vol. 493, 2013, p. 522–5. <doi.org/10.1038/nature11698>
3. Percival, B., Percival, F., *Reinventing the Wheel: Milk, Microbes, and the Fight for Real Cheese*, Oakland, University of California Press, 2019.
4. Donnelly, CW., *Ending the War on Artisan Cheese: The Inside Story of Government Overreach and the Struggle to Save Traditional Raw Milk Cheesemakers*, Vermont, Chelsea Green Publishing, 2019.
5. Australian Government, Federal Register of Legislation, Australia New Zealand Food Standards Code – Standard 4.2.4 – 'Primary Production and Processing Standard for Dairy Products (Australia Only)', 2012. <legislation.gov.au/Details/ F2021C00670>
6. Australian Government, Department of Agriculture, Fisheries and Forestry, 'Raw Milk Cheese', 2022. <agriculture. gov.au/biosecurity-trade/import/ goods/food/type/raw-milk-cheese>
7. Running, CA., Craig, BA., Mattes, RD., 'Oleogustus: The Unique Taste of Fat', *Chemical Senses*, vol. 40, issue 7, Sep 2015, p. 507–16. <doi.org/10.1093/ chemse/bjv036>
8. Andersen, CA., 'What Happens in Your Brain When You Taste Food', Ted Talk, 2019. <ted.com/talks/camilla_arndal_ andersen_what_happens_in_your_ brain_when_you_taste_food>
9. McCalman, M., Gibbons, D., *Mastering Cheese: Lessons for Connoisseurship from a Maître Fromager*, New York, Clarkson Potter/Publishers, 2009.
10. de Araujo, IE., Schatzker, M., Small, DM., 'Rethinking Food Reward', *Annual Review of Psychology*, vol. 71, no. 1, 2020, p. 139-64. <annualreviews. org/doi/full/10.1146/annurev- psych-122216-011643#_i32>

CONVERSION CHARTS

Measuring cups and spoons may vary slightly from one country to another, but the difference is generally not enough to affect a recipe. All cup and spoon measures are level.

One Australian metric measuring cup holds 250 ml (8 fl oz), one Australian metric tablespoon holds 20 ml (4 teaspoons) and one Australian metric teaspoon holds 5 ml. North America, New Zealand and the UK use a 15 ml (3-teaspoon) tablespoon.

LENGTH

METRIC	IMPERIAL
3 mm	⅛ inch
6 mm	¼ inch
1 cm	½ inch
2.5 cm	1 inch
5 cm	2 inches
18 cm	7 inches
20 cm	8 inches
23 cm	9 inches
25 cm	10 inches
30 cm	12 inches

LIQUID MEASURES

ONE AMERICAN PINT	ONE IMPERIAL PINT
500 ml (16 fl oz)	600 ml (20 fl oz)

CUP	METRIC	IMPERIAL
⅛ cup	30 ml	1 fl oz
¼ cup	60 ml	2 fl oz
⅓ cup	80 ml	2½ fl oz
½ cup	125 ml	4 fl oz
⅔ cup	160 ml	5 fl oz
¾ cup	180 ml	6 fl oz
1 cup	250 ml	8 fl oz
2 cups	500 ml	16 fl oz
2¼ cups	560 ml	20 fl oz
4 cups	1 litre	32 fl oz

DRY MEASURES

The most accurate way to measure dry ingredients is to weigh them. However, if using a cup, add the ingredient loosely to the cup and level with a knife; don't compact the ingredient unless the recipe requests 'firmly packed'.

METRIC	IMPERIAL
15 g	½ oz
30 g	1 oz
60 g	2 oz
125 g	4 oz (¼ lb)
185 g	6 oz
250 g	8 oz (½ lb)
375 g	12 oz (¾ lb)
500 g	16 oz (1 lb)
1 kg	32 oz (2 lb)

OVEN TEMPERATURES

CELSIUS	FAHRENHEIT	CELSIUS	GAS MARK
100°C	200°F	110°C	¼
120°C	250°F	130°C	½
150°C	300°F	140°C	1
160°C	325°F	150°C	2
180°C	350°F	170°C	3
200°C	400°F	180°C	4
220°C	425°F	190°C	5
		200°C	6
		220°C	7
		230°C	8
		240°C	9
		250°C	10

IN GRATITUDE

FROM ELLIE

The idea for this book came to me during meditation one morning. I'd told my partner, KJ, about this vision, so when Mary Small from Plum called me the next day and asked, 'Have you ever thought of writing a cheese book?', our jaws hit the floor in awe of my powers of manifestation. From the hatching of this cosmic wish to the calm 'yes' of my response to Mary, and the reality of writing a book Sam and I are both proud of, this project has taken us on one wild journey. And yet, we did it! There may have been a little help from the universe, but there was certainly loads of support from many wonderful people around us. We have a deep gratitude and enormous respect for their talent, inspiration and unyielding love.

Firstly, to Kirsten Jenkins (KJ), my life partner. You are the cheese to my cracker. I could not have taken this crazy ride without you by my side. Thank you for your unwavering support and patience throughout the conception, gestation and birth of two babies in one year – this baby and our beautiful daughter, Stella (both arriving at the same time). Your love was unfaltering and your unwavering presence alongside me was endlessly assuring and uplifting as I wrote while trying to get pregnant, while I was pregnant and post-partum. You are my Taurean earth that I need physically, emotionally and spiritually. You're also my recipe guru, writing and testing on-set! Your talented hands make our food look soooo incredible. Nothing Comtés to you. I love you so much.

A heartfelt thanks to my bro, Sam. You may be an island and I may be a wave, but thank you for your perseverance and for being your authentically cheeky self, right to the end of this queso quest. I could not have done any of this without you.

FROM SAM

To my family: Will, Bonnie, Fleur, Simon, Rosie, Archie, Ellie, KJ and Stella, to whom I owe everything. Thank you for your unconditional love and endless support. You have made good food and life experiences the epitome of my existence. I love you all from the deepest corners of my heart.

To my mates and lovers, be they past, future or present. You have all held my hand through this life journey, taught me valuable lessons and helped me see the beauty in the everyday. For this, I will always hold gratitude and be thankful.

To my dog, Cha Cha, you are strange. I love every aspect of your being. Thanks for being my anchor.

A special thank you to everyone I've met on my cheese journey. You're a bunch of freaks, geeks and misfits who have shown me how to find solace, comfort, community, culture and inspiration in remarkable, nutrient-rich cheese. I love you all – keep fighting the good fight.

To my sister, Ellie, thank you for being unapologetically yourself. I endlessly admire your gumption, work ethic and stubbornness to achieve exactly what you want, as well as your trust in the universe. Thank you for breathing life into this book. I love you.

FROM BOTH OF US

Thanks, Dad (grand high cheese lord), for teaching us all that we know in cheese and indoctrinating us in the magical world of curds and whey. Thank you for correcting the 'facts that are wrong in cheese books' with your real-life knowledge and photographic memory for all things cheese. Thank you, Mum, for always supporting us with your warmth, words, intuition and love. Also, for looking after Stell; you're the best mum and Yia Yia there is.

The warmest of thanks to Mary Small and Jane Winning for believing in us and giving us the opportunity to write. You're kind, talented and compassionate boss humans, who we admire, respect and adore. We deeply appreciate your patience, your nurturing energy and your support of us as siblings and individuals.

To Abigale Ulman, who believed in our Studd Sibling voice from the start and began this journey with us.

To Lara Picone, a pure word magician like no other, who added the extra sparkle to our voice and smoothed out our lumpy words.

To Sarah Watson and Meryl Batlle – the all-star food team. Who knew that such serene and gracious energy in the kitchen could pump out more than 70 recipes to absolute perfection?

Thanks to Lauren Bamford for putting up with us siblings and taking some damn fine photos. You make us look real good!

Thank you also to Lucy Heaver for your keen eye for details and edits, and to Andy Warren for your super-sexy design that encapsulates who we are perfectly.

Thank you to Kerrie McCallum at *delicious.* magazine for seeing our potential and supporting us from day dot.

To our cheese mentor, Cathy Strange, whose sage words 'how can four ingredients speak so many languages?' will echo loudly in our heads forevermore. Thanks also to David Gremmels, Peggy, Sue, Andy Hatch and Mateo, who've paved the way for us and patiently taught us with their utterly infectious passion. To David Brault from Dexpa, thank you for all that you do for the Studd family.

Finally, blessed be the cheesemakers. May we continue to support you in the protection of the diversity of cheeses, preserving ancient traditions and forging new ones, and in creating memories of pleasure one mouthful at a time – now and for future generations.

INDEX

Pan Macmillan acknowledges the Traditional Custodians of country throughout Australia and their connections to lands, waters and communities. We pay our respect to Elders past and present and extend that respect to all Aboriginal and Torres Strait Islander peoples today. We honour more than sixty thousand years of storytelling, art and culture.

A Plum book

First published in 2023 by
Pan Macmillan Australia Pty Limited
Level 25, 1 Market Street,
Sydney, NSW 2000, Australia

Level 3, 112 Wellington Parade,
East Melbourne, VIC 3002, Australia

Text copyright © Ellie and Sam Studd 2023
Design Andy Warren Design copyright © Pan Macmillan 2023
Photography Lauren Bamford copyright © Pan Macmillan 2023, with additional photography © Will Studd, Nicole Cooper, Ellie Studd, Adrian Lander, Kirsten Jenkins, Lucas Tourlier, Alex Carlyle, Riley Hart, Andy Taylor, Alex Drewniak, Quickes, Flore Vallery Radot and Nick Haddow.

The moral right of the authors has been asserted.

Design and illustration by Andy Warren Design
Typesetting by Kirby Jones
Editing by Lucy Heaver
Index by Helena Holmgren
Photography by Lauren Bamford, except for the following images:
- Pages 10–11, 82, 83 (bottom), 119, 132, 135, 139 (top row and bottom left) and 303 by Michael Robinson (courtesy of Will Studd's *Cheese Slices*)
- Pages 7, 33, 38–9, 61–2, 65, 109 and 297 by Nicole Cooper
- Pages 15, 20, 22, 94, 105 (top right and bottom row) and 131 by Ellie Studd
- Pages 17 (top), 29, 83 (middle), 97, 99, 107 and 137 (top right) by Adrian Lander
- Pages 6, 52 and 138 by Kirsten Jenkins
- Pages 21, 24 (top) and 42 by Lucas Tourlier
- Pages 24 (bottom), 33 and 38 by Alex Carlyle
- Pages 14, 41 and 120 by Riley Hart
- Pages 108 and 116 by Andy Taylor
- Pages 36 and 124 by Alex Drewniak
- Pages 142 and 143 (bottom) by Quickes
- Page 104 (top left) by Flore Vallery Radot (Pecora Dairy)
- Page 144 by Nick Haddow (Bruny Island)
Prop and food styling by Kirsten Jenkins
Food preparation by Sarah Watson and Meryl Batlle
Colour reproduction by Splitting Image Colour Studio
Printed and bound in China by 1010 Printing International Limited

A CIP catalogue record for this book is available from the National Library of Australia.

All rights reserved. No part of this book may be reproduced or transmitted by any person or entity (including Google, Amazon or similar organisations), in any form or means, electronic or mechanical, including photocopying, recording, scanning or by any information storage and retrieval system, without prior permission in writing from the publisher.

Wallace & Gromit quote on page 1 from *Wallace & Gromit: A Grand Day Out* by Nick Park, produced by Aardman Studios © 1989. Reprinted by permission of Aardman Studios.

10 9 8 7 6 5 4 3 2 1

The Studd family joke is that their veins run with brie instead of blood, so it's no great surprise that siblings Ellie and Sam Studd share the same passion for cheese as their father, legendary cheese expert, Will Studd. Ellie and Sam spent childhood holidays visiting artisan producers in Europe and snacking on rare mountain cheeses and cave-ripened blues.

Over the last decade, Ellie and Sam have travelled the world, working with celebrated mongers and makers, and learning to make, mature and sell cheese. They are inducted members of the Guilde Internationale des Fromagers and American Cheese Society Certified Cheese Professionals.

Ellie and Sam hand-pick artisan cheeses for the 'Selected by Will Studd' range and are passionate about education, working closely with cheesemongers and chefs, running masterclasses, hosting events and contributing to food media, such as *delicious* magazine. This is their first book.

@thestuddsiblings

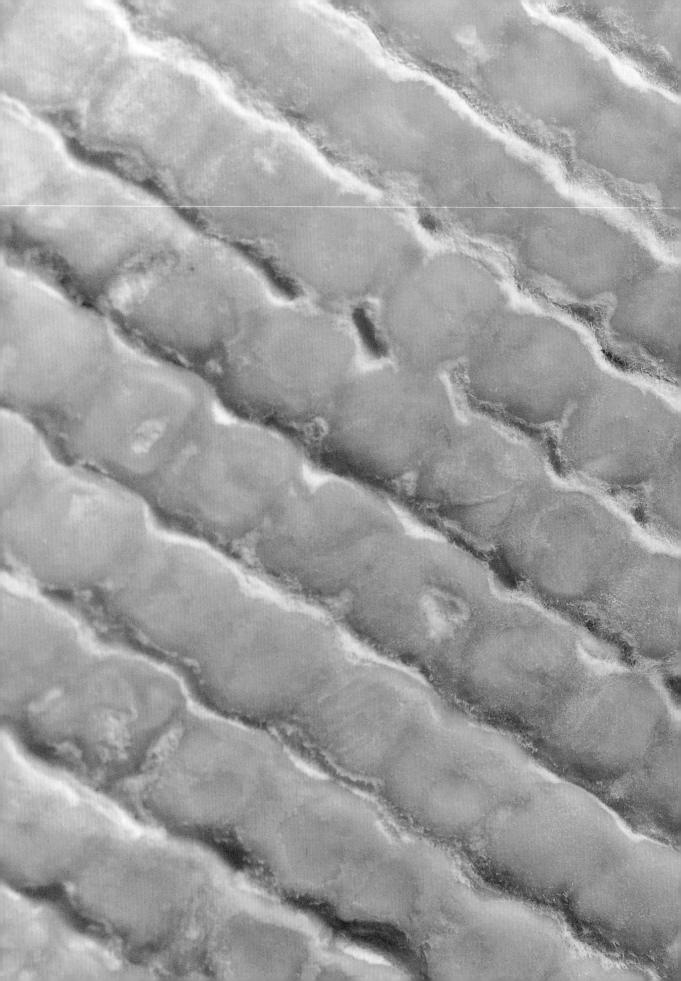